Biotechnology Industries and Entrepreneurs

Biotechnology Industries and Entrepreneurs

P. R. Gilbert

ANMOL PUBLICATIONS PVT. LTD.
NEW DELHI - 110 002 (INDIA)

ANMOL PUBLICATIONS PVT. LTD.

H.O.: 4374/4B, Ansari Road, Darya Ganj
New Delhi-110 002 (India)
Ph.: 23278000, 23261597

B.O.: 1015, Ist Main Road, BSK IIIrd Stage
IIIrd Phase, IIIrd Block
Bangalore - 560 085 (Karnataka)
Ph: 080-41723429, Tel/Fax: 080-2672 3604
Visit us at: www.anmolpublications.com

Biotechnology Industries and Entrepreneurs

First Published, 2008

ISBN 978-81-261-3273-7

PRINTED IN INDIA

Printed at Mehra Offset Press, Delhi.

Contents

Preface

This book entitled "Biotechnology Industries and Entrepreneurs" is designed to acquaint readers with the modern *biotechnology industries and entrepreneurs* at the global level. Industrial biotechnology is the practice of using cells to generate industrially-useful products. Industrial biotechnology has had significant impact on many chemical industries around the world. It might enable national economies to become less dependent on fossil fuels. A significant problem in industrial biotechnology is waste production. A cell may be used to generate desirable carbon dioxide, other cells, and other molecules. It will use energy to accomplish its industrial purpose. Yet it will also use some energy to generate waste (like acetic acid) instead of the desired product or products. Decreasing waste production is a significant goal in industrial biotechnology. Metabolic engineering may help reach that goal.

This book related to technologies being used in modern biotech industries looks at how biotechnology contributes to new and enhanced industrial processes. It examines how biotechnology enables the use of renewable resources in industry, thereby increasing efficiency, decreasing pollution, and reducing energy usage and waste production during various types of industrial processing. Biochemicals are chemicals produced from organic sources known as biomass. They are sometimes called bio-based chemicals, green chemicals, and plant-based chemicals. Biochemicals are chemicals produced from organic sources known as biomass.

Biomass is any living matter that can be naturally and regularly replenished, including agricultural food and feed crop residues, aquatic plants, animal wastes and other waste materials. Biochemicals are sometimes called bio-based chemicals, green chemicals, and plant-based chemicals. Currently, the most popular source for biochemicals is corn. Chemicals like ethyl lactate, succinic acid, and polylactic acid are made from corn components, such as corn starch, and are used to make a variety of products, such as plastics, solvents, clothing fibres, paints, and food additives. Biochemicals are made from the processing of plant sugars. Currently, corn is being used extensively as a starting material for biochemicals. The role of biotechnology in the creation of biochemicals is crucial. Through fermentation technology, biotechnology enables the processing of common crops and crop wastes, such as corn kernels and corn stalks, to make products such as plastics, textiles, and ethanol. Biotechnology also allows the creation of genetically modified bacteria that can convert plant sugars into an ingredient used in clothing, packaging, and plastics.

New enzymes are also being developed for breaking down plant sugars. Biotechnology also helps scientists better understand the biology of bacteria and enzymes that can be used in bioprocessing, which may enable the development of cheaper methods of biochemical production. Currently, biochemical products are often expensive to produce and are not cost-effective enough to compete with traditional products. Biotechnology has impacted the textiles industry through the development of more efficient and more environmentally friendly manufacturing processes, as well as through the design of improved textile materials. Some of biotechnology's key roles have involved the implementation, production, and modification of enzymes for the improvement of textile manufacturing processes. Biotechnology has also facilitated the production of novel and biodegradeable fibres from biomass feedstocks. Synthetic fibres made from renewable sources of biomass are environmentally sustainable, and are becoming increasingly economically sustainable. Biodegradable synthetic polymers include novel fibres such as polyglycolic acid and polylactic acid, which are made from natural starting materials. Not all novel fibres are synthetic; they may also be naturally derived. A prime example of a synthetic biomass fibre is Polylactic Acid (PLA), which is made by fermenting cornstarch or glucose into lactic acid, and then chemically transforming it into a polymer fibre. With properties similar to other synthetic fibres, PLA based materials are durable with a silky feel, and may be blended with wool or cotton. PLA has potential applications in several areas. PLA minimizes environmental waste, as it may be fully biodegraded by microorganisms under appropriate conditions into carbon dioxide and water. Unlike the non-renewable petroleum resources used to make traditional synthetic fibres, the supply of renewable corn biomass needed to make PLA is expected to surpass demand in the anticipated future.

Microbial Enhanced Oil Recovery (MEOR) is the use of microorganisms to retrieve additional oil from existing wells, thereby enhancing the petroleum production of an oil reservoir. In this technique, selected natural microorganisms are introduced into oil wells to produce harmless by-products, such as slippery natural substances or gases, all of which help propel oil out of the well. Because these processes help to mobilize the oil and facilitate oil flow, they allow a greater amount to be recovered from the well. MEOR is used in the third phase of oil recovery from a well, known as tertiary oil recovery. The microorganisms used in MEOR can be applied to a single oil well or to an entire oil reservoir. They need certain conditions to survive, so nutrients and oxygen are often introduced into the well at the same time. MEOR also requires that water be present. Microorganisms grow between the oil and the well's rock surface to enhance oil recovery. So, MEOR is a direct application of biotechnology. It uses biological materials, such as bacteria, microorganisms, and their products of metabolism to facilitate the movement of oil out of a well, thereby enhancing oil recovery. Other applications of biotechnology in MEOR include genetic engineering techniques and recombinant DNA technology, which are used to develop strains of bacteria with improved oil recovery traits. Genetic engineering is being used to develop microorganisms that cannot live in the high temperatures of an oil well, but can also subsist on inexpensive nutrients, remain chemically active, and produce substantial amounts of biosurfactants. Some researchers are developing bacteria that can be grown on inexpensive agricultural waste material, which is abundant in supply and is environmentally friendly.

This book consists of—Biotech Industries and Entrepreneurs: An Introduction; Phylogenetics, Pharmacogenomics and Genomics Research; Bioengineered Food and Stem Cells: Ethical and Safety Issues; and Regulatory Oversight in Biotechnology: A US Case Study etc. besides a large body of list of acronyms, glossary of relevant terms, extensive bibliography, list of websites and links, for further referencing and research.

—Editor

List of Acronyms

ABI	—	Applied Biosystems, Inc.
ABIC	—	Agricultural Biotechnology Intl. Conf.
ABRF	—	Association of Biomolecular Resource Facilities
ACMG	—	American College of Medical Genet.
ACS	—	American Chemical Society
ADA	—	Americans with Disabilities Act
AEC	—	Atomic Energy Commission
AES	—	American Electrophoresis Society
ASCI	—	American Society for Clinical Investigation
ASHG	—	American Society for Human Genetics
BNL	—	Brookhaven National Laboratory
BSCS	—	Biological Sciences Curriculum Study
BS/SCF	—	Biological Sequence/Structure Computational Facility
BTCI	—	BioPharmaceutical Technology Center Institute
CATCMB	—	Center for Advanced Training in Cell and Molecular Biology

CCM	—	Chromosome Coordinating Meeting
CDC	—	Centers for Disease Control
cDNA	—	Complementary DNA
CE	—	Capillary Electrophoresis
CRADA	—	Cooperative Research and Development Agreement
DM	—	Myotonic Dystrophy
DMD	—	Duchenne Muscular Dystrophy
DOE	—	Department of Energy
EEOC	—	Equal Employment Opportunity Commission
EL.B.A.	—	ELectronics and Biotechnology Advanced
EMBL	—	European Mol. Biol. Lab.
EMBO	—	European Molecular Biology Organisation
EMG	—	Encyclopedia of the Mouse Genome
EMS	—	Environmental Mutagen Society
EORTC	—	European Organization for Research and Treatment of Cancer
ERDA	—	Energy Research and Development Administration
ERI	—	Eleanor Roosevelt Institute
ES	—	Embryonic Stem
ESF	—	European Science Foundation
ESHG	—	European Society of Human Genetics
ESI	—	Electrospray Ionization
EST	—	Expressed Sequence Tag

GESTEC	—	Genome Science and Technology Center
GIST	—	Genome Informatics System of Transputers
GLaRGG	—	Great Lakes Regional Genetics Group
GMCRF	—	General Motors Cancer Res. Foundation
GMD	—	Genomic Map Design
GPI	—	Genetics and Public Issues Program
GRAIL	—	Gene Recognition and Analysis Internet Link
GRC	—	Gordon Res. Conf.
HERAC	—	Health and Environmental Research Advisory Committee
HGCC	—	Human Genome Coordinating Committee
HGM	—	Human Genome Meeting
HGMIS	—	Human Genome Management Information System
HGP	—	Human Genome Project
HHMI	—	Howard Hughes Medical Institute
IBF	—	International Business Forum
IBI	—	Institute for Biotechnology Information
ICES	—	International Council of Electrophoresis Societies
ICGEB	—	International Centre for Genetic Engineering and Biotechnology
IMGS	—	Intl. Mammalian Genome Society

INRIA	—	French Natl. Inst. for Research in Computer Science and Control
IOM	—	Institute of Medicine
IOR	—	Institute of Religion
ISAG	—	Intl. Society for Animal Genetics
ISMB	—	Intelligent Systems for Molecular Biology
ISONG	—	Intl. Soc. of Nurses in Genet.
ISQL	—	Interactive Standard Query Language
ISTR	—	Institute for Science Training and Research
IUBMB	—	Intl. Union of Biochemistry and Molecular Biology
IU	—	Indiana University
LBNL	—	Lawrence Berkeley National Laboratory
LLNL	—	Lawrence Livermore National Laboratory
LTI	—	Life Technologies, Inc.
MBC	—	Massachusetts Biotechnology Council
MBL	—	Marine Biological Laboratory
MCD	—	Mouse Cytogenetic Database
MDA	—	Muscular Dystrophy Assoc.
MEMS	—	Microelectromechanical Systems
MGC	—	Mouse Genome Conference
NCSA	—	National Center for Supercomputing Applications

NCSL	—	National Conference of State Legislatures
NCSU	—	North Carolina State University
NLGLP	—	National Laboratory Gene Library Project
NLM	—	National Library of Medicine
NMHCC	—	National Managed Health Care Congress
NORD	—	National Organization for Rare Disorders
NRC	—	National Research Council
NRSA	—	National Research Service Award
NSF	—	Natl. Sci. Foundation
NSGC	—	National Society of Genetic Counselors
OHER	—	Office of Health and Environmental Research
OMIM	—	Online *Mendelian Inheritance in Man*
OPRR	—	Office of Protection from Res. Risks
ORAU	—	Oak Ridge Associated Universities
ORISE	—	Oak Ridge Inst. for Science and Education
ORF	—	open reading frame
ORNL	—	Oak Ridge National Laboratory
OSU	—	Oregon State University
PCR	—	Polymerase Chain Reaction
PFGE	—	Pulsed-field gel electrophresis
PG	—	Plant Genome

PIR	—	Protein Info. Resource
SNP	—	Single Nucleotide Polymorphism
SQL	—	Standard Query Language
SSLP	—	Single-sequence Length Polymorphism
SSR	—	Simple Sequence Repeat
STM	—	Scanning Tunneling Microscope
WHS	—	Wolf-Hirschhorn syndrome
WLMG	—	Wellcome Laboratory for Molecular Genetics
WSES	—	World Scientific and Engineering Society

List of Glossary of Terms

Antigenic switching: The altering of a microorganism's surface antigens through genetic rearrangement, to elude detection by the host's immune system.

Bacteriorhodopsin: Pigmented protein found in the plasma membrane of a salt-loving bacterium, *Halobacterium halobium*; it pumps protons out of the cell in response to light.

Basal lamina (plural basal laminae): Thin mat of extracellular matrix that separates epithelial sheets, and many types of cells such as muscle cells or fat cells, from connective tissue. Sometimes called a basement membrane.

Beta-DNA: The normal form of DNA found in biological systems, which exists as a right-handed helix.

Biosensor: The term "biosensor" is a general designation that denotes either a sensor to detect a biological substance or a sensor which incorporates the use of biological molecules such as antibodies or enzymes. Biosensors are a subcategory of chemical sensors.

Chromatid: Each of the two daughter strands of a duplicated chromosome joined at the centromere during mitosis and meiosis.

Cistron: A DNA sequence that codes for a specific polypeptide; a gene. See DNA, Gene.

Clone: An exact genetic replica of a specific gene or an entire organism. See Cloning.

Competency: An ephemeral state, induced by treatment with cold cations, during which bacterial cells are capable of uptaking foreign DNA.

Concatemer: A DNA segment composed of repeated sequences linked end to end.

Conjugation: The joining of two bacteria cells when genetic material is transferred from one bacterium to another.

Crossing-over: The exchange of DNA sequences between chromatids of homologous chromosomes during meiosis.

Cross-pollination: Fertilization of a plant from a plant with a different genetic makeup.

Crosstalk: Electromagnetic noise transmitted between leads or circuits in close proximity to each other.

Endocrine cell: Specialized animal cell that secretes a hormone into the blood; usually part of a gland, such as the thyroid or pituitary gland.

Endocytosis: Uptake of material into a cell by an invagination of the plasma membrane and its internalization in a membrane-bounded vesicle.

Endophyte: An organism that lives inside another.

Endoplasmic reticulum (ER): Labyrinthine, membrane-bounded compartment in the cytoplasm of eucaryotic cells, where lipids are synthesized and membrane-bound proteins are made.

Enzymes: Proteins that control the various steps in all chemical reactions.

Ethidium bromide: A fluorescent dye used to stain DNA and RNA. The dye fluoresces when exposed to UV light.

Eukaryote: An organism whose cells possess a nucleus and other membrane-bound vesicles, including all members of the protist, fungi, plant and animal kingdoms;

and excluding viruses, bacteria, and blue-green algae. See Prokaryote.

Eurisko: A computer program developed by Professor Douglas Lenat which is able to apply heuristic rules for performing various tasks, including the invention of new heuristic rules.

FIFRA: The Federal Insecticide, Fungicide, and Rodenticide Act. See Environmental Protection Agency.

Fingerprint: A set of molecular markers sufficiently diverse to identify particular individuals with reasonable certainty.

Flanking region: The DNA sequences extending on either side of a specific locus or gene.

Food and Drug Administration (FDA): The U.S. agency responsible for regulation of biotechnology food products. The major laws under which the agency has regulatory powers include the Food, Drug, and Cosmetic Act; and the Public Health Service Act.

Gel, agarose: A substance used to separate DNA or RNA fragments by size. Used for southern and northern blots.

Gel, polyacrylamide: A substance used to separate proteins by size. Used for western blots.

GEM: A genetically engineered microorganism.

Gene amplification: The presence of multiple genes. Amplification is one mechanism through which proto-oncogenes are activated in malignant cells.

Gene cloning: The process of synthesizing multiple copies of a particular DNA sequence using a bacteria cell or another organism as a host. See DNA, Host.

Gene expression: The process of producing a protein from its DNA- and mRNA-coding sequences.

Gene flow: The exchange of genes between different but (usually) related populations.

Gene modification: The chemical repair of a gene's defective DNA sequence. See DNA.

Gene pool: The totality of all alleles of all genes of all individuals in a particular population.

Genetic drift: Random variation in gene frequency from one generation to another.

Genetic engineering: Genetic engineering is the process of manually adding new DNA on a molecular level with the goal of adding one or more new traits that are not already found in that organism. For the purposes of this web site, genetic engineering includes recombinant DNA and gene splicing technologies.

Genetic marker: A gene or group of genes used to "mark" or track the action of microbes.

Genome: The genetic complement contained in the chromosomes of a given organism, usually the haploid chromosome state. The full chromosome set containing all the genes of a particular individual.

Genomics:: The study of the structure and function of genomes. Genomics usually involves high speed sequencing of the DNA and computer searches for sequences that code for genes.

Genotype: The sum total of the genetic information of an organism including the linkage relationships between genes. The genotype, modified by environment, determines the phenotype.

Genus: A category including closely related species. Interbreeding between organisms within the same category can occur.

Germ cell (germ line) gene therapy: The repair or replacement of a defective gene within the gamete-forming tissues, which produces a heritable change in an organism's genetic constitution.

Green revolution: Advances in genetics, petrochemicals, and machinery that culminated in a dramatic increase in crop productivity during the third quarter of the 20th century.

GUI: Graphical User Interface — hardware, software, and firmware that produces the display on modern personal computers.

Heterochromatin: Dark-stained regions of chromosomes thought to be for the most part genetically inactive.

Heteroduplex: A double-stranded DNA molecule or DNA-RNA hybrid, where each strand is of a different origin.

Homologous chromosomes: Chromosomes that have the same linear arrangement of genes—a pair of matching chromosomes in a diploid organism. See Chromosomes.

Homologous recombination: The exchange of DNA fragments between two DNA molecules or chromatids of paired chromosomes (during crossing over) at the site of identical nucleotide sequences.

Homozygote: An organism whose genotype is characterized by two identical alleles of a gene. See Allele, Genotype.

Insulin: A peptide hormone secreted by the islets of Langerhans of the pancreas that regulates the level of sugar in the blood.

Interferon: A family of small proteins that stimulate viral resistance in cells.

Intergenic regions: DNA sequences located between genes that comprise a large percentage of the human genome with no known function.

Introgression: Backcrossing of hybrids of two plant populations to introduce new genes into a wild population.

Intron: A noncoding DNA sequence within a gene that is initially transcribed into messenger RNA but is later snipped out. See Coding, DNA, Messenger RNA, Transcription.

Kilohertz (kHz): One thousand cycles per second.

Kilojoule: Standard unit of energy equal to 1000 joules, or 0.24 kilocalories.

Lag phase: The initial growth phase, during which cell number remains relatively constant prior to rapid growth. See growth phase.

Legume: A member of the pea family that possesses root nodules containing nitrogen-fixing bacteria.

Library, DNA: A large set of clones of DNA fragments from a particular organism. DNA libraries are usually maintained in *E. coli* or in bacteriophages.

Ligation: Joining two fragments of DNA end to end. See sticky ends.

Linked genes/markers: Genes and/or markers that are so closely associated on the chromosome that they are coinherited in 80% or more of cases.

Linker: A short, double-stranded oligonucleotide containing a restriction endonuclease recognition site, which is ligated to the ends of a DNA fragment.

Locus (plural = loci): A specific location or site on a chromosome.

Logarithmic phase (log or exponential growth phase): The steepest slope of the growth curve—the phase of vigorous growth during which cell number doubles every 20-30 minutes.

Lysogen: A bacterial cell whose chromosome contains integrated viral DNA.

Lytic: A phase of the virus life cycle during which the virus replicates within the host cell, releasing a new generation of viruses when the infected cell lyses.

Machine-phase chemistry: The chemistry of systems in which all potentially reactive moieties follow controlled trajectories (e.g., guided by molecular machines working in vacuum).

Macroscale: Larger than nanoscale; often implies a design that humans can directly interact with; too large to be built by a single assembler (one cubic micron of diamond contains 176 billion atoms).

Magnetostrictive material: A material that changes dimension in the presence of a magnetic field or generates a magnetic field when mechanically deformed.

Malignant: Having the properties of cancerous growth.

Manufacturing: The ability to make products, in this case ranging from clothing, to electronics, to medical devices, to books, to building materials, and much more.

Meat Machine: AKA Cabinet Beast. A box containing assemblers and raw material, within which is formed meat [or whatever else it was programmed to make].

Megabyte (MB): 220 (= 1,048,576, or about one million) bytes of information.

Megahertz (Mhz): One million cycles per second

Meiosis: The reduction division process by which haploid gametes and spores are formed, consisting of a single duplication of the genetic material followed by two mitotic divisions.

Metabolism: The biochemical processes that sustain a living cell or organism.

Metallothionein: A protective protein that binds heavy metals, such as cadmium and lead.

Micelles: Micelles are small, spherical structures composed of molecules that attract one another to reduce surface tension. The head of the molecule is hydrophilic, meaning it likes water, while the interior portion is hydrophobic, meaning it avoids water.

Microbial mats (biofilms): Layered groups or communities of microbial populations.

Microelectronics: Narrower terms: MEMS, nanoelectronics, optoelectronics, SED Single Electron Devices. Related terms: molecular electronics, semiconductors

Microencapsulation: Individually encapsulated small particles.

Microinjection: A means to introduce a solution of DNA, protein, or other soluble material into a cell using a fine microcapillary pipet.

Microsystem: A microscale machine that can sense information from the environment and act accordingly. Outside the U.S., it can also refer to microelectromechanical systems (MEMS). [smalltimes glossary, 2002]

Microtubule: A hollow cylindrical tube used for the transport of materials inside cells.

Miller indices: A set of 3 integers (4 for hexagonal) that designate crystallographic planes, as determined from reciprocals of fractional axial intercepts.

Millimeter: One thousandth of a meter, or about 1/26 of an inch.

Mitosis: The replication of a cell to form two daughter cells with identical sets of chromosomes.

Molecular - Nanotechnology: The technology of precisely-constructed molecular-scale machines; from nanometer: a billionth of a meter. For a good introduction, see What is Nanotechnology? or Ralph C. Merkle's nanotechnology page.

Molecular Beam Epitaxy: [MBE] Process used to make compound (multi-layer) semiconductors. Consists of depositing alternating layers of materials, layer by layer, one type after another (such as the semiconductors gallium arsenide and aluminum gallium arsenide).

Molecular biology: The study of the biochemical and molecular interactions within living cells.

Molecular genetics: The study of the flow and regulation of genetic information between DNA, RNA, and protein molecules.

Molecular markers: Genetic traits which are detectable on gels or blots and can be used to construct genetic maps. Molecular markers usually have no known function. RFLPs are molecular markers.

Molecular Wire: A molecular wire—the simplest electronic component—is a quasi-one-dimensional molecule that can transport charge carriers (electrons or holes) between its ends. [Michael D Ward]

Monoclonal antibodies: Immunoglobulin molecules of single- epitope specificity that are secreted by a clone of B cells.

Monoculture: The agricultural practice of cultivating crops consisting of genetically similar organisms.

Monogenic: Controlled by or associated with a single gene.

Mycorrhizae: Fungi that form symbiotic relationships with roots of more developed plants.

Nanoscience: Nanoscience is the science of nanoscale phenomena. This is a very complicated area, since Quantum Mechanics is often needed to describe the physical properties of atoms and molecules properly.

Nitrocellulose: A membrane used to immobilize DNA, RNA, or protein, which can then be probed with a labeled sequence or antibody.

Nitrogen fixation: The conversion of atmospheric nitrogen to biologically usable nitrates.

Occupational Safety and Health Administration (OSHA): One of the U.S. agencies responsible for regulation of biotechnology. The major law under which the agency has regulatory powers is the Occupational Safety and Health Act.

Oncogenesis: The progression of cytological, genetic, and cellular changes that culminate in a malignant tumor.

Open pollination: Pollination by wind, insects, or other natural mechanisms.

Operator: A prokaryotic regulatory element that interacts with a repressor to control the transcription of adjacent structural genes.

Organelle: A cell structure that carries out a specialized function in the life of a cell.

Origin of replication: The nucleotide sequence at which DNA synthesis is initiated.

Paleontology: The study of the fossil record of past geological periods and of the phylogenetic relationships between ancient and contemporary plant and animal species.

Parasitism: The closee association of two or more dissimilar organisms where the association is harmful to at least one. See Commensalism, Parasitism, Symbiosis.

Particle bombardment: Using metal particles to blast DNA into cells for the purpose of genetic engineering. A gene gun is used to propel the metal particles.

Pheromone: A hormone-like substance that is secreted into the environment.

Phosphatase: An enzyme that hydrolyzes esters of phosphoric acid, removing a phosphate group.

Phosphodiester bond: A bond in which a phosphate group joins adjacent carbons through ester linkages. A condensation reaction between adjacent nucleotides results in a phosphodiester bond between 3' and 5' carbons in DNA and RNA.

Phosphorylation: The addition of a phosphate group to a compound.

Piezoelectric material: A ferroelectric material in which an electrical potential difference is created due to mechanical deformation, or conversely, in which the application of a voltage causes dimensional changes in the material.

Population: A local group of organisms belonging to the same species and capable of interbreeding.

Primary cell: A cell or cell line taken directly from a living organism, which is not immortalized.

Primer: A short DNA or RNA fragment annealed to single-stranded DNA, from which DNA polymerase extends a new DNA strand to produce a duplex molecule.

Prokaryote: A bacterial cell lacking a true nucleus; its DNA is usually in one long strand. See Eukaryote.

Pronucleus: Either of the two haploid gamete nuclei just prior to their fusion in the fertilized ovum.

Protease: An enzyme that cleaves peptide bonds that link amino acids in protein molecules.

Protein kinase: An enzyme that adds phosphate groups to a protein molecule at serine, threonine, or tyrosine residues.

Recessive gene: Characterized as having a phenotype expressed only when both copies of the gene are mutated or missing.

Recessive: Refers to the member of a pair of alleles that fails to be expressed in the phenotype of the organism when the dominant member is present. Also refers to the phenotype of an individual that has only the recessive allele.

Rhizobia: Bacteria in a symbiotic relationship with leguminous plants that results in nitrogen fixation. See Nitrogen fixation.

Rhizosphere: The soils region on and around plant roots.

Ribosome: Cellular organelle that is the site of protein synthesis during translation. See Organelle, Translation.

Ribosome-binding site: The region of an mRNA molecule that binds the ribosome to initiate translation.

Risk assessment: Defined as a formalized basis for the objective evaluation of risk in a manner in which assumptions and uncertainties are clearly considered and presented.

RNA: Ribonucleic acid. The three basic types are messenger RNA (mRNA), ribosomal RNA (rRNA), and transfer RNA (tRNA).

Roundup Ready: A trademark for plants that are genetically engineered to be resistant to the herbicide Roundup (technical name: glyphosate).

Salmonella: A genus of rod-shaped, gram-negative bacteria that are a common cause of food poisoning.

Satellite RNA (viroids): A small, self-splicing RNA molecule that accompanies several plant viruses, including tobacco ringspot virus.

Self-pollination: Pollen of one plant is transferred to the female part of the same plant or another plant with the same genetic makeup.

Semiconservative replication: During DNA duplication, each strand of a parent DNA molecule is a template for the synthesis of its new complementary strand. Thus, one half of a preexisting DNA molecule is conserved during each round of replication.

Sequence hypothesis: Francis Crick's seminal concept that genetic information exists as a linear DNA code; DNA and protein sequence are colinear.

Sequence: Noun: the particular order of nucleotides in a DNA or RNA fragment. Verb: to determine the particular order of nucleotides in a strand of DNA.

Sequence-tagged site (STS): A unique (single-copy) DNA sequence used as a mapping landmark on a chromosome.

Sexual reproduction: The process where two cells (gametes) fuse to form one hybrid, fertilized cell. See Asexual reproduction, Gamete, Hybrid.

Signal transduction: The biochemical events that conduct the signal of a hormone or growth factor from the cell exterior, through the cell membrane, and into the cytoplasm. This involves a number of molecules, including receptors, pro- teins, and messengers.

Site-directed mutagenesis: The process of introducing spe- cific base-pair mutations into a gene.

Species: A classification of related organisms that can freely interbreed.

Spore: A form taken by certain microbes that enables them to exist in a dormant stage. It is an asexual reproductive cell. See Asexual reproduction, Dormant.

Susceptibility: When individual or species will become ill or possibly die in the face of the stressful event or circumstances.

Transgenic plant: Genetically engineered plant or offspring of genetically engineered plants. The transgenic plant usually contains material from at least one unrelated organisms, such as from a virus, animal, or other plant. See Transgenic.

Upstream: The region extending in a 5' direction from a gene.

Vaccinia: The cowpox virus used to vaccinate against smallpox and, experimentally, as a carrier of genes for antigenic determinants cloned from other disease organisms.

Variable surface glycoprotein (VSG): One of a battery of antigenic determinants expressed by a microorganism to elude immune detection.

Variation: Differences in the frequency of genes and traits among individual organisms within a population.

Vasculocyte: In medical nanorobotics, a theorized (nanorobotic) device capable of performing repairs of an injured vascular luminal surface.

Vasculography: A physical description (and mapping) of the human vascular system.

1

Biotech Industries and Entrepreneurs: An Introduction

Biotechnology Industry Statistics

- There are 1,457 biotechnology companies in the United States, of which 342 are publicly held.
- Market capitalization, the total value of publicly traded biotech companies at market prices, was $224 billion as of early May 2002.
- The biotechnology industry has more than tripled in size since 1992, with revenues increasing from $8 billion in 1992 to $27.6 billion in 2001.
- The U.S. biotech industry spent $15.6 billion on research and development in 2001.

Antibiotics

- New antibiotics through genetic modification

  Many antibiotics that were once highly effective are now proving to be useless as the disease-causing microorganisms develop resistance.
- Antibiotics and antibiotic resistance

  Antibiotics are chemicals produced naturally by microorganisms in the environment that kill, or prevent the growth of other microorganisms.

- New antibiotics

  A soil bacterium – *Streptomyces* – is a source of antibiotics, immunosuppressants, anti-cancer and anti-parasitic agents, and natural herbicides. It is possible to generate new compounds by changing the blueprint – switching some of the genes, and thus some of the units, around.

  http://www.jic.bbsrc.ac.uk/exhibitions/bio-future/medbiotech.htm

Environment

- Transgenic foods such as papaya, soybeans and corn are already in the market. Hundreds of biopesticides and other agricultural products are being used to improve the food supply and to reduce our dependence on conventional chemical pesticides.

  http://www.bio.org/er/statistics.asp

- Ready to enter the market: Wheat in North Dakota

Animal Husbandry

- Enzymes, such as amylases and proteases, are being added to animal feed to supplement the animals' own enzymes and improve digestion. Most animal feedstuffs are plant-derived and contain 'anti-nutritional factors' that interfere with digestion in a variety of ways. Many of these factors are non-starch polysaccharides, from cereal grains. Adding enzymes (beta-glucanases and arabinoxylanase) to feedstuffs increases the nutritional value of feeds by breaking down these factors, aiding digestion and making nutrients more easily absorbed. Phytic acid is another anti-nutritional compound found in plant cereals that prevents dietary absorption of essential minerals such as iron and zinc. It also pollutes the environment because it is excreted as phosphorus in manure. Addition of phytase in the diet helps digestion, but until it was recently cloned this enzyme was not available in sufficient quantities for widespread use.

- Enviropigs:
- Each contains an enzyme in its saliva which helps digest food better and so creates less smell and pollution through its manure.

Cows

- New Zealand's AgResearch, a government-owned research company, put extra copies of the genes for beta-casein and kappa-casein (milk proteins) into laboratory cow cells. The cells were cloned, and then implanted. Nine of the eleven cows born produce milk with 8% to 20% more beta casein and twice as much kappa casein.
- Food and Drug Administration has asked that milk or meat from cloned animals not be sold while it develops a policy on such products.

Industry Entrepreneurs, Scientists, and Biotechnology

In 1988, Zucker and Marilynn B. Brewer began a study at the University of California, Los Angeles (UCLA) of elite scientists and the founding of biotech firms, and of the effect of commercial involvement on the productivity of those bioscientists. They defined star scientists for their project as those who by 1990 had recorded more than 40 genetic-sequence discoveries or had authored at least 20 articles reporting such discoveries. GenBank collected discoveries and articles internationally without regard to language or location of publication, so this definition did not favor any particular nationality. By the time Darby joined the collaboration in 1992, Zucker and Brewer had hand-collected all the genetic-sequence articles by these 327 star scientists, coded the names of all their co-authors (whether another star or a collaborator), located all of these scientists by affiliation on each article, coded data in all U.S. universities, and collected extensive data on all the firms that had entered biotechnology in the United States. Since 1992, the relational database has been greatly extended to cover articles up to 1994, has added extensive data on Japanese firms and universities, and has added some initial data on European firms and universities. A parallel database is nearly complete for semiconductors and one has been started for interactive media. The quantitative studies based on this data have all been informed by fieldwork and case studies in which more than 100 scientists, executives, and government and university officials have been interviewed across the United States, Japan, Europe, and Australia.

Until recently, economists and sociologists studying science and technology have been averse to viewing scientists — particularly top scientists — as pursuing private motives, viewing them instead as disinterested contributors to a shared common pool of knowledge. Our results suggest that star scientists often are better viewed as entrepreneurial individuals who value both financial rewards and the pleasure, recognition, and resources that come from being the first to make a significant new discovery. Collaborations expected to lead to higher valued discoveries, for example, are more likely to be limited to authors from a single organization, and increased use of single-organization collaborations retards the rate of diffusion to new scientists. One of our interviewees, when asked about delays of publication to enable patenting, responded, "In the university, it's hardly unknown to hold off publishing a breakthrough until. The key role of star scientists in commercialization of their discoveries is suggested by some of our early results but confirmed more strongly in our most recent analysis. Where and when star scientists are actively publishing scientific articles is a key determinant of where and when firms enter into biotechnology in the United States. This result seems to support the "geographically localized knowledge spillovers model" in which those nearby — for example, within Route 128 (in Massachusetts) or in Silicon Valley — hear first of breakthrough discoveries as the scientists give the knowledge away in seminars or barroom gossip. However, this model is inconsistent with our interviews, which suggest that the stars are fully cognizant of the value of their discoveries and use it either as the basis for starting their own firms or trading with existing firms. Our database permits us to see which star scientists have published with scientists from firms — generally agreed by the scientists to be an indicator of both bench-science collaboration and alignment of interests. When we consider the success of California firms in terms of new products in development, there is an apparent value to being located in the same region as universities with star scientists who have many publications. However, this turns out to result entirely from the large positive effects on firm success of those firms that have jointly authored articles with university stars. The large impact of these articles is apparent in other measures of success such as products on the market and employment growth. We have since replicated these results in work underway for the United States and in Japan, in which we substituted number of patents granted for unavailable data on employment growth. In the United States, linked articles appeared by 1985 for 9 of the 10 most successful (to date) new biotech firms, as measured by market valuation. An initial working hypothesis of the project — and one still popular in the literature — is that a star scientist who becomes involved in commercialization of his or her discoveries is a loss to the progress of science. We have found instead that the scientists who are more involved in commercialization and patenting are more productive scientifically during their period of involvement. To compare the extreme cases, for example, up until 1990, stars who were ever affiliated with firms and had some patents had an average annual citation rate in genetic-sequence discovery articles 9.17 times that of pure academic stars who neither patented nor ever published with, or as an employee, of a firm. It could be that only the most successful of the stars have the opportunity to work with existing firms or to obtain financial backing to start their own firms, but by examining their publication history before, during, and after publishi tists publish significantly more articles with significantly higher citation rates during than before or after firm ties. (Japanese stars also publish significantly more while tied to firms, but their increase in citation rate is not statistically significant.)

Thus, we conclude that stars who are involved commercially use part of their gains to advance their independent scientific careers: they are partly venture capitalists, rather than wholly tied to the National Institutes of Health or the National Science Foundation. Because university star links to firms are important in determining both the firms that will be successful and the rate of advancement of the underlying science base, we examine that process in our work with Maximo Torero. We find that the probability that the first article published with, or as, a firm employee will occur in a given period increases with the academic star's total citations to articles written to date, the percentage of co-authors in other institutions, the number of nearby firms, and, notably, the increase in research productivity of other nearby stars who have already established such commercial ties. Again, the most productive stars are the most desirable to firms and those stars respond not only to the financial but also to the scientific rewards of commercial involvement.

In collaboration with Shingo Kano of the University of Tokyo; Takuma Takahashi of Nomura Research Institute, Limited; and Kazuo Ueda of the Bank of Japan, we are currently preparing a monograph examining the adoption of biotechnology in Japan, with particular emphasis on how institutional differences have caused that process to differ from what has been observed in the United States. Two key institutional differences are: In Japan, until recently, financial market regulations precluded the venture capital and initial public offering processes that have financed so many U.S. startups, so that virtually all Japanese adoption of the technology has been by pre-existing firms. Japanese national university professors have been precluded from starting firms on the side, but generally they have been able to patent in their own name any discoveries made in their universities.

As a result, star-firm collaborations generally occur in Japanese university laboratories, as opposed to U.S. collaborations, in which the work is frequently done in firm laboratories to secure the property rights. As a result, we see that although stars' publishing still plays the leading role in determining where and when Japanese firms enter, the stars' impact is significantly less and the impact of pre-existing economic structure is significantly greater than in the United States. As indicated earlier, the effects of university star-firm collaborations on firm success appear to be about as potent in Japan as in the United States, but because Japanese firms send their employees to work in the university laboratories, the stars' economic impact is not nearly so geographically localized as in the United States.

The breakthrough technology in the United States has led to a transformation of the pharmaceutical industry, earliest and most importantly through the creation of new firms but also through the transformation of existing firms. Many of the previous incumbent firms have disappeared and others have successfully transformed themselves, even as new entrants have become important players in the drug-discovery part of the business or, in a few cases, full-fledged pharmaceutical firms. Our Japanese collaborators are examining both the transformation of Japanese incumbent pharmaceutical firms and successful and unsuccessful entry by pre-existing firms from other industries. We have recently found evidence that the European reliance on national research institutes instead of research universities may have disadvantaged European commercial adoption of biotechnology. Although Europe has a substantial percentage of the world's stars, it has fewer than 10 percent of those who have written articles with or as firm employees. Across countries, the correlation of percentage of stars with firm ties and percentage of stars in research institutes is large, significant, and negative. Also, the United States and Japan, with the largest percentages of stars tied to firms, have been drawing stars from the rest of the world, a process that has continued in the 1990s.

The new growth theory or endogenous growth models generally treat discoveries as a sort of software, "knowledge or information that can be stored in a form which exists outside of the brain," and is therefore nonrivalrous (and possibly nonexcludable) so that public good issues arise. Our evidence for biotechnology indicates instead that the relevant knowledge or information — at least in the breakthrough stage we are investigating — has important elements that are tacit and must be learned by working, directly or indirectly, with discovering scientists. Ultimately, the knowledge diffuses widely and earns only the normal rate of return on the cost of learning it in any reputable graduate program. But between initial discovery and the long run, natural excludability implies extraordinary financial and scientific returns to scientists adept in discovery and ensures that discoveries are normal rivalrous goods. To the ess, revisions in the new growth theories are required. Policy analysts find our research of interest because by clarifying the potentially important role of star scientists in commercializing their work — and the virtuous circles through which that accelerates scientific advance — we are able to identify particular institutions or policies that facilitate or interfere with that process. Examples include across-university variations in rights of professors to serve as principals or consult for companies on the side, research institute rules that effectively insulate scientists from direct commercial involvement, and the role of the Bayh-Dole Act and similar rules in providing incentives for commercialization.

Nanotech Related Intellectual Property Rights Issues

Over the past two decades the role of intellectual property in all areas of science and technology has exploded globally—primarily due to rules prescribed by the World Trade Organization's Trade-Related Aspects of Intellectual Property (TRIPs) and by bilateral/regional trade agreements. The TRIPs agreement obligates all WTO member countries to adopt and enforce minimum standards of intellectual property. WTO has 150 members, and claims that it accounts for over 97% of all world trade.50 In 1996 the World Intellectual Property Organization (WIPO) and WTO established a collaborative relationship in order to implement the TRIPs Agreement. (WIPO has 182 member states, which represents over 90% of the world's countries.) Among other IP rules, WTO members must allow patenting in *all* fields of technology. The initial grace periods and flexibility allowed by TRIPs for developing country members have nearly expired. By 2006, the so-called "least developed countries" are required to adopt the WTO/TRIPs standards. Over the past decade, civil society, social movements, the UN Human Rights Commission and some governments have warned of the inequities of IP for the global South. Recently, even at WIPO – the UN body whose mission is to promote and protect intellectual property – the uneven IP playing field and the negative impacts of TRIPs have become undeniable and untenable for many developing nations. In September 2004 the "Geneva Declaration on the Future of the World Intellectual Property Organization" warned that current IP regimes are having negative impacts in the developing world, resulting in lack of access to essential medicines, anticompetitive practices that hinder innovation and the misappropriation of social and public goods. At WIPO's General Assembly meeting (September 27-October 5, 2004), Brazil and Argentina, supported by 14 developing country co-sponsors, proposed that WIPO adopt a "development agenda," stating that Intellectual property protection cannot be seen as an end in itself, nor can the harmonization of intellectual property laws leading to higher protection standards in all countries, irrespective of their levels of development. The role of intellectual property and its impact on development must be carefully assessed on a case-by-case basis. IP protection is a policy instrument the operation of which may, in actual practice, produce benefits as well as costs, which may vary in accordance with a country's level of development. Action is therefore needed to ensure, in all countries, that the costs do not outweigh the benefits of IP protection. WIPO's General Assembly adopted the decision to welcome a development agenda. But the US, UK and other industrialized nations are balking at the decision to give development concerns a higher profile within WIPO, acknowledging only that WIPO should give greater technical assistance to developing countries.52 Reports will be prepared and the issue will be considered at WIPO's General Assembly meeting in September 2005.53 Meanwhile, developing nations are now facing a new technology wave – and the requirement to accommodate nanotechnology-related inventions – even while still grappling with unresolved controversies over biotechnology and information technologies. By next year, ready or not, most of the world's developing nations will be obligated to evaluate and enforce nanotech patents. ETC Group is not suggesting that nanotech, unencumbered by patents, will provide solutions for the South's most pressing needs. On the contrary, ETC Group believes that a technological fix can never right social wrongs. However, much ink has been spilled of late on the benefits nanotech will bring to developing nations while ignoring the realities of technology transfer and intellectual property.54 Multinational corporations, universities and nanotech start-ups (primarily in the OECD countries) have already secured numerous patents on essential nanotech tools, materials and processes. To the extent that these are "foundational" patents – that is, seminal breakthrough inventions upon which later innovations are built, researchers in the developing world could be shut-out. Nanotech patent thickets are already causing concern in the US and Europe. Researchers in the global South are likely to find that participation in the proprietary "nanotech revolution" is highly restricted by patent tollbooths, obliging them to pay royalties and licensing fees to gain access. Ultimately, nanotech will profoundly impact the South's economy, regardless of its level of direct participation or its handling of intellectual property. Nano-scale manufacturing platforms could make geography, raw materials, as well as labour, irrelevant. By employing nanotech to build from the bottom-up rather than processing down, the quantity of raw materials required could be sharply reduced. In short, nano-scale technologies are poised to become the strategic platform for global control of materials, food, agriculture and health in the immediate years ahead. Intellectual property monopoly is a crucial and powerful tool for realizing that strategy. As a starting place for further debate, ETC Group offers the following recommendations related to nanotech IP.

Six "Pro-South Science" Policy Proposals:

1. Poor applause: When the G8 meets in July to discuss its dubious "Pro-Poor Science" strategy, leaders of rich nations shouldn't ignore the restrictions implicit in intellectual property that make it difficult or impossible for the South to develop its own independent technology solutions and to have access to the useful technologies of others. A truly "Pro-South" science policy would establish a global ten-year sunset clause on all monopoly patents.

2. Patent pause: WIPO should initiate a global suspension of patent approvals related to any applications that meet the US PTO's Class 977 standard (the criteria for nanotechnology patents) until further social review, including wide public debate, is undertaken on the impacts of nanotech IP.

3. Technology flaws: In close cooperation with social movements, including trade unions, the Food and Agriculture Organization (FAO) and the United Nations Conference on Trade and Development (UNCTAD) should cooperate with WIPO in producing a study on the impact of nanotech-related intellectual property on monopoly practices, technology transfer and trade. The UNCTAD Commission on Science and Technology for Development, also in conjunction with social movements, should examine the implications for technology transfer and the needs and interests of developing countries.

4. TRIPs clause: South governments and countries-in-transition should suspend any Class 977 equivalent patent grants or applications pending a full evaluation of their impacts. In particular, governments should determine whether or not such patents compromise access to the basic elements of nature or contravene national legislation or international agreements, such as WTO TRIPs, concerning intellectual property over living material.

5. Ordre public laws: National governments and relevant international organizations such as WIPO and UNCTAD should examine the social and *ordre public* significance of Class 977 equivalent patents that could compromise access to the fundamental components of nature.

6. Diversity laws: With input from indigenous peoples and peasant farmers' organizations, the Convention on Biological Diversity (CBD), the Commission on Sustainable Development (CSD) and FAO should consider the impact of intellectual property on fundamental elements of nature with respect to biodiversity and national sovereignty over genetic resources (especially in such fields as synthetic biology or nanobiotechnology). In a wider context, either the CBD or the CSD should adopt a permanent agenda item to monitor developments in nano-scale technologies.

Opportunities and Challenges of Biotechnology in Agricultural

Over the past decade, traits developed using modern biotechnology have been introduced into U.S. agricultural commodities including corn, soybeans, cotton, and canola. They have been adopted rapidly by American farmers, and also are being grown by farmers in other countries. The new varieties were intended to provide increased productivity, profitability, and improved environmental management (e.g., reduced pesticide use and expanded conservation tillage).

Most of the new varieties were developed to be incorporated into existing undifferentiated commodities. Genetically engineered traits have been part of a multifaceted biotechnology research milieu in which enhanced breeding, a greater focus on germplasm improvement, and advances in understanding the molecular basis of growth, productivity and disease resistance jointly have led to substantial increases in agricultural productivity. In the United States, these transgenic varieties are largely undifferentiated and fully integrated into commodity markets. In 2005, 52% of corn, 87% of soybeans, and 79% of cotton planted in the United States was genetically engineered, according to the National Agricultural Statistics Service.

In addition, in 2005 transgenic crops were planted globally on about 222 million acres, roughly 5.8% of the estimated 3.8 billion acres devoted to crops. Transgenic varieties thus far in the marketplace have been beneficial to farmers and the environment, but have not provided marketing advantages to food retailers or improved nutrition or taste to attract consumers. In some countries, there have been increased risk management requirements as well as opposition to introduction of the transgenic seed varieties and the foods produced from those crops. Food processors and retailers have been reluctant to introduce food products developed from transgenic crops in markets where there is a requirement for mandatory labeling of food products and/or perceived consumer resistance to genetic engineering technology. The resistance stems in part from some governments' and consumers' perception that there are unknown risks associated with genetically engineered foods and an absence of obvious consumer benefits. The development of new transgenic products, controversies related to such products, varying national requirements, and different consumer preferences have driven numerous market responses, including the development of segregated markets and differentiated product streams (genetically engineered and non-engineered). Other market responses have included regionalized production and ingredient sourcing, new testing methods, new systems for identity preservation and certification, and the development of marketing and risk management tools. AC21's earlier report, entitled, "Global Traceability and Labeling Requirements for Agricultural Biotechnology-Derived Products: Impacts and Implications for the United States," describes in greater detail strategies developed to meet various traceability and labeling requirements.

In Future

It is impossible to predict exactly which new modern biotechnology-derived plants or animals will be ready for the marketplace over the next decade. Some possibilities include:

- Genetically engineered plant varieties that provide improved human nutrition (e.g., soybeans enriched in omega-3 fatty acids);
- Products designed for use in improved animal feeds (providing better nutritional balance by increasing the concentration of essential amino acids often deficient in some feed components, increased nutrient density, or more efficient utilization of nutrients such as phosphate that could provide environmental benefits);
- Crops resistant to drought and other environmental stresses such as salinity;
- Crops resistant to pests and diseases (e.g., fusarium-resistant wheat; chestnut-blight resistant chestnut; plum pox resistance in stone fruit; various insect resistant crops);

- Additional crops containing a number of transgenic traits incorporated in the same plant (stacked traits);
- Crops engineered to produce pharmaceuticals, such as vaccines and antibodies;
- Crops engineered for particular industrial uses (e.g., crops having improved processing attributes such as increased starch content, producing useful enzymes that can be extracted for downstream industrial processes, or modified to have higher content of an energy-rich starting material such as oil for improved utilization as biofuel); and
- Transgenic animals for food, or for production of pharmaceuticals or industrial products (e.g., transgenic salmon engineered for increased growth rate to maturity, transgenic goats producing human serum factors in their milk, and pigs producing the enzyme phytase in their saliva for improved nutrient utilization and manure with reduced phosphorus content).

There are several factors beyond whether a genetically engineered crop or animal can be developed and found efficacious which will help determine whether it is successful as a marketable product. For each such possibility, before any product reaches the marketplace, the federal government must ensure it is safe for human consumption, safe for the environment, and will not adversely affect the food supply. To appropriately manage risk, the government might impose additional measures on developers, farmers, or others throughout the food and feed chain that may affect the economic or technical viability of the product and the realization of potential benefits. AC21 members have diverse views about the appropriate role of plant and animal products derived from modern biotechnology in the food and agricultural marketplace. Members recognize that new products will be entering a world that is very different from the one that existed a decade ago when the first agricultural products of modern biotechnology were introduced:

- Many of the "first-generation" transgenic organisms developed in the United States have now been adopted by farmers in other nations, including developing nations;
- Some of the transgenic plant varieties intended for food use developed over the next few years will likely emerge from the developing world. For example, if transgenic rice varieties (probably insect-resistant varieties) that have been developed in the developing world (e.g., in China or India) are commercialized, this could have a significant impact on the global genetic engineering debate because large populations of humans will be consuming a staple transgenic whole food;
- Some of the "next generation" of transgenic varieties and products may need to be produced under identity preservation conditions or require strict segregation from food or feed product streams;
- Media coverage and public debate have made consumers more aware of genetically engineered products than when the first crops were adopted. Increased awareness along the food and feed chain will continue to influence the acceptance of new products derived from modern biotechnology;
- Genomic information is being used to enable the development of improved crops and animals through both transgenic and non-transgenic approaches;
- National regulatory systems for evaluating the safety of new transgenic products are being developed and

implemented in many countries around the world, eliminating some uncertainties but, in some cases, complicating the path to market;

- Many countries now require mandatory labeling for food products derived from modern biotechnology, and some require traceability of those products throughout the food and feed chain. Food manufacturers who do not want to label their products as containing transgenics are sourcing non-transgenic crops, further segmenting the marketplace;
- U.S. regulations are evolving slowly and many governing statutes were written before modern agricultural biotechnology was developed. That system may not be optimal to meet the needs of producers and consumers.
- The commercialization of a transgenic plant or animal product is affected by considerations beyond the safety of the product. Technical challenges may arise when turning a beneficial trait into a marketable food. New products must gain acceptance by consumers and trading partners;
- Sometimes social and ethical concerns may influence decisions about commercialization. For example, the development of transgenic animals may generate, for some people, higher levels of concern than those for plant breeding;
- Some international agreements specific to modern biotechnology, e.g., the Cartagena Protocol on Biosafety, and standards related to modern biotechnology under Codex Alimentarius, now exist. Additional efforts under these bodies are continuing, but their future outcomes are uncertain;

- There is an ongoing trade dispute over modern biotechnology-derived products between the EU and a number of complainants, including the United States, nearing a final report from the World Trade Organization;
- Technology producers, food producers and processors increasingly recognize the global interdependence of markets and the importance of resolving genetic engineering- related issues;
- With the increased use of genetically engineered organisms, other issues such as testing, liability, coexistence, and intellectual property rights, have emerged.

Achieving AC21's shared vision of a safe and abundant food supply and a diversified agricultural marketplace that can meet the needs and preferences of customers and consumers will require national and international regulatory systems with several characteristics. These characteristics include assurance that the food and feed supply is safe for humans and animals, that the environment is protected, and that the regulatory processes maintain commercial viability of products and engender public trust. An effective international marketplace also requires agreement to and enforcement of fair, clearly defined trading rules. All recognize that achieving the vision will be a worthwhile but not an easy endeavor. AC21 has discussed a number of topics that some or all members believe are relevant to USDA's efforts to adapt to this changing world and ensure that American agricultural products, including current and future transgenic products, remain competitive in the global marketplace. The following are brief descriptions of those topics, some of which were discussed at considerable length by the AC21. While none of these descriptions completely captures the extent and richness of committee discussions on the topics, the Committee is willing to provide further information to the Secretary on any that are of particular interest.

The extent of domestic and global adoption of transgenic crops has influenced, and may increasingly influence, U.S. producers and agricultural production patterns. The adoption of genetically engineered corn, soybeans, cotton and canola has influenced cropping patterns in the United States. The availability of genetically engineered crops is one of the major factors affecting production of other crops for which transgenic varieties are not currently commercially available. For example, a recent North Dakota State University study[3] suggests that availability of genetically engineered corn and soybeans, along with other variables, has corresponded with an increase in acres planted to those crops in the Dakotas and Minnesota, replacing acres planted to wheat. Adoption of transgenic crops in other countries, including Argentina and Brazil, also has contributed to changes in cropping patterns in the United States. Such changes could have important implications on market access, food security, research programs, biodiversity and competitiveness.

Farmer demand has become a driver for the continued development of new agricultural traits derived from modern biotechnology because benefits have been delivered to the production segment of the food and feed chain. Since the first commercial transgenic crop traits were introduced in the United States, herbicide tolerant crops and insect protected (Bt) crops have generated substantial production benefits including: improved soil conservation through enhanced use of no-till or minimal tillage systems; lowered pesticide use; improved flexibility and ease in pest management, which has been documented in at least one instance to result in greater net returns for farmers; and improved crop quality of Bt corn in those cases where decreased insect damage leads to decreased fungal damage and reduced levels of natural mycotoxins. Most farmers who have grown transgenic crops anticipate growing varieties containing new traits. This demand will help drive the development of new traits. However, some farmers believe that there are downsides to modern biotechnology and that similar benefits can be attained through other methods.

Crops with energy specific traits may be developed to help meet the growing demand for renewable alternative fuels. Currently, commodity crops (e.g., corn and soybeans), a substantial portion of which are genetically engineered for agronomic purposes, are being increasingly used for energy. In the future, genetic engineering could be employed to engineer traits in both food and non-food crops (e.g., grasses and trees) that specifically relate to energy production. The large scale production of such energy crops could have tremendous implications for U.S. agricultural systems. As with other genetically engineered crops, all regulatory and safety issues must be addressed before commercialization. Bioenergy uses will be visible to consumers and their scale alone could raise concerns for them, although meeting bioenergy needs using genetically engineered crops could be seen by consumers as a benefit as well.

The private sector provides most of the funding for research and development of new genetically engineered crops, and this funding is largely directed toward major crops that offer a substantial return on the research investment. Privately funded research and private sector development of genetically engineered crops are driven by potential profitability. Publicly funded research aimed at development of new varieties has remained static over the past several years. As a result, crops that do not appear to offer substantial market returns are deprived of adequate research funding and are not able to attract research personnel. Advances through biotechnology could provide improvements in some specialty crops, including forest trees, vegetables and fruits, yielding public benefits, if adequate research funding were available.

The application of modern biotechnology to specialty crops continues to be limited by the cost of product development and the unique characteristics of specialty crops. Nearly all of the genetically engineered crops currently on the market are major commodity crops such as corn, soybean, and cotton as opposed to "specialty crops" (a term defined by Congress to mean "fruits, vegetables, tree nuts, dried fruits, and nursery crops [including floriculture]"). The public could potentially benefit from modern biotechnology-derived innovation of specialty crops, but the extent of commercialization of transgenic specialty crop is currently limited by multiple characteristics. Those characteristics include, but are not limited to, the small market size of specialty crops, access to intellectual property, acceptable return on investment, unique or individual biological characteristics of specialty crops, the dynamics of the marketplace, and other commercial challenges.

There is a need for more publicly sponsored data collection and peer-reviewed analyses on the use and broad impacts of transgenic organisms. Such data and analyses should be publicly available. USDA has a unique role in collecting primary data and providing information to the public in a fair, understandable, and factual way. Relevant topics include not only environmental impacts (e.g., on pesticide use patterns, pest resistance management, soil loss, etc.), but also social and economic impacts (e.g., on net farm income, distribution of benefits, economic opportunities, etc.). USDA also has an important role in encouraging external, independent peer-reviewed analyses of the data it gathers.

Some of the gene manipulation technologies that are

being employed or are under development may produce organisms that are not regulated by the U.S. government under the current biotechnology regulatory framework or may require development of new assessment methodologies. Some technologies to remove, mutate or silence the expression of particular genes arguably do not produce "transgenic" organisms. In addition, new transgenic organisms may result in substantially different types of products than have thus far been reviewed by U.S. regulatory agencies. In either case, some of these organisms may not be regulated under the current regulatory system, while others may require new or modified regulatory assessment methodologies or may pose challenges for the traditional boundaries of agency responsibility. As a result, this new generation of biotechnologies may influence the debate on genetic engineering.

There are concerns that food crops genetically engineered to produce medical or industrial products never intended for food or feed use could inadvertently end up in a food or feed product. New genetically engineered organisms designed for medical and industrial markets could offer substantial health and economic benefits. There are a number of new products under active development in these categories, and some of those being produced in plants have been engineered for production using important food crops. Consumers generally do not want such substances in their food. One group of committee members believes that the federal government should not approve the use of food crops for the production of medical and industrial substances, even if the substances are deemed safe, because no regulatory process or containment system can assure that these products will never enter the food supply. Other committee members believe that adequate regulatory oversight of crops producing medical or industrial products utilizing a tiered risk-based approach can ensure the safety and integrity of the food and feed supply. These members believe that at small scale, complete segregation from food products can be ensured by a combination of physical and biological containment strategies. As scale or potential risk increases, food safety assessment may be required in addition to stringent containment procedures. Still another group prefers the use of non-food crops for such products. They believe that, if food crops are to be used, it is impossible to guarantee the absolute absence of such substances in the food supply. Therefore, in their view, no food crop should be used without thorough regulatory review of food safety and the establishment of stringent safeguards to prevent intermingling with the food supply. For the last two groups, the Federal government's ability to successfully address the issues of containment and public confidence in that containment system remains critical for the development of these products.

There is no clear, comprehensive federal regulatory system to assess the environmental and food safety of transgenic animals before they are commercialized. The next generation of genetically engineered products will include transgenic animals developed for food and non-food purposes. The federal government has not clearly indicated how and under which laws and regulations transgenic animals will be regulated. The Office of Science and Technology Policy (OSTP) published a package of regulatory case studies in 2001, one of which described a prospective pathway for the regulation of transgenic salmon using FDA's "new animal drug" authorities under the Federal Food Drug and Cosmetic Act. FDA indicated in that case study that it "...intends to publish draft guidance on how the new animal drug provisions of the FFDCA pertain to transgenic animals, and on procedures by which companies developing transgenic animals can comply with those provisions." However, the government has issued no further guidance on the scope or implementation of such a policy. If FDA's new animal drug regulatory process is used to regulate transgenic animals, there are concerns about the lack of transparency and public participation in the process. There are also concerns about whether FDA has adequate legal authority to assess and address the full range of environmental risks that could arise. In 2003, USDA indicated that it was reviewing whether it might have the legal authority to regulate certain transgenic animals. As research involving transgenic animals moves toward commercialization, a credible, appropriate and transparent federal regulatory framework applicable to genetically engineered food and non-food animals is increasingly important.

There is no comprehensive domestic policy regarding adventitious presence of transgenic events in seed, grain, or food. In the context of modern plant biotechnology, adventitious presence (AP) refers to unintentional, low levels of transgenic material (or a specific transgenic event) in seed, grain, or food and feed products. AP can arise from transgenic organisms that have satisfactorily completed all regulatory procedures or those that have not. Such adventitious presence can result in regulatory, contractual, and/or consumer issues. Although federal policies address some aspects of AP, the federal government has not set forth comprehensive policies, guidelines, or standards regarding the adventitious presence of transgenic events.

The concerns of some people about genetically engineered products are not addressed by a regulatory system designed to assess and manage health and safety risks. In addition to safety, some people consider other factors in their food purchasing decisions. They also may be concerned with a product's origins and whether the foods are "wholesome," "pure" or "natural." Some consumers may raise moral or ethical issues about certain products. As one example, some find the genetic engineering of animals to be ethically problematic and may object to the presence of meat and milk from these animals if they enter the food supply. These concerns may continue to impact the marketplace and, if so, may influence the development and acceptance of aspects of modern agricultural biotechnology.

Transparency in the regulatory system is important for stakeholders including the consuming public, in the United States and around the world, to have confidence in the safety of genetically engineered organisms. Transparency enables the public to learn about, and gain access to key information on the regulatory requirements established to ensure food, feed, and environmental safety of new products. In a transparent system, organizations and individuals would have the ability to gain timely access to information about the regulatory process and to the safety information submitted in support of new products. In addition, the public would have information about the basis for federal regulatory actions and the regulatory systems and structures from which they derive, and would be able to comment on proposed actions. Although aspects of the federal regulatory system have been very transparent, other portions could improve in this area.

The success of some future food products derived from transgenic plants or animals will be influenced by whether food processors and retailers embrace these products. Their purchasing decisions will, in turn, be influenced by whether customers and consumers perceive that the resulting genetically engineered food products provide value to them. Most transgenic crops currently on the market were developed primarily for advantages they confer on productivity and agricultural management. They have produced some environmental benefits. However, there are no foods now on the market that use genetically engineered traits to provide retail consumers with improved quality, nutrition or particular safety benefits, such as reduced pathogens or allergenicity. There are some such products under development, although the appeal of these products for consumers is difficult to assess and anticipate. Polling data indicate a wide variety of responses to questions regarding genetically engineered food, complicating assessment of consumer response to future transgenic products. Typically, consumers' choices on product purchases involve a diverse array of considerations including not only price, convenience, safety, and nutrition, but taste, familiarity, appearance, wholesomeness and in some cases, considerations of morality and ethics. Many future transgenic products may be major components of foods or may in themselves constitute a whole food. Products designed to offer consumer-specific improvements, such as improved nutrition or health benefits, may also be more visible and therefore potentially more controversial. Food processors and retailers are responsive to consumer preferences and are likely to play an increasing role in determining whether, when and how such new products reach the marketplace.

While all AC21 members agree that ensuring the food and feed safety of transgenic crops is important, members differ in their views about whether the current FDA regulatory system for transgenic crops is adequate to ensure safety and public acceptance. For foods and feeds derived from transgenic crops, FDA employs a voluntary consultative process to review safety data. While FDA does not require pre-market approval of these products, FDA does require pre-market approval of food additives regardless of method of production. In considering this system, some AC21 members have noted that all foods from biotechnology-derived plants that are on the market today have successfully completed the FDA's pre-market consultation process and that the same safety standards apply to all foods regardless of their source, so that the consultation process mirrors the voluntary process widely used by the food industry to notify FDA prior to marketing new conventionally-produced substances that are "generally recognized as safe." The submissions reviewed by FDA scientists under the consultation process provide the basis for the developer's conclusion that the food is as safe as conventionally-produced counterpart foods and may lawfully proceed to market. The biotechnology and food industries understand that, although the FDA consultation process is technically voluntary, marketing a food from a biotechnology-derived plant without completing a consultation with FDA is simply not a viable commercial option, making the FDA process effectively mandatory. These members support making this consultation process mandatory. Other AC21 members believe the Federal government needs to establish a mandatory pre-market approval process for transgenic crops eaten by humans and animals. They note that those crops receive such treatment in virtually every developed country where such crops are marketed. With the next generation of transgenic crops poised to include more scientifically complex products as well as crops developed in other countries and imported into the United States, a regulatory system that provides mandatory pre-market assessment for environmental and agricultural concerns related to those crops but not a similar food safety assessment is not protective of the public that will consume those crops. These members further note that, when informed that there is no mandatory pre-market safety approval for foods regulated by FDA, most Americans respond that they are unaware and that they would be more inclined to accept the foods if there were such a process.

AC21 members have different points of view regarding how strongly consumers feel about having information about whether their food is genetically engineered and whether the food should be labeled as such. AC21 members agree that consumers are interested in having access to more information about their food and that, food issues are more visible and discussed more frequently. The first group thinks that American consumers have a fundamental right to know about the origin and makeup of ingredients in their food. Having information about whether foods are, or are derived from, genetically engineered organisms included on the label would allow consumers to choose to purchase or avoid those products without being restricted to limited or higher priced options. The EU and other governments require such information on labels and members of this group do not understand why US consumers should not also get that information. In addition, these members believe that consumers are more likely to be uncomfortable with or opposed to some future genetically engineered products, especially milk and meat derived from transgenic animals. Unlike the first generation of products that have been largely invisible because virtually all are used as animal feed or ingredients in processed foods, future modifications may be more controversial. For example, even if consumers accept that genetically engineered animals are safe, they may want to avoid them because they have moral or religious objections to altering sentient animals. These members believe màndatory labeling of products of modern biotechnology is the middle ground: allowing such products to come to market but making it possible for consumers to avoid products they oppose. Other AC21 members believe consumer interest is not focused on whether food products are derived through agricultural biotechnology or contain genetically engineered ingredients. They assert that those consumers who do have an interest in whether products are developed from genetic engineering, have multiple means of finding this information, including the Internet, calling the company and other avenues. Some specialty or niche markets have been developed for those consumers who want to avoid these products. Consumer preference can be addressed by market driven voluntary labeling that provides truthful, non-misleading and verifiable information to consumers and allow market forces to operate. These members also believe that the majority of American consumers are primarily interested in food quality, safety and cost. To mandate labeling of products generally has led to avoidance of such ingredients, reformulation of food products and limited choice in the marketplace. They also believe that mandatory labeling would send the wrong message regarding safety of these products – potentially and erroneously confusing consumers.

Public ballot or legislative initiatives at the state and/ or local level in the United States to establish moratoria on certain uses of transgenic organisms or to regulate them will lead to regulatory differences across the country and will impact the use of these products. Regulation of genetically engineered agricultural products is a role that has been filled primarily by the federal government. Recent initiatives have been launched in certain states and counties seeking to regulate locally the commercial use of transgenic plants or animals. Some members believe that local regulation is not necessary in light of federal regulation and think that a potential patchwork of additional regulations will significantly increase costs throughout the system, impede commerce, deny choice, and slow the development of new products. Other members think that state and local involvement with the regulation of transgenic organisms is a reaction to inadequate federal regulation and may lead to greater safety, increased information to the public, a more transparent and participatory regulatory process and a regulatory system that is more responsive to the public's concern.

As transgenic organisms developed in other countries and products made from them are imported into the United States, it is important to have adequate U.S. regulatory systems in place to address their safety. U.S. regulations and procedures for evaluation of an increasing number of imported transgenic crops and their products into the United States must ensure their food, feed, and environmental safety and be implemented and enforced in a manner that maintains confidence in the U.S. food and feed system. In addition, when imports of agricultural products are allowed from countries developing and approving new transgenic events, a new potential consideration is raised: the adequacy of the U.S. regulatory system to address adventitious presence (AP) of events that have not completed all applicable regulatory procedures in the United States.

Managing the coexistence of different agricultural products and production methods intended to meet different market specifications has become more complex with the emergence of genetically engineered crops. Commingling of different classes of conventional crops (e.g., yellow corn in a white corn shipment) has been addressed for many years in the marketplace through tolerances, title transfers, and testing. Currently, rules and procedures appropriate to address commingling of genetically engineered crops with other crops are evolving in the marketplace. The use of Identity Preservation (IdP) systems, including those for organic production methods and genetically engineered plant varieties, is expanding. These systems enable producers to participate in new value-added markets, some of which depend on the ability of producers to achieve high standards of purity. This has resulted in questions as to which party should bear responsibility for managing production practices, defining the specifications for different products, and assuring the level of crop purity in different systems.

Commercial differentiation between conventional and transgenic agricultural products is creating opportunities and challenges for the U.S. marketing system. The current U.S. commodity handling system is extremely efficient at managing commodity streams segregated by distinct functional characteristics as long as there are commercially-viable tolerances for off-types and AP. Segregation of transgenic products that do not have distinct functional characteristics may be difficult. The cost, complexity, and time involved in differentiating between transgenic and non-transgenic products increase when contractual specifications detail stringent segregation requirements.

To reduce the commercial risks associated with supplying grain and grain products based on transgenic testing results, improved standards for testing and common sampling methods are required to address issues associated with such tests. Many of the currently available testing methods to detect transgenic traits in numerous crops, plants and foods, are not accepted internationally and have not been validated based on international standards. The commercial risk associated with providing grain and grain products based on transgenic testing results could be reduced if international organizations would foster the development of mutually recognized reference materials, validated method performance criteria, and common sampling protocols that reflect the test method being applied, the material being tested, and any specified detection levels.

Adventitious presence remains a significant trading issue internationally for the food and feed supply chain. Adventitious presence of transgenic varieties in commodities for food or feed use can occur with transgenic events not yet approved in export markets, events unapproved in all markets, or events present in conventionally sourced specialty programs. The development of country-specific AP policies that do not encompass considerations of international trade is unlikely to satisfactorily resolve trade issues. Development of global, commercially viable AP policies that also ensure food, feed and environmental safety might minimize trade disruptions in the food and feed supply chain. The adoption of different approaches to AP by different countries hinders the flow of food and feed products and exposes trade to shipment rejections and substantial costs. Situations in which no AP of a particular transgenic event is allowed carry the risk that even after multiple tests at origin have tested negative, a subsequent positive test at destination may place a shipment out of compliance. This is an important and complicated issue requiring input from a broad range of interested stakeholders.

The emergence of markets that seek only non-transgenic products has introduced a new level of commercial risk, creating additional liability and insurance implications for some participants in the food/feed chain. Certain insurance companies have exclusions in their policies for claims arising from the presence of transgenic material. This creates uncertainty as to which agents in the food and feed chain will bear the liability for a transgenic-related claim. Additionally, the rules for apportioning liability along the food/feed chain are still evolving in certain situations: (1) when shipments tested at origin meet transgenic specifications but then test outside transgenic specifications at destination; and (2) when transgenic trait testing is imposed under commercial contracts for products produced under an identity-preserved process providing a verification "paper trail."

As more transgenic events become commercially available and enter the global marketplace, the issue of asynchronous approvals will become increasingly important. Trade of modern biotechnology derived crops commercialized in the U.S. and other countries has encountered obstacles stemming from asynchronous regulatory approvals. Asynchrony of regulatory approvals will continue in some cases to affect market access and the acceptance and adoption of crops and products derived from modern biotechnology. Resolving how the marketplace addresses events that have satisfactorily completed regulatory procedures in some countries but not others and are present in commodity food and feed or present in conventionally-sourced specialty products is important. The market impact of asynchronous approvals may be reduced through the development of commercially viable thresholds for AP in food and feed markets.

Other governments' moratoria on allowing the entry of new transgenic crops or *de facto* moratoria on reaching decisions on such crops are limiting the ability of the United States to sell those transgenic crops and other commingled varieties. Market access for transgenic varieties and derived products that have completed U.S. regulatory review is required for those goods to reach a broad cross-section of users, including consumers. However, some governments, such as those in the European Union, have effectively prevented trade in some products through *de facto* moratoria on approvals of particular transgenic varieties. Such moratoria can affect not only the import or growing of transgenic varieties, but also the import and use of the wider range of derived food and feed ingredients. The existence of such moratoria is a disincentive for the commercialization of new transgenic varieties and even for trade with some other nations without moratoria. Some members believe that the incorporation of political or socioeconomic criteria into some nations' regulatory evaluation processes, as has been done in Argentina and South Africa, are factors that could also inhibit the development and deployment of potentially useful new crops. Other members believe that conditioning regulatory decisions based on social and economic considerations is a legitimate exercise of sovereign authority. These members see no evidence that socioeconomic considerations within the regulatory process have prevented a transgenic crop from being commercialized and believe there are ways that those issues can be addressed by those governments without impacting trade from the United States. Addressing these barriers for transgenic crops and derived products will directly impact trade, technology advancement, and diffusion.

As new transgenic organisms are developed in the United States and enter the international marketplace, US embassy staff will be approached with questions about the safety of those organisms and how they are regulated in the United States. Increasingly, the questions that arise regarding new transgenic organisms require detailed knowledge, but U.S. officials with the appropriate expertise are not always available at embassies to answer questions about the safety of those organisms and the U.S. regulatory system. Science officers and agricultural attaches who serve as primary conduits for information between foreign interests and domestic experts are typically generalists who may have neither the time nor the specialized training to adequately answer questions about transgenic organisms. Continued prominence of modern biotechnology in agricultural developments in the United States will lead to further questions to embassy staff regarding biotechnology and products of biotechnology, placing increasing claims on embassy priorities, knowledge and expertise.

The least developed countries often lack capacity to

address scientific and regulatory issues related to modern biotechnology. The least developed countries are formulating national biosafety regulatory systems to address organisms developed through modern biotechnology, but they often lack sufficient capacity to address many of the relevant scientific and regulatory issues. There is an ongoing need to provide them with assistance to develop their regulatory systems. If countries have their own trained scientists, technical experts, and policymakers, they will be able to make informed decisions, about both policy options and the safety of individual organisms and products. The United States participates in capacity-building efforts in these areas, but there are also vital roles for international organizations. USDA has a role to play in encouraging effective and appropriate efforts.

Protection of intellectual property (IP), in key international markets and elsewhere, is essential for the capture of sufficient product value to justify and recoup costs of developing and marketing transgenic organisms. The cost of developing and marketing new transgenic varieties is substantial. Other costs are likely to mount as new varieties increasingly require the assembly of IP from multiple sources and as gaining access to such IP becomes increasingly complex. Recouping costs for new product development depends on effective IP protection, nationally and internationally. The ability and/or willingness of foreign governments to protect IP associated with transgenic varieties have been highly variable. For some markets and uses, IP protection is likely to be ineffective or non-existent in the foreseeable future. Nonetheless, the overall level of IP protection internationally and the effectiveness of U.S. efforts to promote adherence to IP standards by other nations will influence technology transfer and investments in developing and in some cases marketing new transgenic crop and animal varieties.

Humanitarian use licenses are important for the transfer of transgenic technologies and transgenic plant and animal varieties to the poorest, most food-insecure nations. It is sometimes difficult to secure all the necessary licenses for these transfers. Future transgenic crop and animal varieties, especially those intended for humanitarian uses, are likely to involve an increasingly complex mixture of intellectual property from many sources, both public and private. The priorities and attitudes of IP holders towards contributing to humanitarian use licenses vary.

Genetically Modified Watermetions: A Case Study

Questions abound regarding the safety of genetically manipulated agricultural products. These questions and concerns are usually focused on laboratory or "genetically engineered" products and not those developed through traditional plant breeding technologies involving the manipulation of traits using hand pollination. While selective breeding and the production of food by microorganisms have been around for thousands of years, some people may find it mysterious or worrisome to move genetic material from one cell into another cell that may also be derived from a different species. Some of their questions range from concerns about allergic reactions, protecting the environment, the transfer of antibiotic resistance from one species to another, to fears about reducing the amount of biodiversity in the world.

The Environmental Protection Agency (EPA), the US Department of Agriculture (USDA) and the Federal Drug Adminisitration (FDA) all have regulations that impact agricultural biotechnology. Which agency or agencies are involved depends on the type of technology used. An introduction of new genetic material into a different species will likely involve additional restrictions and pre-market testing than does the use of more traditional methods such as selective breeding. Most of these regulations relate to genetically engineered materials where genes from one cell have been inserted to create a new variety. Field testing for new varieties produced by selective pollination are not usually required to demonstrate consumer safety. The U.S. Department of Agriculture (USDA) and the Environmental Protection Agency (EPA) have the roles of imposing safety regulations and/or performance standards for pesticides, herbicides and genetically engineered crops. An example is the insertion of genetic material into plants to convey resistant to the herbicide, Roundup®(Monsanto). Roundup® can be sprayed on fields to eliminate weeds and other unwanted plants while not affecting the desired crop.

Genetically Modified Lactic Acid Bacteria: A Case Study

Ever since human domestication took place approximately 10,000 years ago, parts of our food supply have been cultured in order to support survival of the human population. In our current times, the main objectives of agriculture are still the same, the assurance of efficient food supply in the first place, and the increase of quality of the supplied foods for the consumer in the second place. Modern biotechnology, using recombinant DNA technology, offers ample opportunities to further improve food production in the expanding world of today. Within the United States of America there is not much public resistance towards the use of genetically modified organisms, GMOs, in food. However, in other areas of the world, for instance Oceania and Europe, the production of novel foods using GMOs is subject to strong debate.

For example, within the European Union the scientific community states that there is sufficient legislation to guarantee that such novel foods are safe for the consumer and the environment, but green groups in many cases state an opposite opinion. The support for the use of GM crops and foods among the European population has recently increased in some countries. Yet at the same time a majority of Europeans do not support agri-food biotechnology (Gaskell et al. 2003). In the current debate about the application and safety of GMOs in the food industry no clear distinction is made between GMOs derived from animal, plant, or microbial origin. Moreover, ethical aspects could play a role in the debate about GMOs from animal or plant origins, but these are considered less relevant in the discussion about genetically modified micro-organisms. Apart from this, the current European legislation on novel foods and the use of GMOs in food production processes, as laid down in the regulation EC No 258/97, amended in regulation 1829/2003, directive 2001/18/EC (revised directive 90/220/EC), directive 90/219/EC, and Commission Recommendation 97/618/EC, generates a framework for what should and what should not be permitted by law. The legislation, however, is not yet completely clear on a number of important scientific matters. First of all, the legislation predominantly focuses on the methodology rather than on the end product and hence, holds too strongly to the definition of GMOs. Consequently, organisms in which the genetic material has been altered by recombinant DNA techniques in a way that does occur naturally, for instance by point mutations or small deletions, are considered to be GMOs. Secondly, foods with a new structure which date from before 1997 are not considered as novel foods. Thirdly, self cloning (Box 2) of non-pathogenic micro-organisms is not considered to lead to a GMO as long as containment of the organism is guaranteed (directive 90/219/EC).

However, the same self-cloned micro-organism when used in products (deliberate release) is considered to be a

GMO (directive 2001/18/EC). Moreover, the market introduction of foods with organisms that have been improved via classical breeding or random mutagenesis is currently acceptable without profound safety analysis[1], but it could be questioned whether these foods are more safe than GMO-derived novel foods. The new regulation 1829/2003 (amending 258/97) regulates the approval and the labelling, and distinguishes between products from GMO, and products which are produced with help of GMO. Foods, ingredients, additives, flavours as well as feedstuffs, which contained or are GMO, or which were produced from GMO are in the scope of the regulations. The labelling of these products is also process-oriented. Products produced with help of GMO are not in the scope of the regulations. It is still unclear if the regulations can be applied on the use of GMO (micro-organisms) within fermentation (Jany and Schuh, 2005). The rationale for food safety regulations is the assurance to prevent any adverse effects on human health or on the environment. The starting point for a food safety approach is the comparison between the new foods and the conventional counterparts that have a history of safe use, both for the food produced and for the micro-organism that is modified. This approach leads to identification of new or altered hazards relative to the conventional counterpart (substantial equivalence, Box 3) is essential (OECD, 1993).

This document will analyse the current situation within Europe with regard to the safe use of novel foods derived from genetically modified lactic acid bacteria (GM-LAB). The application and safety assessment of genetically modified yeast and fungi are not discussed; neither is the use of GMOs derived from plants (Kuiper et al. 2001) or animals. Genetically modified microbial inoculants for use in agriculture, such as biological control agents, biofertilisers, or phytostimulators is reviewed elsewhere (Amarge, 2002;

Morrissey et al. 2002). An overview will be given of the specific genetic techniques that generate GM-LAB and the advantages that the novel foods fermented with GM-LAB may bring to the consumer or the producer. Moreover, the current safety assessment procedures are considered and further suggestions are made for an adequate risk analysis when GM-LAB are applied in food production. Careful analysis of the properties of GM-LAB combined with a profound safety assessment procedure for foods that are produced through the actions of GM-LAB, are essential for comparing the safety of such products with traditional foods. Finally, based upon the principle of assuring food safety for the consumer, it could be argued to make no distinction between foods produced by LAB that have been altered in an uncontrolled way, for instance by random mutagenesis, or a more directed way, such as GM-LAB. This could imply that all foods fermented by LAB should be subjected to a safety assessment procedure, before commercialisation can occur. Recently, such issues have been considered for non-GM-LAB in a draft document introducing the concept of Qualified Presumption of Safety (QPS), which will be discussed below (EU, 2003). Furthermore, we will examine the value of the principle of a long and safe history of use of traditionally used LAB and discuss whether this could be a starting point for the acceptance of GM-LAB.

Lactic Acid Bacteria and Genetic Engineering

LAB have a long history of use by man for food production and food preservation. LAB are Gram-positive, non-spore forming bacteria and naturally present in raw food material and in the human gastro-intestinal tract. The heterogeneous group of LAB includes the rod-shaped bacteria like lactobacilli, and cocci such as streptococci, lactococci, pediococci and leuconostocs. LAB are widely used as starter cultures for fermentation in the dairy, meat and other food industries.

Their properties have been used to manufacture products like cheese, yoghurts, fermented milk products, beverages, sausages, and olives. These food-grade bacteria can also improve the safety, shelf life, nutritional value, flavour and quality of the product. Moreover, LAB can be used as cell factories for the production of food additives and aroma compounds. It is further assumed that LAB may function as probiotics and contribute to the general health of the consumer upon consumption. The use of probiotics falls currently within a grey area between food and medicine and many health claims assigned to probiotics are not yet scientifically proven.Another application - the use of LAB in the production of proteins for application in health care or for development of new vaccines (Mercenier et al. 2000) – is more related to pharma than to food. In the future it is predicted that knowledge about the interaction between LAB and the human host will open new avenues for developing LAB which support human health. The uncontrolled genetic alterations of LAB that occur during random mutagenesis may lead to strains with improved traits. These may be either attractive for the manufacturer of fermented foods, or have benefits for the consumer. Both directed and uncontrolled genetic alterations result in a change of the genetic code of the micro-organism that may affect the transcription and translation processes and, consequently, may influence metabolic processes in the cell. However, it seems that in the current legislation regarding the use of GMOs in food industry, the nature of the DNA modification could dictate the necessity for the novel food product to be subjected to a safety assessment procedure.

Uncontrolled Genetically Altered LAB

Spontaneous mutations may occur in LAB by natural events such as insertion sequence elements (Visser et al. 2004), radiation, erroneous DNA replication or transcription, and other factors. The level of such mutations depends upon the growth conditions. By screening of natural isolates of LAB, strains with improved fermentation characteristics can be selected. The frequency of mutations can be further increased by exposing LAB to mutagenic conditions such as UV light or chemicals like N-methyl-N'-nitro-N-nitrosoguanidine (NNG), or ethyl methyl sulphonate. Specific screening for desired traits may result in the identification of new strains with improved utility for the food industry.

Examples of LAB Selected After Uncontrolled Genetic Alterations

Selection of strains that have been subjected to uncontrolled genetic alterations is used in the dairy industry to improve certain intrinsic characteristics of the fermented end product, like flavour, structure, nutritional value, or phage resistance. Spontaneous mutations in single genes can lead to altered lactose metabolism, citrate uptake, and increased proteolytic activity. In *Lactobacillus bulgaricus* a spontaneous insertion sequence (IS) element-mediated deletion of the *lacZ* gene altered lactose metabolism resulting in limited fermentation capacity. As a consequence, yoghurt, made with these altered *L. bulgaricus*, is not suffering from post-fermentation acidification during the shelf life period (Mollet and Delley, 1990). A gene inactivation method for several lactic acid bacteria has been described that is mediated via IS elements that may integrate into a gene, resulting in inhibition of function (Maguin et al. 1996). According to current legislation, however, strains with inactivated genes obtained by this latter IS-based strategy are considered to be GMOs. *L. lactis* strains that are involved in the fermentation of Roquefort cheeses were randomly mutated, and selection was based on carbon dioxide production that improves the quality of the cheese (El Attar et al. 2000). In a similar way LAB defective in lactate production, but with increased production levels of the butter flavour compound diacetyl were selected after random mutagenesis with the mutagen NNG (Boumerdassi et al. 1997). The selection of a spontaneously mutated *L. lactis* strain that overproduced diacetyl, responsible for the butter flavour in many fresh dairy products, is described by Monnet et al. 2000. A stronger and more direct selection procedure was applied by the temporarily introduction of a plasmid that generates valine prototrophy in the bacterium (Curic et al. 1999). After selection of the desired mutation in the *aldB* gene, encoding a-acetolactate decarboxylase, the plasmid was removed, leading to strain that did not contain any foreign DNA. Nevertheless, under the actual EU legislation this strain is still considered as a GMO after release in the environment (Henriksen et al. 1999). This last case is a perfect example of possible inconsistencies in the current legislation. The nutritional value of fermented foods can also be improved by (over)production of healthy components, like vitamins, in the fermenting bacteria. To increase vitamin B2 (riboflavin) production levels in the dairy starter bacterium *L. lactis*, bacterial cells were exposed to increasing concentrations of roseoflavin. This resulted in the selection of a roseoflavin-resistant strain with deregulated riboflavin biosynthesis and increased production levels of riboflavin, up to 1 mg/L.

Food products obtained from fermentation with this modified *L. lactis* will contribute strongly to the daily recommended intake (DRI) of 1.3 mg for riboflavin. Partial analysis of the genome of this mutant revealed a mutation in a supposed regulatory sequence just upstream of the first gene of the riboflavin gene cluster (Burgess et al. 2003). LAB can also be selected for the removal of undesirable compounds from raw food materials. In traditional yoghurt fermentation, the undesirable sugar lactose is degraded only partially. One of the degradation products is galactose which may be harmful for people suffering from galactosemia and which also may cause cataract problems (Liu et al. 1998). Vaughan describes the selection of spontaneous galactose-fermenting mutants of *Streptococcus thermophilus*, that contain up-mutations in the *gal* operon and that may assist in removal of undesired galactose from the food matrix (Vaughan et al. 2001). The selection of a double mutant strain of *L. lactis* with an inactivated glucose uptake system deficient in glucokinase could also reduce the concentrations of lactose and galactose during fermentation. Moreover, this strain could also be used as natural sweetener due to the excretion of the undegradable lactose moiety glucose (Thompson et al. 1985).

Controlled Genetic Alteration of LAB

An alternative for random mutagenesis is targeted or directed modification of the DNA. Renault (2002) has evaluated the potential benefit to society and the possible risks associated with the use of genetically modified lactic acid bacteria in food and health applications. It was concluded that risk assessment and expected benefits will determine the future use of modified bacteria in the domains of food technology and health. Controlled genetic modifications vary from single base pair substitutions, mutations, insertions of genes into the chromosomes, or removal of DNA from the chromosome (deletions) resulting in inactivation of specific enzymes.

According to the current legislation, all such directed genetic alterations lead to strains that are considered as GMOs, except for strains obtained by self-cloning, transduction and conjugation. A variety of techniques has been developed to generate GM-LAB, such as cloning systems, chromosome modification systems and expression systems (de Vos, 1999). The most popular transformation system for generating directed genetic alterations in LAB is electroporation with self-replicating vectors. Alternative systems are conjugation and transduction (Gasson, 1990). Besides efficient cloning systems, adequate expression systems have been developed allowing the controlled expression of homologous and heterologous genes. Controlled constitutive expression is possible by using a system of synthetic promoters (Solem and Jensen, 2002), whereas a nisin induced controlled expression system (NICE) allows the gradual over expression of genes (Kleerebezem et al. 1997). Other systems are controlled by promoters based on sugar utilisation, e.g. the lactose operon promoter (Payne et al. 1996), by presence of salt, *e.g. gadC* promoter (Sanders et al. 1997), pH decrease (Madsen et al. 1999), or temperature up-shifts (Nauta et al. 1997) (reviewed by de Vos, 1999). Targeted gene replacement or removal and inactivation of genes can also be applied via (non-replicating) vectors using the natural event of crossing-over during cell division and DNA replication (Leenhouts et al. 1996). Compared to the use of replicating vectors in GM-LAB that result in new or enhanced cellular behaviour, the deletion of genes after double cross-over events (by using a non replicating plasmid) does not result in the addition of any DNA to the genetic content of the cell.

A specific aspect related to the application of vectors in industrial strain improvement is the use of selection markers. The use of antibiotic resistance markers might result in transfer of antibiotic resistance from one organism to another. As a consequence, the practical value of antibiotics that are used for human health or in veterinary practice will be severely reduced. Hence, food-grade resistance markers are preferred. Currently there are many food-grade selection markers for vector cloning in LAB. For instance, transfer of the á-galactosidase gene (*aga*) and a gene coding for a putative transcriptional regulator from the LacI/GalR family (*galR*) of *Lactococcus raffinolactis* ATCC 43920 into *L. lactis* and *Pediococcus acidilactici* strains modifies the sugar fermentation profile from melibiose negative (Mel(-)) to melibiose positive (Mel(+)) (Boucher et al. 2002). A similar food-grade vector is based on complementation of the lactose operon in *L. lactis* NZ3600 or *L. casei* by introduction of *lacF*, or *lacG,* respectively, enabling growth on lactose (MacCormick et al. 1995; Platteeuw et al. 1996, Takala et al. 2003). An alternative system is based on a suppressor tRNA allowing growth in milk of a purine auxotrophic strain (Dickely et al. 1995). A newly developed food-grade marker is characterised by the requirement of D-alanine in the medium to enable growth of the micro-organisms (Bron et al. 2004). An overview of general strategies for constructing food-grade markers has previously been reported (de Vos, 1999). As mentioned before, the current use of these food-grade markers if constructed via self-cloning techniques is restricted to applications with contained use. Other targeted modifications of the genetic content of DNA may occur via conjugation and transduction (Gasson, 1990). These processes are considered natural events. According to the current legislation, bacteria that are changed by using these transfer systems are not considered as GMOs.

Examples of GM-LAB Engineered Via Directed Genetic Alterations

Directed mutagenesis is widely applied in research to improve fermented food products. The following paragraphs will provide an overview of successful examples of metabolic engineering aimed at the improvement of certain characteristics of food products, like flavour, structure, shelf life, nutritional value, or product performance in general. A schematic overview of GM-LAB. The flavour and flavour stability of buttermilk was improved by inactivation of the *aldB* gene encoding á-acetolactate decarboxylase (Swindell et al. 1996). The over expression of peptidase genes in LAB via self-replicating plasmids could also enhance flavour formation and cheese ripening. Peptidolytic activity can be increased by overproduction of peptide degrading enzymes originating from the same species or from other species. An example of the self-cloning strategy is the overproduction of an aminopeptidase (PepN) by *L. lactis* (Gasson and de Vos, 1994). GM-LAB with increased proteolytic propertied are generated by the over expression of the genes encoding PepN, PepX, PepC and PepI peptidases from a highly proteolytic *L. helveticus* strain (Joutsjoki et al. 2002) or PepI, PepL, PepW, and PepG from *L. delbrueckii* (Wegmann et al. 1999) into *L. lactis*. Moreover, the expression of *gdh* from *Peptoniphilus asaccharolyticus*, encoding glutamate dehydrogenase, into *L. lactis* increases the production of á-ketoglutarate (Rijnen et al. 2000). This enhances the degradation of amino acids, which also benefits the cheese ripening process. Food fermentation processes that, because of size, cannot be operated under strict axenic conditions, may suffer from bacteriophage infections resulting in lysis of starter bacteria. The transformation of industrially important strains with phage resistance genes from other LAB could generate new phage resistant strains. Engineering of starter strains aimed at inhibiting phage development is possible by creating a system of lethal gene induction upon phage infection (Djordjevic et al. 1997) or by production of antisense RNA inhibiting translation of phage RNA (Kim et al. 1992; Walker and Klaenhammer, 1998). The inactivation of a phage infection protein, *pip*, involved in phage adsorption and DNA injection resulted also in a phage resistant *L. lactis* strain (Monteville et al. 1994). The lactococcal abortive infection mechanisms AbiA and AbiG were introduced into *Streptococcus thermophilus*, and a range of phages capable of infecting this host were sensitive to these mechanisms (Tangney and Fitzgerald, 2002). The quality of food fermentation processes could be further improved when they are protected from spoilage by other bacteria. The expression of the food-grade lantibiotics in dairy starter strains could prevent spoilage from Gram positive bacteria during the process of cheese ripening (Horn et al. 1999). The production of lantibioticsto prevent growth of *Listeria monocytogenes* and *Lactobacillus fermentum,* during the production of cheese was also achieved via the non-GMO approach of conjugation (Hugenholtz and de Veer, 1991; O'Sullivan et al 2003). Bacteriophage-resistant dairy starter cultures were also selected after the natural event of transduction (Hill et al. 1989; Gasson, 1990) or after conjugation (stacking) of plasmids with phage resistant genes (Mills et al. 2002).

The event of phage induced cell lysis is undesirable during early stage of cheese making, but cell lysis in a later stage of the fermentation can actually decrease ripening time and enhance flavour due to the release of many enzymes. The controlled production of lysin and holin by bacteria has created the possibility to induce cell lysis at desired states of food fermentation (de Ruyter et al. 1997). Another important feature of food products is texture. Complete gene clusters, encoding exopolysaccharide producing enzymes have been transformed from one LAB strain to another one. The newly generated strains could influence viscosity and texture of the fermented product (Germond et al. 2001). In *S. thermophilus* the phosphoglucomutase gene was inactivated resulting in improved exopolysaccharide production enhancing the viscosity of the fermented food product (Levander et al. 2002). Engineering of exopolysaccharide production in *L. lactis* was also achieved by using a self-cloning strategy.Genetic engineering using genes from non related micro-organisms could also be used to produce high added value products, such as l-alanine. By introduction of a *Bacillus subtilis* (formerly *B. natto*) alanine dehydrogenase gene into a *L. lactis* strain deficient in lactate production, pyruvate conversion was pushed in the direction of alanine. The subsequent inactivation of the host gene encoding alanine racemase leads to the production of the stereo specific and thus highly valuable l-alanine (Hols et al. 1999). The nutritional value of fermented foods can be improved via use of GM-LAB. It was shown that by overexpressing the complete riboflavin gene cluster (four genes) via a multi copy plasmid and strong promoter, riboflavin production reached levels as high as 8 mg/L (Burgess et al. 2003). With this production level in fermented dairy products, average servings would already contain the DRI of riboflavin. Another important vitamin in the human diet is folate. This B-vitamin decreases the risks of neural tube defects in newborns and lowers the concentration of homocysteine in the blood, which is a risk factor for the occurrence of cardiovascular diseases. Nowadays, a large part of the population in both developed and under-developed countries does not meet the DRI of folate (200-400 μg). By the overexpression of all the genes encoding for the folate biosynthesis pathway in *L. lactis*, folate levels ranging from 5 - 8 mg/L can be achieved (Sybesma et al. 2003a). This could result in fermented food products that require an intake of less than 100 ml to meet the DRI for folate. It should be stated here that both riboflavin and folate-overproducing strains were developed as proof of principles, and in the current state contain plasmids with chloramphenicol resistant markers. These strains could only be applied in food fermentations after the substitution of the antibiotic resistance marker with a food-grade marker. Another line of research focuses on control of the bioavailability of folate produced in fermented foods. In nature, folate predominantly exists as polyglutamyl folate, however folate is absorbed as monoglutamyl folate. Several studies show that the bioavailability of monoglutamyl folate, which does not need enzymatic deconjugation, is higher than that of polyglutamyl folate. The overexpression of the first enzyme in the folate biosynthesis pathway increases the production of monoglutamyl folate (Sybesma et al. 2003a; Sybesma et al. 2003b).

Recently, the engineering of a *L. lactis* strain was described that contributes to the formation of lactose-free and naturally sweetened foods. By the deletion of three genes involved in glucose uptake and degradation, and introduction of the genes for lactose-PTS and tagatose-6P pathway, the strain can grow on lactose. The galactose-moiety of lactose is used as a C-source, whereas the glucose moiety is completely excreted (Pool et al. 2003). This GM-LAB obtained by self-cloning has identical properties to the earlier selected non-GM-LAB of Thompson (Thompson et al. 1985). However, the genetic background of the latter strain was spontaneously altered and, except for the desired mutations, it is likely that several non-anticipated mutations have occurred (de Vos and Hugenholtz, 2004). An example of the use of recombinant DNA technology in the development of probiotic strains is in removal of undesirable sugars from the gastro-intestinal tract. á-Galactosides such as raffinose and stachyose, that are present in raw agromaterials like soy, cause digestion problems in a lot of people. Because humans do not produce intestinal á-galactosidases, these sugars pass into the lower GI-tract where they are fermented by gas-producing bacteria, rendering intestinal pain and flatulence.

The expression of genes encoding enzymes that are able to degrade raffinose, stachyose, etc, such as á-galactosidases (Boucher et al. 2002; Silvestroni et al. 2002), in certain LAB, results in the (extracellular) production of sugar-degrading enzymes. Consequently, upon passage of these sugars through the GI tract, they will be degraded by the probiotic LAB and not by the resident gas-forming bacteria (Piard, 2003). In the feed industry, strain improvement can also be successfully applied. *Lactobacillus plantarum* is used as an inoculum in grass silage and vegetable products due to its pH lowering effect, which allows preservation of the products (Seale, 1986; Daeschel et al. 1987). The cloning of the phytase gene, *phyC*, from *Bacillus subtilis* in *Lb. plantarum* has recently been described (Kerovuo and Tynkkynen, 2000). Phytases are enzymes which hydrolyse phytate. These enzymes have a significant value as feed additives. The application of a phytase-producing silage strain in feed preparation may improve the nutritional value of feed and, at the same time, reduce the environmental phosphate pollution following consumption by monogastric production animals. Another GM-LAB designed to improve the nutritional value of feed is an amylolytic *L. plantarum* silage strain with improved starch degrading capacity (Fitzsimons et al. 1994).

Risk Factors for Use of Genetically Modifed Lactic Acid Bacteria

The process of introducing novel traits into LAB by the addition, substitution, removal, or rearrangement of defined DNA sequences, including the DNA sequences used for the maintenance or transfer of the new DNA into the recipient strain could lead to the generation of LAB with novel genetic properties and a modified cellular behaviour. It is anticipated that this will result in the intended effects. However, unintended effects, that could be a consequence of the modification, could also occur in the newly generated LAB. A distinction can be made between the predictable and unexpected effects that differ in their origin. Predictable effects are a foreseeable and direct consequence of the intended genetic alterations and unexpected effects are caused by unintended genetic alterations, or they may occur as a consequence of predictable effects.

The Predictable Unintended Effects

The predictable unintended effects could occur as a consequence of directed genetic alterations. For example, by insertion or modification of genes that are located in an operon, the expression of adjacent genes that are present in the same operon may be affected (polar effects). Also the expression of the inserted gene and subsequent production of a protein may result in potential toxicity or allergenicity of this protein, especially when posttranslational modifications in the recipient micro-organism may be different from the original host of the new protein. Another kind of predictable unintended effect may arise as a result of the synthesis of a chimeric protein (fusion protein), due to the insertion of foreign DNA. These new proteins may provoke a different type of cellular behaviour, but they might also lead to toxicity or allergic responses by the consumer because of their different chemical structure. Careful analysis of the genomic organization prior to and following the directed genetic alterations could be used to avoid the occurrence of such predictable unintended effects. For instance, the use of well-characterised loci for the insertion of the new DNA may prevent the effects on expression levels of adjacent genes. It should be noted that despite the fact that strains obtained via random mutagenesis are not considered as GMOs, the occurrence of such predictable unintended effects is very likely to occur within such mutant strains as well. In addition, it is possible that DNA elsewhere in the genome will also be affected by random mutagenesis. This could result in synthesis of modified enzymes and altered metabolite production (unexpected unintended effects), which might affect the health of the consumer. Therefore, it is not unlikely that certain GM-LAB may have a lower risk profile than LAB isolated after random mutagenesis.

The Unexpected Unintended Effects

The occurrence of unexpected and unintended effects could be a consequence of unintended genetic alterations. However, these effects could also be caused by the direct intended effect or by the predictable unintended effects of the alterations. The overproduction of certain desired metabolites or blocking pathways preventing the production of specific metabolites in the cell may result in unexpected and undesired cellular responses. For instance, a LAB defective in lactate dehydrogenase capacity may produce other acids and alcohol under certain environmental conditions. Increased concentrations of desired metabolites may also result in feedback inhibition of parallel biosynthetic pathways in the cell. Hence, a careful analysis of alterations in metabolism is desirable. Recently it was shown that inactivation of *ldhD* (responsible for the formation of D-lactate) in *Lactobacillus johnsonii*, primary and secondary end products were not easily redirected in high amounts to other pathways (Lapierre et al. 1999). Another unexpected and unintended effect may occur when the overproduction of one product inhibits the production of another compound. For instance, the biosynthesis of the vitamins folate and riboflavin starts with GTP as a substrate. An increased flux through the riboflavin biosynthesis pathway, as found with *L. lactis* producing increased riboflavin levels (Burgess et al. 2003), might reduce the concentration of GTP available for folate biosynthesis. As a consequence, folate production levels may be decreased. Another class of unexpected unintended effects is the change of the microbial population when GM-LAB are applied in mixed cultures. Several starter strains may grow simultaneously or in succession. For instance, during yoghurt fermentation, *S. thermophilus* grows prior to *L. bulgaricus* which only starts growing after acidification of the milk by the *S. thermophilus*. During the fermentation of sauerkraut, heterofermentative bacteria such as *Leuconostoc mesenteroides* initiate the fermentation, and after 3 to 7 days it is usually succeeded by the more acid-tolerant homofermentative *Lactobacillus* species, while *Lactobacillus plantarum* completes the fermentation (Lu et al. 2003). Hence, the synthesis of new metabolites, specifically those with antimicrobial activity, may disturb the balance in a mixed culture resulting in unintended changes in the final product. The phenomenon of gene transfer can probably be seen as one of the most important unexpected unintended effects. In the previous section many examples are given about self-replicating vectors to introduce additional DNA in the LAB cell. The production and consumption of GM-LAB will result in their contact with micro-organisms in the environment, including the intestinal microbiota of the consumer. Consequently, transfer of DNA between these micro-organisms may occur (horizontal gene transfer) (Jain et al. 2002; Doolittle et al. 2003). Transfer between the GM-LAB and the consumer has not been demonstrated (Genereux and Logsdon, 2003). Horizontal gene transfer is not restricted to plasmid-based DNA, as other modes of gene transfer such as those mediated by transposons, phages, or naked DNA, can also take place (Droge et al. 1998). In case a selective advantage is conferred by transferred DNA, the likelihood of stable gene transfer may be higher. For this reason the use oftransferable antibiotic resistance markers in fermenting micro-organisms should not be allowed, because these could provide a selective advantage following transfer to intestinal micro-organisms as soon as consumers are treated with antibiotics. This is a realistic scenario since there is evidence indicating that gene transfer of antibiotic resistance genes has occurred to bacteria that are present in traditionally fermented foods (Teuber et al. 1999). In contrast, the inactivation of genes by deletion does not result in the addition, but in the omission of DNA. Consequently, any discussion about potential gene transfer in GM-LAB with inactivated genes is void. It should be noted that the potential for the occurrence of unintended effects is not restricted to the use of recombinant DNA techniques. Rather, it is an inherent and general phenomenon that can also occur in the development of strains using traditional genetic techniques and procedures, or from exposure of micro-organisms to the intentional or unintended selected pressure. An overview of these concerns and other potential effects of food-related genetically modified micro-organisms is provided by von Wright and Bruce (2003).

Considerations for Restrictions in Development GM-Lab

Partially following earlier recommendation (Wymer, 1998), and to ensure the safety of humans and the environment, the following restrictions regarding the uncontained use ofGM-LAB are recommended: 1. Only LAB with a qualified presumption of safety (see below, EU, 2003) should be used as a recipient; 2. The use of transferable antibiotic resistance markers should not be permitted; 3. The expression of distantly related genes in LAB is acceptable under contained use only, unless the inserted gene will not induce growth or survival advantages to other micro-organisms after potential horizontal gene transfer; 4.The strain engineering should never result in production of toxic or allergic compounds or generation of a pathogenic strain that may affect human health.

Food-Grade Micro-Organisms

The use of micro-organisms in food production is accepted when they have a long history of safe use. However it is not scientifically defined what is a long history and what is a safe use. Moreover, a recent draft document (EU, 2003) suggests that only micro-organisms that have a long and safe history of use in food and that also have a qualified presumption of safety status (see below) should be applied in the food industry. These strains could be used as recipients for genetic modification. The use of pathogenic micro-organisms should not be allowed. However, the history of safe use in food should not be an everlasting guarantee that the strain could always be applied in food fermentation processes. If new research shows that strains with a long history of safe use are producing toxic components in levels that may harm human health, these strains should not be accepted anymore for use in food fermentations. For instance, certain LAB have an unblemished history of safety in food fermentation, but, as was discovered later, may produce unfavourable amines under some conditions (Ten Brink et al. 1990; Cantoni et al. 1994; Faeth and Radler, 1994). Evidently these strains should not be used in preparation of foods without a profound safety assessment, that, especially in this case, also investigates the actual concentrations of the harmful compound to which the consumer will be exposed.

Transferable Antibiotic Resistance Markers

The use of transferable antibiotic resistance markers in LAB used in food production may increase the risk of their transfer to human intestinal flora, and cannot be allowed. The use of safe and sustainable food-grade selection markers is recommended (de Vos, 1999). However, contrarily to current legislation, the use of antibiotic resistance markers in intermediate strains that are used for the generation of new bacterial strains with improved characteristics, and that are completely removed before the final production strain is developed, should not be rejected on the basis of reasons related to antibiotic resistance. For instance, the selection of the earlier described GM-LAB with inactivated á-acetolactate decarboxylase (Curic et al. 1999) should be allowed, because the vector containing the antibiotic resistance gene was removed from the selected strain. It is noteworthy that antibiotic resistance could also occur spontaneously. Well known examples include resistance to streptomycin and rifampicin that are a consequence of point mutations in rRNA or RNA polymerase genes, respectively. A specific case is resistance to vancomycin. Strains carrying transferable vancomycin resistance genes should not be used for food fermentations. Related Gram-positive bacteria like enterococci can spontaneously acquire vancomycin resistance. In such vancomycin resistant strains, spontaneous mutations in genes encoding cell wall synthesizing enzymes may result in altered peptidoglycan intermediates bearing D-alanine–D-lactate termini that confer vancomycin resistance (Arthur et al. 1996; Baptista et al. 1997). Similarly, LAB that produce D-lactic acid show endogenous resistance to vancomycin. These naturally occurring phenomena however, are not a reason to exclude such strains from consideration as recipients in constructing GM-LAB, since this endogenous resistance is not transmissible. Specific consideration needs to be given to tolerance to antibiotics that is caused by certain classes of transporters. Many of these are naturally present in LAB and may be essential for their survival in certain environments, where they could be involved in export of toxic compounds. It is conceivable that these transporters also export structurally related compounds, such as some antibiotics. This is likely to be the case for the endogenous tetracycline resistance found in many lactobacilli. In most cases the level of antibiotic resistance is far from that found in clinically relevant antibiotic-resistant pathogens. Hence, there appears to be no need for specific precautions when such antibiotic tolerant LAB strains are used as recipients. It should be further noted that the eventual selective pressure on these transporters caused by antibiotics used during medical treatment is not as dominant as the selective pressure caused by all the (natural) compounds that exist in nature. Therefore, it is likely that the risk of antibiotic resistance transfer via genes coding for transporter proteins from harmless bacteria to clinically important bacteria is much higher in nature than in the situation where fermenting bacteria are consumed.

Expression of Homologous or Heterologous Genes

The potential event of horizontal gene transfer following expression of foreign genes in LAB used in food fermentations is one of the major concerns that affect the safety assessment for consumer and environment. When the applied genetic elements originate from LAB that have a long and safe history of use in food, it is often said that no new risks are introduced. Although this argumentation is very logical, it does not mean that fermented foods are by definition safe. Therefore, adequate safety assessment remains necessary. However, it could eliminate the risk of negative consequences for the environment. For microbiota in complex natural habitats it is generally assumed that all genetic information is already omni-present, but that natural constraints drive selection. Thus, fear of negative consequences after the release of engineered LAB (containing genetic elements of other LAB species in the environment is unfounded. Evidently this is also valid for strains that have been subjected to spontaneous DNA modifications, or deletions of DNA. The introduction of more distantly related genes in micro-organisms is likely to occur in nature at much lower frequencies compared to the transfer of related genes. The cloning of such genes on a plasmid can be regarded as a potential risk factor since horizontal gene transfer could lead to selective advantage in specific niches. Therefore, some precautions are suggested for the expression of heterologous genes in LAB from non-microbial origin. As long as heterologous genes are only inserted in the chromosome via double cross over, and the inserted heterologous gene does not lead to evolutionary advantages and survival of such strains, there are no reasons to fear the consequences of potential gene transfer. Containment of such engineered strains may prevent interactions with the environment. In addition, survival in the environment can be limited by using host strains with a strict dependency on growth factors or special temperature or pH -requirements (Steidler et al. 2003). Genes that may cause pathogenicity (*e.g.* generation of virulence factors) or that encode for enzymes that are known to be involved in synthesis of toxic or allergic compounds, or precursors of toxic or allergic compounds, should *a priori* be excluded as targets for genetic engineering. Finally, one should consider avoiding the use of sequences that mediate integration into other genomes in the development of genetic constructs. Although in nature such sequences widely exist, and their use in strain development could be regarded as safe, it is better not to accelerate and support the process of gene transfer by the use of these sequences.

Considerations of the Safey Assessment Procedures for Foods Devided from Traditional Lab and GM-LAB

With the exception of those LAB not previously used in the preparation of a human food within the EU, LAB for food use are not subject to EU regulation. Implicit in this absence of any formal requirement for a safety assessment is the recognition that there has been a long history of presumed safe use. The long and safe history of LAB usage is in itself an arbitrary criterion and may need further consideration. If the long history of safe use is based on the absence of reports of the occurrence of adverse effects on consumers of fermented foods, it can be questioned whether this could also apply to certain GM-LAB. This would include LAB obtained by self cloning, or LAB that were subjected during their production process to recombinant DNA techniques, but that did not maintain the foreign DNA. This would imply the immediate acceptance of all such non-pathogenic GM-LAB for food production. However, is this whole debate not made for the assurance of safety for the society? Before regulation about food safety was an issue, society decided autonomously that it wanted to consume certain fermented foods, probably based on positive experience. These facts could be a convincing social, but less scientific, argument that LAB with a long history of safe use may be accepted in food fermentations until adverse effects are reported. The European Food and Feed Culture Association (EFFCA) has produced a list of starter species for which a documented history for use in food manufacture exists. Documented history of use is defined by the EFFCA as cultures sold for human consumption in quantities exceeding 100 kg of freeze dried culture. Although for many species belonging to LAB the safety documentation is sufficient, it is remarkable that the list also contains species that are potentially pathogenic.

Qualified Presumption of Safety

Within the EU it is proposed to introduce a system similar in concept and purpose to the GRAS (Generally Recognized As Safe) definition used in the USA, which could be applied to micro-organisms and their products. Such a system should lead to a listing of qualified micro-organisms that will not have properties that may adversely affect human health or the environment (EU, 2003). For this purpose, Qualified Presumption of Safety (QPS) is being introduced as an assumption based on reasonable evidence. It aims to provide a qualified generic approval for non-genetically modified micro-organisms, without requiring all organisms used in food production with a long history of safe use to be subjected to a full and unnecessary safety review. A case-by-case safety assessment then could be limited to only those aspects that are relevant to the organism in question. A pre-requisite for QPS would be that identity is unambiguously established at the taxonomic level claimed. Appropriate and state of the art biochemical and molecular biological methods must be applied to realise this. For organisms not commonly used in food production or without a long history of safe use, this implies the need for experimental data on the genetics of the taxonomic unit and the growth and biochemical characteristics of the component strain under a variety of relevant environmental conditions. For some groups of organisms, such as those used as biocontrol agents for plant protection, a consideration of the impact on the wider environment may be appropriate. However, this could exclude organisms considered either to be of uncompromised origin and regularly introduced into the wider environment or originating from soil or water. In both cases the organisms are naturally occurring and therefore free of any need for an environmental impact assessment. The QPS could only be valid for bacteria that enter the food chain and that are free of any acquired resistance to antibiotics of importance in clinical and veterinary medicine. The presence of antibiotic resistance determinants would not exclude their safe use for production purposes provided that only the fermentation products are retained in the final product. A decision scheme relating to the concept of QPS has been proposed and is presently subject to discussion (Figure 1) (EU, 2003). It is worthwhile mentioning that this QPS decision protocol might be subjected to modifications before its implementation. The decision step questioning other concerns related to safe use of micro-organisms, which are not involved with pathogenicity or toxicity, is currently not well defined. Many industrial strains will be the product of mutagenesis and selection programs designed to improve their phenotype for a particular purpose. These cryptic mutations will not affect taxonomic status. As a consequence, following the QPS decision tree, strains that are not produced via genetic modification, but contain altered DNA sequences that may cause predictable or unexpected unintended effects, will be accepted for use in food preparation without a further safety assessment. The next paragraph considers whether such strains of LAB should be subject to similar scrutiny as GM-LAB.

Due to the long history of use of many LAB, the resultant fermentation products are obviously not systematically assessed for safety. Moreover, food products containing improved strains obtained after random mutagenesis are not assessed either. It could be reasoned that the omission of adequate safety assessment in the past does not render the fermented foods safe for the consumer and the environment in the future. However, in the debate about safety of food derived from genetically modified microorganisms, the point is not to demonstrate that novel foods are completely risk-free, but that the risks are comparable to those associated with traditional foods. The safety assessments that have been conducted thus far are primarily aimed at discrete chemical entities such as food additives, or specific chemical or microbial contaminants that pose identifiable hazards and risks. It is likely that unintended effects could always occur in the development of strains using traditional (non-recombinant DNA) techniques, or from exposure of micro-organisms to selective pressure or certain environmental conditions, or just by natural events. This would justify that each new natural LAB strain should undergo the same safety assessment procedure as engineered strains. Whether this is a viable approach is currently being investigated by analysing differences at the global transcriptional level in strains isolated by random mutagenesis and by directed mutagenesis (Renault, 2001). The development of GM-LAB for use in food should be focused on minimizing the occurrence of unintended effects with adverse consequences on human health. Risk assessment studies using new technologies should focus on global response in cellular metabolism as a tool to identify unintended effects. It could be considered that in the future the decision to grant a QPS status to strains that are isolated after spontaneous or induced random mutagenesis, or to assess those strains using a profound safety assessment procedure as obliged for novel foods, would be taken after the performance of representative comparative profiling studies. These may include transcriptomics, proteomics, and metabolomics, between the mentioned strains and their natural conventional counterparts. In case of no relevant differences between the strains, the QPS protocol could be applied. In analogy with the outcome of these studies, the profiling of engineered strains obtained by directed genetic alterations may result in a more scientific food safety assessment procedure for novel foods derived from these GM-LAB, in which not the technical aspects, but the final products are assessed.

Consideration of Safety Assessment Procedures of GM-LAB and Novel Foods

The safety assessment of food produced by GM-LAB should comprise analysis of the intended effect, the nature of the modification, and detectable unintended effects that may occur in the micro-organism or in the food that is producedby the fermenting micro-organism. Furthermore, issues that are specific to the use of recombinant GM-LAB include the genetic stability, the potential for gene transfer (see above), the colonisation of the gastrointestinal tract and the persistence therein, interactions that the recombinant-DNA micro-organism may have with the gastrointestinal flora or the mammalian host, and any impact of the recombinant-DNA micro-organism on the immune system. The development of modern genetic techniques could enhance the safety assessment, and the follow up by post market surveillance may also contribute to the safety assessment and increase the consumers' trust. Furthermore, the safety assessment procedure should encompass the obligations stated in directive 2001/18/EC and Commission Recommendation 97/618/EC.

Toxicity and Allergenicity

Because the nucleic acid techniques enable the introduction of DNA that can result in the synthesis of new substances in the LAB, specific attention should be paid to the toxicity and allergenicity of the newly synthesised compounds (proteins and metabolic products). When a substance is new to foods or food processing, the use of conventional toxicology studies or other applicable studies on the new substance will be necessary. In the case of proteins, the assessment of potential toxicity and allergenicity should focus on amino acid sequence similarity between the new protein and the known protein and anti-nutrient activities (*e.g.* protease inhibitors, lectins) as well as stability to heat or processing and to degradation in appropriate representative gastric and intestinal model systems. Appropriate oral toxicity studies may need to be carried out in cases where the protein present in the food is not similar to proteins that have been previously consumed safely in food, taking into account the biological function of the protein in the donor organism where known. At present there is no definitive test that can be relied upon to predict allergic response in humans to a newly expressed protein. However, it could first be assessed whether a newly expressed protein is one to which certain individuals may already be sensitive as well as whether a protein new to the food supply is likely to induce allergic reactions in some individuals as could be predicted by amino acid sequence homology and sera screenings. The Codex Alimentarius (2003) proposes that IgE-cross-reactivity between the newly expressed protein and a known allergen should be considered a possibility when there is more than 35% identity in a segment of 80 or more amino acids. The development of international serum banks would enhance efficient testing for allergic potential of the newly expressed proteins. Strategies such as stepwise contiguous identical amino acid segment searches may also be performed for identifying sequences that may represent linear epitopes. The size of the contiguous amino acid search should be based on a scientifically justified rationale in order to minimise the potential for false negative or false positive results. Moreover, resistance to pepsin degradation has been observed in several food allergens and was found to correlate with the allergic potential of the protein under scrutiny. Therefore, the resistance of a protein to degradation in the presence of pepsin under appropriate conditions indicates that further analysis should be conducted to determine the likelihood of the newly expressed protein being allergic. Potential toxicity of substances that have not been safely consumed in food before should be assessed case-by-case on the basis of the identity, concentration, and biological function of the substance and dietary exposure. The type of studies to be performed may include evaluations of metabolism, toxicokinetics, chronic toxicity/carcinogenicity, impact on reproductive function, and teratogenicity. It is important that in such studies the stability of recombinant DNA in lactic acid bacteria is also considered. It is also important to ascertain the impact of changes on the overall nutrient profile and to verify to what extent the modified nutrients are bioavailable and remain stable during processing and storage. Recombinant LAB that remain viable in foods may interact with the immune system in the gastrointestinal tract. Closer examination of these interactions will depend on the types of differences between the recombinant-DNA micro-organism and its conventional counterpart.

Modern DNA Techniques, Genomics, Transcriptomics, Proteomics, and Metabolomics

The rapid development of genetic and biochemical techniques can be applied to increase reliable, fast and profound safety assessment of the fermenting micro-organisms and the derived foods, in accordance with the concept of substantial equivalence. It is preferable that the unintended effects could be foreseen at an early stage so that potential harmful effects could be analysed beforehand. The presence of new proteins or the change in concentrations of certain proteins could point to the altered activity of biochemical pathways that may result in changed metabolite content. The analysis of the complete set of metabolites in the cell could also provide information about potential toxicity and about the general nutritional value. Genome wide analysis of modified strains and of their natural counterparts, for instance by using fingerprint techniques, or by complete sequencing of the genome, can reveal all loci in the genome where mutations have occurred that could result in unintended effects. Transcriptome analysis, by using DNA array or DNA chip technology, could provide information about altered expression patterns of the new micro-organisms compared to the wild-type strain. The observation of altered expression levels of genes not involved in the targeted effect of the genetic engineering could be a starting point for the analysis of the reaction products of the enzymes coded for by the genes of interest. This might be done by studying the literature and by application of bioinformatics, and, if a harmful compound may be produced, subsequent biochemical analysis could be performed to measure the presence of these metabolites. More relevant for food safety assessment is an analysis of the proteome and metabolome of the modified micro-organisms. Proteome analysis, by using 2D-gel electrophoresis, 2D-HPLC or advanced mass spectrometry, provides information on altered protein concentration and content produced by the modified micro-organisms. Likewise the outcome of the transcriptome analysis, the reaction products of the new proteins or increased protein concentrations themselves could be predicted and analysed.

The value of proteomics has already been proven in genetically modified rice that was engineered to produce more storage proteins. SDS-PAGE analysis revealed an unexpected increased level of prolamins (Kubo, 2000). Metabolome analysis, by using a wide range of chromatographic and spectroscopic techniques, could provide information about the presence of new metabolites or altered concentrations of existing metabolites. Increased concentrations of known metabolites could be compared with current acceptable daily intake levels to assure the consumer's safety. Likewise, decreased concentrations of vital components could reduce the nutritional value of a new product. The identification of new proteins, or altered protein levels, new metabolites, or altered metabolite levels, could be a starting point for further toxicological studies. To strengthen the safety assessment, transcriptome, proteome and metabolome analyses under food processing and GI-tract conditions should be performed in case the new engineered strains have potential for survival in the human gut. The outcome of these data analyses will also provide information on the occurrence of the intended and, if present, of the unintended effects. The conclusion of the analysis should be the assurance that neither the intended effects, nor the unintended effects, have adverse effects on human health, because no harmful components or proteins with allergic characteristics are being produced. In the near future it is possible to develop a universal proteome and metabolome reference frame consisting of all proteins and compounds produced by fermenting micro-organisms. The proteome and metabolome reference frame should contain information on potential allergenicity of proteins, based on amino acid sequence comparison with known allergens, and information about acceptable maximum and minimum levels of all compounds present in food. The changed protein and metabolome content of any new engineered strain can then be easily compared with the reference frame. Comparison of the proteome and the metabolome of the new engineered strains with the reference frame could be a starting point for further food safety assessment procedures and could ensure that further safety assessment remains proportional to the perceived risks. For instance, if it could be verified that proteins or metabolites are not produced in harmful concentrations and that the nutritional value is not adversely affected, no further safety assessment would be required for the fermenting micro-organisms and the fermenting food.

Post-market Surveillance

A post-market surveillance (PMS) on novel foods, involves the observation of (health) effects on the consumer over a longer period of time after release of the novel food on the market. It could be questioned whether, after approved pre-market safety assessments of genetically modified foods, the use of post-market surveillance would still be necessary. However, theoretically, novel foods may contain undetected anti-nutrients or toxicants which may lead to (delayed) adverse effects on the health of humans and animals. Moreover, various other factors may also be involved in determining the safety of food in the long run, such as the consumption conditions and the genetic profile of the consumer. Therefore, to further protect the general public, including specific sub-populations such as immuno-compromised individuals, infants and the elderly, and to provide additional information on long term effects, PMS could be applied in the form of a recording and investigation system by national health services, perhaps similar to the adverse drug effects reporting systems used by physicians. Up to now only a few food additives have been subjected to PMS, including the artificial sweetener aspartame (Butchko et al. 1994) and the fat replacer olestra (Slough et al. 2001). Recently within the EU, PMS has started on a novel food related to the use of phytosterol-esters in yellow fat spreads that is assumed to have cholesterol lowering effects in the consumer (Lea, 2002). However, it may be difficult to introduce PMS over a longer time period if the food consumption pattern of individuals is not consistent. It should be taken into account that some consumers might be exposed to newly introduced components from different sources during their daily consumption pattern and consequently might be at risk because of overexposure to certain compounds. PMS could also be used to verify the conclusions about the absence of potential consumer health effects, and it could eventually monitor changes in nutrient intake levels that could occur by the introduction of foods that are likely to significantly change the nutritional status. Although the application of PMS to food products raises significant technical issues, particularly for active surveillance, passive surveillance based on spontaneous reports could be utilised. Apart from this, it could be considered that for novel foods derived from GM-LAB that are substantially equivalent to LAB with a QPS status, PMSwould not be necessary. An effective PMS contains the following elements (Health Council of the Netherlands,

2002): i) Setting up a government supported line for all consumer complaints associated with health and foods. This would enable any side effects produced by a product to be traced, provided that they arise soon after consumption and that they attract attention. One such example is food allergies. This monitoring system will not reveal any causal relationships; however, it can be used to generate a hypothesis. In this way it would alert people to health problems, leading on to a focused follow-up study; ii) Continuous monitoring of consumption of foodstuffs, carried out jointly by government and industry. One precondition is that this must facilitate a detailed breakdown of data on individual products into information on their ingredients (down to the molecular biology level in the case of genetically modified foods); iii) Long term epidemiological, prospective, cohort studies into the relationship between chronic diseases and diet; and iv) An active market monitoring program carried out by companies on novel foods that contain bio-active ingredients. The aim here is to check the accuracy of the presumed (safe) intake of the target group (Health Council of the Netherlands, 2002). It may be concluded that PMS could only prove its value by signalling hazardous events resulting in immediate withdrawal of the concerned food. PMS could not be seen as a safety assessment, but as an early warning system that operates better as the adverse effects are stronger. Moreover, it could be employed if increased confidence by the consumer to use novel foods evolves, and if the principle and reasoning for setting up PMS is well communicated to the consumer.

Suggestions for Cost Accountability of Safety Assessments for Novel Foods

The development, approval and subsequent market release of novel fermented foods involves many economical issues for industry, consumers and society in general.

Investments in research and development by the food industry will provide opportunities for employment and the development of new scientific technologies. The consumption of novel foods with added value will benefit the consumer. The introduction of products with proven health claims, may especially contribute to the generation of a healthier community, and this is expected to decrease public health costs. The costs associated in the development of novel foods can only be worthwhile in a society that accepts and buys these novel foods. The introduction of traits that decrease production costs for the manufacturer could be the impetus to reduce the price as a way to generate an additional advantage for the consumer.Conversely, the introduction of traits that benefit the consumer might lead to added value of the product that may justify a price increase to the consumer. Moreover, novel traits could also be developed that have a lower environmental load and that bring advantages to the society as a whole. It is expected that any obligation to perform a profound safety assessment, before the launching of any novel food, could significantly add to the initial costs to be made by industry. The question is, who should cover these costs: the industry, the consumer, national authorities, or supra national authorities? Finally, although each food producer is responsible for the safety of the products placed in the market, in many countries food safety is principally an issue for the regulating authorities. Therefore, it could be proposed that public money could be used to set up the complete infrastructure required for food safety assessment as stated in the paragraphs above, including development of profiling techniques based on transcriptomics, proteomics, and metabolomics. Consequently, it would also be the task of regulatory authorities to control and conclude the whole safety assessment protocol. On the other hand, the industry might be expected to participate as well in the process of assessing novel foods derived from GM-LAB. After approval of the novel food, PMS would remain acombined matter for the society and the industry. The high costs associated with the development and assessment of novel foods may be a limitingfactor for the industry to develop novel foods, especially those with interesting traits based on health benefits for the consumers. Therefore the industry should be allowed to promote novel foods with scientifically proven advantages over traditional foods by use of labelling and other forms of publicity. Currently the possibilities for promoting scientifically proven functional foods are limited and not harmonised within various EU countries. It is evident that the consumer should be protected by prohibiting the labelling of untrue claims. However, not permitting the labelling of true health claims is equally wrong (Katan and de Roos, 2003). The future EU regulation, as proposed in its working paper of 2002 about nutritional and functional claims (EU/SANCO, 2002), seems to provide a good solution for both consumer and industry by allowing and regulating the labelling of health claims.

The Consumer's Preparation

Consumer's perception is an extremely important factor for successful introduction of new technologies in the market. Leisner (2005) described the obstacles for the introduction of pasteurization and starter cultures in the late 19th century to indicate that the gap between industry, consumers and pressure groups is not an entirely new issue. Genetic alteration of plants and animals is sometimes seen as interference with nature that could have unknown and potentially disastrous interactions with human genetics and natural ecosystems. Moreover, many consumers are extremely aware of health threats caused by unknown risks in the food supply. Green groups have been raising several questions about the environmental risks of genetically altered crops and animals. Environmental risks include the evolution of GM-plants into "super weeds," cross-pollination introducing herbicide resistance into existing weeds or introducing undesirable genetic traits into neighbouring crops, and harm to non-target populations caused by toxins introduced to create insect resistance. In the present work we have shown that the consequences of development and use of GM-LAB are different compared to GMO from plant or animal origins. The potential intended and unintended effects and related risks can be predicted more accurately and can be verified. In combination with profound safety assessments, safety for consumers and safety for the environment can be assured. The occurrence of unintended effects is not unique for GM-LAB, but also occurs in LAB used in conventional food fermentations. Logically, this is no reason to ban GM-LAB, but it could be a reason to analyse the unintended effects of traditionally used strains in food fermentation by genomics-based profiling methods. A further response to the public concern is to strengthen the pre-marketing data requirements and to introduce post-launch surveillance program to confirm safety, as described above.

Besides an approval of the safety assessment, the GM-LAB designed for use in food production is probably more acceptable for the consumer if a clear correlation with consumer benefits can be made. Therefore, labelling on food products should emphasise the benefits (eventually health claims) of the novel foods. Evidently, product labels should also inform the consumer about the nature of the (genetically modified) bacteria, the risk assessment procedure, and the nature of the conventional counterpart. However, it is questionable why, according to the new EU legislation, food and feed products and additives that are derived from GM-LAB should be labelled with such a characteristic when there is no DNA or protein derived from a GM-LAB detectable in the final product. A parallel strategy that could be adapted to increase trust among consumers relates to the liability of the manufacturers in case of damage caused by novel foods. Despite profound pre-market safety assessment that is expected to be conducted before the introduction of novel foods onto the market, unpredicted adverse effects directly related to the consumption of the novel food can theoretically not be excluded. The industry and its products would probably gain support if they accept the liability for such events. However, it would not be reasonable to establish an unlimited liability for the industry. Therefore the liability for predictable adverse effects associated with the consumption of novel foods could be placed onto the consumer as long as the labelling includes warnings for the specified adverse effects that could occur in sub-populations. Moreover, the free choice of the consumer should be respected. Thus, alternative similar products, although they will not possess the introduced advantageous traits, should be widely available on the market. A complex and harmonised legislation and regulation system seems at present times the only correct response to consumer demand for protection from the perceived harms that could be caused by GMOs. However, it remains to be seen if the consumers would accept that as a guarantee for the safe consumption of novel foods. For the future it could be recommended to set up governmental sponsored research programs with the ultimate goal of further reducing the uncertainty and mistrust within society. Educating the public on these matters may help to overcome the negative emotions related to the use of certain GMOs.

The low degree of trust by the general public in the (food) industry, in the regulatory authorities and in the (food) scientific community is a major element contributing to the general negative perception of GMOs in the EU. The set up of an infrastructure by the regulatory authorities to subject all fermenting micro-organisms and fermented foods to a new and profound risk assessment procedure might be the extra step that is currently needed to convince all parties involved that novel foods are as safe as traditional foods. A distinction within the discussion and legislation between food safety assessment procedures for fermented foods (dealing especially with LAB), and GMOs derived from plant and animal origin, is necessary in the current controversy. As a starting point, the QPS protocol (EU, 2003), based on taxonomy and on the history of safe use of LAB applied in food, could in the near future be applied to any kind of LAB or GM-LAB provided that a series of modern profiling methods are used to verify the absence of unintended effects by altered LAB that may cause harm to the health of the consumer. Objective safety assessments of GM-LAB could be a way to improve the current legislation. It is expected that knowledge of genome evolution and profiling studies will reveal that in many organisms the genetic material, that is naturally or spontaneously changed, has been modified more than can be established by directed alterations, including genetic modification.

The assessments of foods derived from modern biotechnology should be reviewed to ensure that the emerging scientific information is incorporated into the risk analysis. In conclusion, broad evaluation of the nature of novel foods derived from GM-LAB, which should be considered as a specific group of GMOs, could be a starting point to bridge the gap between industry, consumers and green groups. This may lead to acceptance of GM-LAB derived novel foods to provide for a better quality of life in today's society.

Direct genetic engineering, including self-cloning, generates targeted modifications that can be much better controlled and evaluated than strains that are exposed to random mutagenesis approaches. If such strains are accepted in food fermentations via QPS status, the acceptance by society of GM-LAB obtained via directed genetic alterations could be improved. In line with current legislation, safety issues should dominate the acceptability of GM-LAB in food industry. A targeted approach should be based upon analysis of key compounds in the new food, such as proteins, carbohydrates, fats, vitamins, minerals, as well as upon analysis of toxicity and allergenicity. A non-targeted approach should use to profile methods to detect global responses to the new food. Global expression profiles will reveal whether changes additional to those expected have occurred. The expression of any new or altered gene in LAB, that is either randomly mutated or self cloned, may affect the transcriptome, proteome, and metabolome profiling and could tell if the expression of the new gene results in any (undesirable) side effects.

2

Phylogenetics, Pharmacogenomics and Genomics Research

Systematics and Molecular Phylogenetics

Have you ever noticed that when you see an insect or a bird, there is real satisfaction in giving it a name, and an uncomfortable uncertainty when you can't? Along these same lines, consider the bewildering number and variety of organisms that live, or have lived, on this earth. If we did not know what to call these organisms, how could we communicate ideas about them, let alone the history of life? Thanks to taxonomy, the field of science that classifies life into groups, we can discuss just about any organism, from bacteria to man. Carolus Linnaeus pioneered the grouping of organisms based on scientific names using Latin. His system of giving an organism a scientific name of two parts, sometimes more, is called binomial nomenclature, or "two-word naming". His scheme was based on physical similarities and differences, referred to as characters. Today, taxonomic classification is much more complex and takes into account cellular types and organization, biochemical similarities, and genetic similarities. Taxonomy is but one aspect of a much larger field called systematics. Taxonomic ranks approximate evolutionary distances among groups of organisms. For example, species belonging to two different superkingdoms are most distantly related (their common ancestor diverged in the distant past), with progressively more exclusive groups indicated by phylum, class and so on, down to infraspecific ranks, or ranks occurring within a species. Infraspecific ranks, such as subspecies, varietas, and forma, denote the closest evolutionary relationship. See the simplified classification of humans below. Taxonomists, scientists who classify living organisms, define a species as any group of closely related organisms that can produce fertile offspring. Two organisms are more closely "related" as they approach the level of species, that is, they have more genes in common. The level of species can be further divided into smaller segments. A population is the smallest unit of a species and is made up of organisms of the same species. Sometimes, a population will physically alter over time to suit the needs of its environment. This is called a cline and can make members of the same species look different.

Carolus Linnaeus was also credited with pioneering systematics, the field of science dealing with the diversity of life and the relationship between life's components. Systematics reaches beyond taxonomy to elucidate new methods and theories that can be used to classify species based on similarity of traits and possible mechanisms of evolution, a change in the gene pool of a population over time. Phylogenetic systematics is that field of biology that does deal with identifying and understanding the evolutionary relationships among the many different kinds of life on earth, both living (extant) and dead (extinct). Evolutionary theory states that similarity among individuals or species is attributable to common descent, or inheritance from a common ancestor. Thus, the relationships established by phylogenetic systematics often describe a species' evolutionary history and, hence, its phylogeny, the historical relationships among lineages or organisms or their parts, such as their genes. Charles Darwin was the first to recognize that the systematic hierarchy represented a rough approximation of evolutionary history. However, it was not until the 1950s that the German entomologist Willi Hennig proposed that systematics should reflect the known evolutionary history of lineages as closely as possible, an approach he called phylogenetic systematics. The followers of Hennig were disparagingly referred to as "cladists" by his opponents, because of the emphasis on recognizing only monophyletic groups, a group plus all of its descendents, or clades. However, the cladists quickly adopted that term as a helpful label, and nowadays, cladistic approaches to systematics are used routinely.

Understanding the Evolutionary Process

Evolution is not always discrete with clearly defined boundaries that pinpoint the origin of a new species, nor is it a steady continuum. Evolution requires genetic variation which results from changes within a gene pool, the genetic make-up of a specific population. A gene pool is the combination of all the alleles —alternative forms of a genetic locus—for all traits that population may exhibit. Changes in a gene pool can result from mutation—variation within a particular gene—or from changes in gene frequency—the proportion of an allele in a given population.

Every organism possesses a genome that contains all of the biological information needed to construct and maintain a living example of that organism. The biological information contained in a genome is encoded in the nucleotide sequence of its DNA or RNA molecules and is divided into discrete units called genes. The information stored in a gene is read by proteins, which attach to the genome and initiate a series of reactions called gene expression. Every time a cell divides, it must make a complete copy of its genome, a process called DNA replication. DNA replication must be extremely accurate to avoid introducing mutations, or changes in the nucleotide sequence of a short region of the genome. Inevitably, some mutations do occur, usually in one of two ways; either from errors in DNA replication or from damaging effects of chemical agents or radiation that react with DNA and change the structure of individual nucleotides. Many of these mutations result in a change that has no effect on the functioning of the genome, referred to as silent mutations. Silent mutations include virtually all changes that happen in the non-coding components of genes and gene-related sequences. Mutations in the coding regions of genes are much more important. Here we must consider the importance of the same mutation in a somatic cell compared with a germ line cell. A somatic cell is any cell of an organism other than a reproductive cell, such as a sperm or egg cell. A germ cell line is any line of cells that gives rise to gametes and is continuous through the generations. Because a somatic cell does not pass on copies of its genome to the next generation, a somatic cell mutation is important only for the organism in which it occurs and has no potential evolutionary impact. In fact, most somatic mutations have no significant effect because there are many other identical cells in the same tissue. On the other hand, mutations in germ cells can be transmitted to the next generation and will then be present in all of the cells of an individual who inherits that mutation. Even still, mutations within germ line cells may not change the phenotype of the organism in any significant way. Those mutations that do have an evolutionary effect can be divided into two categories, loss-of-function mutations and gain-of-function mutations. A loss-of-function mutation results in reduced or abolished protein function. Gain-of-function mutations, which are much less common, confer an abnormal activity on a protein. The randomness with which mutations can occur is an important concept in biology and is a requirement of the Darwinian view of evolution, which holds that changes in the characteristics of an organism occur by chance and are not influenced by the environment in which the organism lives. Beneficial changes within an organism are then positively selected for, whereas harmful changes are negatively selected.

Selection, Drift, and Founder Effects

We just discussed that new alleles appear in a population because of mutations that occur in the reproductive cells of an organism. This means that many genes are polymorphic, that is, two or more alleles for that gene are present in a population. Each of these alleles has its own allele or gene frequency, a measure of how common an allele is in a population. Allele frequencies vary over time because of two conditions, natural selection and random drift.

Natural Selection

> **"Natural Selection"** is the principle by which each slight variation, if useful, is preserved.
>
> *Charles Drawin*

Natural selection is the process whereby one genotype, the hereditary constitution of an individual, leaves more offspring than another genotype because of superior life attributes, termed fitness. Natural selection acts on genetic variation by conferring a survival advantage to those individuals harboring a particular mutation that tends to favor a changing environmental condition. These individuals then reproduce and pass on this "new" gene, altering their gene pool. Natural selection, therefore, decreases the frequencies of alleles that reduce the fitness of an organism and increases the frequency of alleles that improve fitness. It is important to point out that natural selection does not always represent progress, only adaptation to a changing surrounding, that is, evolution attributable to natural selection is devoid of intent— something does not evolve to better itself, only to adapt. Because environments are always changing, what was once an advantageous mutation can often become a liability further down the evolutionary line.

Random Drift

The term random drift actually encompasses a number of distinct processes, sometimes referred to as outcomes. They include indiscriminate parent sampling, the founder effect, and fluctuations in the rate of evolutionary processes such as selection, migration, and mutation. Parent sampling is the process of determining which organisms of one generation will be the parents of the next generation. Parent sampling may be discriminate, that is, with regard to fitness differences, or indiscriminate, without regard to fitness differences. Discriminate parent sampling is generally considered natural selection, whereas indiscriminate parent sampling is considered random drift.

Suppose a population of red and brown squirrels share a habitat with a color blind predator. Although the predator is color blind, the brown squirrels seem to die in greater numbers than the red squirrels, suggesting that the brown squirrels just seem to be unlucky enough to come into contact with the predator more often. As a result, the frequency of brown squirrels in the next generation is reduced. More red squirrels survive to reproduce, or are sampled, but it is without regard to any differences in fitness between the two groups. The physical differences of the groups do not play a causal role in the differences in reproductive success. Now, lets say that the predator is not color blind and can now see the red squirrels better than the brown squirrels, resulting in a better survival rate for the brown squirrels. This would be a case of discriminate parent sampling, or natural selection.

Founder Effect

Another important cause of genetic drift is the founder effect, the difference between the gene pool of a population as a whole and that of a newly isolated population of the same species. The founder effect occurs when populations are started from a small number of pioneer individuals of one original population. Because of small sample size, the new population could have a much different genetic ratio than the original population. An example of the founder effect would be when a plant population results from a single seed. Thus far, we have discussed natural selection and random drift as events that occur in isolation from one another. However, in most populations, the two processes will be occurring at the same time. Furthermore, there is great debate over whether, in particular instances and in general, natural selection is more prevalent that random drift.

Phylogenetic Trees

Systematics describes the pattern of relationships among taxa and is intended to help us understand the history of all life. But history is not something we can see—it has happened once and leaves only clues as to the actual events. Scientists use these clues to build hypotheses, or models, of life's history. In phylogenetic studies, the most convenient way of visually presenting evolutionary relationships among a group of organisms is through illustrations called phylogenetic trees.

- **Node:** represents a taxonomic unit. This can be either an existing species or an ancestor.
- **Branch:** defines the relationship between the taxa in terms of descent and ancestry.
- **Topology**: the branching patterns of the tree.

- **Branch length**: represents the number of changes that have occurred in the branch.
- **Root**: the common ancestor of all taxa.
- **Distance scale**: scale that represents the number of differences between organisms or sequences.
- **Clade**: a group of two or more taxa or DNA sequences that includes both their common ancestor and all of their descendents.
- **Operational Taxonomic Unit (OTU)**: taxonomic level of sampling selected by the user to be used in a study, such as individuals, populations, species, genera, or bacterial strains.

A phylogenetic tree is composed of nodes, each representing a taxonomic unit (species, populations, individuals), and branches, which define the relationship between the taxonomic units in terms of descent and ancestry. Only one branch can connect any two adjacent nodes. The branching pattern of the tree is called the topology, and the branch length usually represents the number of changes that have occurred in the branch. This is called a scaled branch. Scaled trees are often calibrated to represent the passage of time. Such trees have a theoretical basis in the particular gene or genes under analysis. Branches can also be unscaled, which means that the branch length is not proportional to the number of changes that has occurred, although the actual number may be indicated numerically somewhere on the branch. Phylogenetic trees may also be either rooted or unrooted. In rooted trees, there is a particular node, called the root, representing a common ancestor, from which a unique path leads to any other node. An unrooted tree only specifies the relationship among species, without identifying a common ancestor, or evolutionary path. Phylogenetic trees, a convenient way of representing evolutionary relationships among a group of organisms, can be drawn in various ways. Branches on phylogenetic trees may be scaled (*top panel*) representing the amount of evolutionary change, time, or both, when there is a molecular clock, or they may be unscaled (*middle panel*) and have no direct correspondence with either time or amount of evolutionary change. Phylogenetic trees may be rooted (*top* and *middle panels*) or unrooted (*bottom panels*). In the case of unrooted trees, branching relationships between taxa are specified by the way they are connected to each other, but the position of the common ancestor is not. For example, on an unrooted tree with five species, there are five branches (four external, one internal) on which the tree can be rooted. Rooting on each of the five branches has different implications for evolutionary relationships. Two major groups of analyses exist to examine phylogenetic relationships: phenetic methods and cladistic methods. It is important to note that phenetics and cladistics have had an uneasy relationship over the last 40 years or so. Most of today's evolutionary biologists favor cladistics, although a strictly cladistic approach may result in counterintuitive results.

Phenetic Method of Analysis

Phenetics, also known as numerical taxonomy, involves the use of various measures of overall similarity for the ranking of species. There is no restriction on the number or type of characters (data) that can be used, although all data must be first converted to a numerical value, without any character "weighting". Each organism is then compared with every other for all characters measured, and the number of similarities (or differences) is calculated. The organisms are then clustered in such a way that the most similar are grouped close together and the more different ones are linked more distantly. The taxonomic clusters, called phenograms, that result from such an analysis do not necessarily reflect genetic similarity or evolutionary relatedness. The lack of evolutionary significance in phenetics has meant that this system has had little impact on animal classification, and as a consequence, interest in and use of phenetics has been declining in recent years.

Cladistic Method of Analysis

An alternative approach to diagramming relationships between taxa is called cladistics. The basic assumption behind cladistics is that members of a group share a common evolutionary history. Thus, they are more closely related to one another than they are to other groups of organisms. Related groups of organisms are recognized because they share a set of unique features (apomorphies) that were not present in distant ancestors but which are shared by most or all of the organisms within the group. These shared derived characteristics are called synapomorphies. Therefore, in contrast to phenetics, cladistics groupings do not depend on whether organisms share physical traits but depend on their evolutionary relationships. Indeed, in cladistic analyses two organisms may share numerous characteristics but still be considered members of different groups. Cladistic analysis entails a number of assumptions. For example, species are assumed to arise primarily by bifurcation, or separation, of the ancestral lineage; species are often considered to become extinct upon hybridization (crossbreeding); and hybridization is assumed to be rare or absent. In addition, cladistic groupings must possess the following characteristics: all species in a grouping must share a common ancestor and all species derived from a common ancestor must be included in the taxon. The application of these requirements results in the following terms being used to describe the different ways in which groupings can be made:

- A monophyletic grouping is one in which all species

share a common ancestor, and all species derived from that common ancestor are included. This is the only form of grouping accepted as valid by cladists.

- A paraphyletic grouping is one in which all species share a common ancestor, but not all species derived from that common ancestor are included.
- A polyphyletic grouping is one in which species that do not share an immediate common ancestor are lumped together, while excluding other members that would link them.

Molecular Phylogenetics

Macromolecular data, meaning gene (DNA) and protein sequences, are accumulating at an increasing rate because of recent advances in molecular biology. For the evolutionary biologist, the rapid accumulation of sequence data from whole genomes has been a major advance, because the very nature of DNA allows it to be used as a "document" of evolutionary history. Comparisons of the DNA sequences of various genes between different organisms can tell a scientist a lot about the relationships of organisms that cannot otherwise be inferred from morphology, or an organism's outer form and inner structure. Because genomes evolve by the gradual accumulation of mutations, the amount of nucleotide sequence difference between a pair of genomes from different organisms should indicate how recently those two genomes shared a common ancestor. Two genomes that diverged in the recent past should have fewer differences than two genomes whose common ancestor is more ancient. Therefore, by comparing different genomes with each other, it should be possible to derive evolutionary relationships between them, the major objective of molecular phylogenetics. Molecular phylogenetics attempts to determine the rates and patterns of change occurring in DNA and proteins and to reconstruct the evolutionary history of genes and organisms. Two general approaches may be taken to obtain this information. In the first approach, scientists use DNA to study the evolution of an organism. In the second approach, different organisms are used to study the evolution of DNA. Whatever the approach, the general goal is to infer process from pattern: the processes of organismal evolution deduced from patterns of DNA variation and processes of molecular evolution inferred from the patterns of variations in the DNA itself.

Molecular Phylogenetic Analysis

Nucleotide and protein sequences can also be used to generate trees. DNA, RNA, and protein sequences can be considered as phenotypic traits. The sequences depict the relationship of genes and usually of the organism in which the genes are found.

As we just discussed, macromolecules, especially gene and protein sequences, have surpassed morphological and other organismal characters as the most popular forms of data for phylogenetic analyses. Therefore, this next section will concentrate only on molecular data. It is important to point out that a single, all-purpose recipe does not exist for phylogenetic analysis of molecular data. Although numerous algorithms, procedures, and computer programs have been developed, their reliability and practicality are, in all cases, dependent upon the size and structure of the dataset under analysis. The merits and shortfalls of these various methods are subject to much scientific debate, because the danger of generating incorrect results is greater in computational molecular phylogenetics than in many other fields of science. Occasionally, the limiting factor in such analyses is not so much the computational method used, but the users' understanding of what the method is actually doing with the data. Therefore, the goal of this section is to demonstrate to the reader that practical analysis should be thought of both as a search for a correct model (analysis) as well as a search for the correct tree (outcome). Phylogenetic tree-building models presume particular evolutionary models. For any given set of data, these models may be violated because of various occurrences, such as the transfer of genetic material between organisms. Therefore, when interpreting a given analysis, a person should always consider the model used and entertain possible explanations for the results obtained. For example, models used in molecular phylogenetic analysis methods make "default" assumptions, including:

- The sequence is correct and originates from the specified source.
- The sequences are homologous—all descended in some way from a shared ancestral sequence.
- Each position in a sequence alignment is homologous with every other in that alignment.
- Each of the multiple sequences included in a common analysis has a common phylogenetic history with the other sequences.
- The sampling of taxa is adequate to resolve the problem under study.
- Sequence variation among the samples is representative of the broader group.
- The sequence variability in the sample contains phylogenetic signal adequate to resolve the problem under study.

A straightforward phylogenetic analysis consists of four steps:

1. Alignment—building the data model and extracting a dataset.
2. Determining the substitution model—consider sequence variation.
3. Tree building.
4. Tree evaluation.

Key Features of DNA-based Phylogenetic Trees

Studies of gene and protein evolution often involve the comparison of homologs, sequences that have common origins but may or may not have common activity. Sequences that share an arbitrary level of similarity determined by alignment of matching bases are homologous. These sequences are inherited from a common ancestor that possessed similar structure, although the ancestor may be difficult to determine because it has been modified through descent.

Homologs are most commonly defined as orthologs, paralogs, or xenologs.

> **Orthologs** are homologs produced by speciation—they represent genes derived from a common ancestor that diverged because of divergence of the organism. Orthologs tend to have similar function.
>
> **Paralogs** are homologs produced by gene duplication and represent genes derived from a common ancestral gene that duplicated within an organism and then diverged. Paralogs tend to have different functions.
>
> **Xenologs** are homologs resulting from the horizontal transfer of a gene between two organisms. The function of xenologs can be variable, depending on how significant the change in context was for the horizontally moving gene. In general, though, the function tends to be similar.

This tree shows the relationship between four homologous genes: A, B, C, and D. The topology of this tree consists of four external nodes (A, B, C, and D), each one representing one of the four genes, and two internal nodes (e and f) representing ancestral genes. The branch lengths indicate the degree of evolutionary differences between the genes. This particular tree is unrooted—it is only an illustration of the relationships between genes A, B, C, and D and does not signify anything about the series of evolutionary events that led to these genes. The second depicts three rooted trees that can be drawn from the unrooted tree shown above, each representing the different evolutionary pathways possible between these four genes. A rooted tree is often referred to as an inferred tree. This is to emphasize that this type of illustration depicts only the series of evolutionary events that are inferred from the data under study and may not be the same as the true tree or the tree that depicts the actual series of evolutionary events that occurred. To distinguish between the pathways, the phylogenetic analysis must include at least one outgroup, a gene that is less closely related to A, B, C, and D than these genes are to each other (panel below). Outgroups enable the root of the tree to be located and the correct evolutionary pathway to be identified. Let's say that the four homologous genes used in the previous tree examples come from human, chimpanzee, gorilla, and orangutan. In this case, an outgroup could be a gene from another primate, such as baboon, which is known to have branched away from the four species above before the common ancestor of the species.

Gene Trees Versus Species Trees

It is assumed that a gene tree, because it is based on molecular data, will be a more accurate and less ambiguous representation of the species tree than that obtainable by morphological comparisons. This may indeed be the case, but it does not mean that the gene tree is the same as the species tree. For this to be true, the internal nodes in both trees would have to be precisely equivalent, and they are not. An internal node in a gene tree indicates the divergence of an ancestral gene into two genes with different DNA sequences, usually resulting from a mutation of one sort or another. An internal node in a species tree represents what is called a speciation event, whereby the population of the ancestral species splits into two groups that are no longer able to interbreed. These two events, mutation and speciation, do not always occur at the same time.

- **Monophyletic:** two or more DNA sequences that are derived from a single common ancestral DNA sequence.
- Clade: a group of monophyletic DNA sequences that make up all of the sequences included in the analysis that are descended from a particular common ancestral sequence.
- **Parsimony:** an approach that decides between different tree topologies by identifying the one that involves the shortest evolutionary pathway. This is the pathway that requires the smallest number of nucleotide changes to go from the ancestral sequence, at the root of the tree, to all of the present-day sequences that have been compared.
- **Molecular Clock Hypothesis:** states that nucleotide substitutions, or amino acid substitutions if proteins are being compared, occur at a constant rate, that is, the degree of difference between two sequences can be used to assign a date to the time at which their ancestral sequence diverged. The rate of molecular change differs among groups of organisms, among genes, and even among different parts of the same gene. Furthermore, molecular clocks require calibration with fossils to determine timing of origin of clades, and thus their accuracy is crucially dependent on the fossil record, or lack thereof, for the groups under study. Fossil DNA older than about 25,000–50,000 years is virtually empty of phylogenetic signal except in rare instances, and therefore traditional morphological studies of extinct and extant organisms remain a crucial component of phylogenetic analysis.

Systematics and NCBI

The purpose of NCBI's Taxonomy Project is to build a consistent phylogenetic taxonomy for the NCBI sequence databases. The Taxonomy Database contains the names and lineages of every organism represented by at least one nucleotide or protein sequence in the NCBI genetic databases. As of February 2003, this total is over 250,000 taxa. For current information, visit NCBI's Taxonomy Statistics Web page. The database is recognized as the standard reference by the international sequence database collaboration (GenBank, EMBL, DDJB, and Swiss-Prot). The Taxonomy Browser is an NCBI-derived search tool that allows an individual to search the Taxonomy database. Using the browser, information may be retrieved on available nucleotide, protein, and structure records for a particular species or higher taxon. The Taxonomy Browser can be used to view the taxonomic position or retrieve sequence and structural data for a particular organism or group of organisms. Searches may be made on the basis of whole, partial, or phonetically spelled organism names, and direct links to organisms commonly used in biological research are also provided. The Entrez Taxonomy system has the ability to display custom taxonomic trees representing user-defined subsets of the full NCBI taxonomy. TaxPlot, another component of the Taxonomy project, is a research tool for conducting three-way comparisons of different genomes. Comparisons are based on the sequences of the proteins encoded in that organism's genome. To use TaxPlot, one selects a reference genome to which two other genomes will be compared. The TaxPlot tool then uses a pre-computed BLAST result to plot a point for each protein predicted to be included in the reference genome.

BLAST: Detecting New Sequence Similarities

Currently, the characters most widely used for

phylogenetic analysis are DNA and protein sequences. DNA sequences may be compared directly, or for those regions that code for a known protein, translated into protein sequences. Creating phylogenies from nucleotide or amino acid sequences first requires aligning the bases so that the differences between the sequences being studied are easier to spot. The introduction of NCBI's BLAST, or The Basic Local Alignment Search Tool, in 1990 made it easier to rapidly scan huge databases for overt homologies, or sequence similarity, and to statistically evaluate the resulting matches. BLAST works by comparing a user's unknown sequence against the database of all known sequences to determine likely matches. In a matter of seconds, the BLAST server compares the user's sequence with up to a million known sequences and determines the closest matches. Specialized BLASTs are also available for human, mouse, microbial, and many other genomes. A single BLAST search can compare a sequence of interest to all other sequences stored in GenBank, NCBI's nucleotide sequence database. In this step, a researcher has the option of limiting the search to a specific taxonomic group. If the full scientific name or relationship of species of interest is not known, the user can search for such details using NCBI's Taxonomy Browser, which provides direct links to some of the organisms commonly used in molecular research projects, such as the zebrafish, fruit fly, bakers yeast, nematode, and many more. BLAST next tallies the differences between sequences and assigns a "score" based on sequence similarity. The scores assigned in a BLAST search have a well-defined statistical interpretation, making real sequence matches easier to distinguish from random background hits. This is because BLAST uses a special algorithm, or mathematical formula, that seeks local as opposed to global alignments and is therefore able to detect relationships among sequences that share only isolated regions of similarity. Taxonomy-related

BLAST results are presented in three formats based on the information found in NCBI's Taxonomy database. The Organism Report sorts BLAST comparisons, also called hits, by species such that all hits to a given organism are grouped together. The Lineage Report provides a view of the relationships between the organisms based on NCBI's Taxonomy database. The Taxonomy Report provides in-depth details on the relationship between all the organisms in the BLAST hit list.

COGs: Phylogenetic Classification of Proteins

The database of Clusters of Orthologous Groups of proteins (COGs) represents an attempt at the phylogenetic classification of proteins, a scheme that indicates the evolutionary relationships between organisms, from complete genomes. Each COG includes proteins that are thought to be orthologous, or connected through vertical evolutionary descent. COGs may be used to detect similarities and differences between species, for identifying protein families and predicting new protein functions, and to point to potential drug targets in disease-causing species. The database is accompanied by the COGnitor program, which assigns new proteins, typically from newly sequenced genomes, to pre-existing COGs. A Web page containing additional structural and functional information is now associated with each COG. These hyperlinked information pages include: systematic classification of the COG members under the different classification systems; indications of which COG members (if any) have been characterized genetically and biochemically; information on the domain architecture of the proteins constituting the COG and the three-dimensional structure of the domains if known or predictable; a succinct summary of the common structural and functional features of the COG members, as well as peculiarities of individual members; and key references.

HomoloGene

HomoloGene is a database of both curated and calculated orthologs and homologs for the organisms represented in NCBI's UniGene database. Curated orthologs include gene pairs from the Mouse Genome Database (MGD) at the Jackson Laboratory, the Zebrafish Information (ZFIN) database at the University of Oregon, and from published reports. Computed orthologs and homologs are identified from BLAST nucleotide sequence comparisons between all UniGene clusters for each pair of organisms. HomoloGene also contains a set of triplet clusters in which orthologous clusters in two organisms are both orthologous to the same cluster in a third organism. HomoloGene can be searched via the Entrez retrieval system.

> **UniGene** is a system for automatically partitioning GenBank sequences into a non-redundant set of gene-oriented clusters. Each UniGene cluster contains sequences that represent a unique gene, as well as related information, such as the tissue types in which the gene has been expressed and map location.

Entrez Genome

The whole genomes of over 1,200 organisms can be found in Entrez Genomes. The genomes represent both completely sequenced organisms and those for which sequencing is in progress. All three main domains of life—bacteria, archaea, and eukaryotes— are represented, as well as many viruses, viroids, plasmids, and eukaryotic organelles. Data can be accessed hierarchically starting from either an alphabetical listing or a phylogenetic tree for complete genomes in each of six principle taxonomic groups. One can follow the hierarchy to a variety of graphical overviews, including that of the whole genome of a single organism, a single chromosome, or even a single gene. At each level, one can access multiple views of the data, pre-computed summaries, and links to analyses appropriate for that level. In addition, any gene product (protein) that is a member of a COG is linked to the COGs database. A summary of COG functional groups is also presented in tabular and graphical formats at the genome level. For complete microbial genomes, pre-computed BLAST neighbors for protein sequences, including their taxonomic distribution and links to 3D structures, are given in TaxTables and PDBTables, respectively. Pairwise sequence alignments are presented graphically and linked to NCBI's Cn3D macro-molecular viewer that allows the interactive display of three-dimensional structures and sequence alignments.

PDBeast: Taxonomy in MMDB

NCBI's Structure Group, in collaboration with NCBI taxonomists, has undertaken taxonomy annotation for the three-dimensional structure data stored in the Molecular Modeling Database (MMDB). A semi-automated approach has been implemented in which a human expert checks, corrects, and validates automatic taxonomic assignments in MMDB. The PDBeast software tool was developed by NCBI for this purpose. It pulls text descriptions of "Source Organisms" from either the original entries or user-specified information and looks for matches in the NCBI Taxonomy database to record taxonomy assignments.

> The Molecular Modeling Database (MMDB) is a compilation of three-dimensional structures of biomolecules obtained from the Protein Data Bank (PDB). The PDB, managed and maintained by the Research Collaboratory for Structural Bioinformatics, is a collection of all publicly available three-dimensional structures of proteins, nucleic acids, carbohydrates, and a variety of other complexes experimentally determined by X-ray crystallography and NMR. The difference between the two databases is that MMDB records reorganize and validate the information stored in the database in a way

that enables cross-referencing between the chemistry and the three-dimensional structure of macromolecules. By integrating chemical, sequence, and structure information, MMDB is designed to serve as a resource for structure-based homology modeling and protein structure prediction.

The Importance of Molecular Phylogenetics

The field of molecular phylogenetics has grown, both in size and in importance, since its inception in the early 1990s, attributable mostly to advances in molecular biology and more rigorous methods for phylogenetic tree building. The importance of phylogenetics has also been greatly enhanced by the successful application of tree reconstruction, as well as other phylogenetic techniques, to more diverse and perplexing issues in biology. Today, a survey of the scientific literature will show that molecular biology, genetics, evolution, development, behavior, epidemiology, ecology, systematics, conservation biology, and forensics are but a few examples of the many disparate fields conceptually united by the methods and theories of molecular phylogenetics. Phylogenies are used essentially the same way in all of these fields, either by drawing inferences from the structure of the tree or from the way the character states map onto the tree. Biologists can then use these clues to build hypotheses and models of important events in history. Broadly speaking, the relationships established by phylogenetic trees often describe a species' evolutionary history and, hence, its phylogeny—the historical relationships among lineages or organisms or their parts, such as their genes. Phylogenies may be thought of as a natural and meaningful way to order data, with an enormous amount of evolutionary information contained within their branches. Scientists working in these different areas can then use these phylogenies to study and elucidate the biological processes occurring at many levels of life's hierarchy.

Pharmacogenomics

Adverse Drug Reaction. These three simple words convey little of the horror of a severe negative reaction to a prescribed drug. But such negative reactions can nonetheless occur. A 1998 study of hospitalized patients published in the *Journal of the American Medical Association* reported that in 1994, adverse drug reactions accounted for more than 2.2 million serious cases and over 100,000 deaths, making adverse drug reactions (ADRs) one of the leading causes of hospitalization and death in the United States. Currently, there is no simple way to determine whether people will respond well, badly, or not at all to a medication; therefore, pharmaceutical companies are limited to developing drugs using a "one size fits all" system. This system allows for the development of drugs to which the "average" patient will respond. But, as the statistics above show, one size does NOT fit all, sometimes with devastating results. What is needed is a way to solve the problem of ADRs before they happen. The solution is in sight though, and it is called pharmacogenomics.

The way a person responds to a drug (this includes both positive and negative reactions) is a complex trait that is influenced by many different genes. Without knowing all of the genes involved in drug response, scientists have found it difficult to develop genetic tests that could predict a person's response to a particular drug. Once scientists discovered that people's genes show small variations (or changes) in their nucleotide (DNA base) content, all of that changed—genetic testing for predicting drug response is now possible. Pharmacogenomics is a science that examines the inherited variations in genes that dictate drug response and explores the ways these variations can be used to predict whether a patient will have a good response to a drug, a bad response to a drug, or no response at all.

- **Pharmacogenomics** refers to the general study of all of the many different genes that determine drug behavior.
- **Pharmacogenetics** refers to the study of inherited differences (variation) in drug metabolism and response.

  The distinction between the two terms is considered arbitrary, however, and now the two terms are used interchangeably.

  DNA sequencing is the determination of the order of nucleotides (the base sequence) in a DNA molecule.

Right now, there is a race to catalog as many of the genetic variations found within the human genome as possible. These variations, or SNPs (pronounced "snips"), as they are commonly called, can be used as a diagnostic tool to predict a person's drug response. For SNPs to be used in this way, a person's DNA must be examined (sequenced) for the presence of specific SNPs. The problem is, however, that traditional gene sequencing technology is very slow and expensive and has therefore impeded the widespread use of SNPs as a diagnostic tool. DNA microarrays (or DNA chips) are an evolving technology that should make it possible for doctors to examine their patients for the presence of specific SNPs quickly and affordably. A single microarray can now be used to screen 100,000 SNPs found in a patient's genome in a matter of hours. As DNA microarray technology is developed further, SNP screening in the doctor's office to determine a patient's response to a drug, prior to drug prescription, will be commonplace. SNP screenings will benefit drug development and testing because pharmaceutical companies could exclude from clinical trials those people whose pharmacogenomic screening would show that the drug being tested would be harmful or ineffective for them. Excluding these people will increase the chance that a drug will show itself useful to a particular population group and will thus increase the chance that the same drug will make it into the marketplace. Pre-screening clinical trial subjects should also allow the clinical trials to be smaller, faster, and therefore less expensive; therefore, the consumer could benefit in reduced drug costs. Finally, the ability to assess an individual's reaction to a drug before it is prescribed will increase a physician's confidence in prescribing the drug and the patient's confidence in taking the drug, which in turn should encourage the development of new drugs tested in a like manner.

Pre-screening should allow clinical trials to be smaller, faster, and less expensive; therefore, the consumer could benefit in reduced drug costs.

The explosion in both SNP and microarray data generated from the human genome project has necessitated the development of a means of cataloging and annotating (briefly describing) these data so that scientists can more easily access and use it for their research. NCBI, always on the forefront of bioinformatics research, has developed database repositories for both SNP (dbSNP) and microarray (GEO) data. These databases include either descriptive information about the data within the site itself and links to NCBI and external information resources. Access to these data and information resources will allow scientists to more easily interpret data that will be used not only to help determine drug response but to study disease susceptibility and conduct basic research in population genetics. Right now, in doctors' offices all over the world, patients are given medications that either don't work or have bad side effects. Often, a patient must return to their doctor over and over again until the doctor can find a drug that is right for them. Pharmacogenomics offers a very appealing alternative. Imagine a day when you go into your doctor's office and, after a simple and rapid test of your DNA, your doctor changes her/his mind about a drug considered for you because your genetic test indicates that you could suffer a severe negative reaction to the medication. However, upon further examination of your test results, your doctor finds that you would benefit greatly from a new drug on the market, and that there would be little likelihood that you would react negatively to it. A day like this will be coming to your doctor's office soon, brought to you by pharmacogenomics.

GENOMICS

Selling DNA Data

Human cells are almost ridiculously tiny and efficient. Every one of them has an entire genetic instruction set - three billion As, Cs, Gs and Ts - packed into a nucleus one hundredth of a millimeter across. And a few cents worth of carbon, nitrogen and phosphorus will keep millions of cells happy in a dish, reproducing themselves and their DNA data. Incyte Pharmaceuticals, Inc. (Palo Alto, Calif.) also stores DNA data, but in a way that is somewhat less compact and far more likely to impress a computer geek. Ground-zero for Incyte is a highly air-conditioned room filled with scores of black, towering supercomputers worth up to a million dollars each. Nine of the ten largest pharmaceutical companies in the world each pay Incyte ~$5 million per year to look at the data on those computers. The money has brought an expanding workforce - from 160 to 675 employees in the last two and a half years - and a frantic effort to keep generating more and more information. "We're maybe a year away from going bankrupt if we don't pursue new technologies at any one point," says Tod Klingler, Director of Research Bioinformatics at Incyte. The manpower and computer power is needed to tame an ever-growing mountain of DNA sequence information. "We now have 24 organisms completely sequenced we have their entire genetic message written down," says Temple Smith of Boston University.

"This information allows us to get information about one organism and use that to understand another."

AFLP MARKERS COTTON GENETIC DIVERSITY: A CASE STUDY

Amplified fragmentlength polymorphism (AFLP) markers have been used to ascertainthe intensity of inherent diversity and relatedness in cotton (*Gossypium* spp.) plants. The effectiveness of this method to distinguish inter and intra specific difference in cotton could be handy in cultivar recognition and in marker assisted parental selection tool for plant breeders. Twenty cotton cultivars belonging to *Gossypium hirsutum L.*, and *G. arborium L.* from the Pakistan and US origin were used for AFLP based genetic diversity estimates. The objective of this study was to assess the level of genetic variation among some cotton cultivars belonging to the old and new world species of cotton. Four *Eco*RI-*Mse*I primer-pair combinations were used forthe AFLP analysis. The AFLP data assigned the genotypes into groups that corresponded with their origin and lineage relationships and showed a narrow genetic base among these cultivars.

Cotton and cotton products occupy a pivotal position in the world economy. Pakistan is the fifth largest producer of cotton in the world, the third largest exporter of raw cotton, the fourth largest consumer of cotton, and the largest exporter of cotton yarn. It was important to study the genetic diversity of Pakistan's present cotton cultivars and hybrids, which will be used for the development of new cotton genotypes. Previous studies (Wendel, 1989; Brubacker and Wendel, 1994; Multani and Lyon, 1995; Tatineni et al. 1996) revealed that cultivated cotton displays a very low level of genetic diversity. While need for cultivar specific DNA markers in a cottonbreeding program for cultivar registration, plant patents,and breeder's right protection and early detection of agronomic and economic traits as an aid to marker assisted selection is still needed (Brubaker and Wendel, 1994). Polymerase chain reaction (PCR) technology has promoted the development of a range of molecular assay systems which detect polymorphism at the DNA level and offer an alternative to the hybridization-based method of RFLP. In this study we will use the most widely adopted PCR-based marker technologies, AFLPs for characterizing the natural variations of cotton cultivars. The AFLP technique is based on the amplification of short restriction endonuclease digested genomic DNA fragments onto which adaptors have been ligated at both ends. Primers complementary to the adaptors and possessing 30 selective nucleotides of one to four bases are used in a selective amplification reaction. The presence or absence of these selective nucleotides in the genomic fragments being amplified provides the basis for revealing polymorphism. AFLPs tend to generate dominant markers due to the differences in the DNA sequence in the selective 30 nucleotides immediately adjacent to the restriction enzyme site. AFLPs have been used to estimate genetic relationships in many studies including cotton (Pillay and Myers, 1999) lentil (Sharma et al. 1996), soybean (Maughan et al. 1996), and barley (Becker et al. 1995). The objective of this study was to evaluate the genetic diversity in cotton cultivars and hybrids by the use of AFLP marker technology. Plants used in this study were consisted of 19 accessions of *G. hirsutum* and one accession from *G. arborium*. Seed material wasobtained from the cotton-breeding program at Bahauddin Zakaryia University, Multan and Cotton Research Institute, Faisalabad, Pakistan.

Cultivars and Their Special Characters

Rohi old world cotton belonging to *G. arborium.* AC134 (obsolete local cultivar), B557 (obsolete local cultivar), FH87 (high oil content), S14 (high ginning outturn), SA100 (red leaves), these are belongs to the new world *G. hirsutum L.*

Crosses

Laokra 5.5 x SA100, SA100 x Laokra 5.5, S14 x SA100, SA100 x S14, SA100 x Stoneville 857, Stoneville 857 x SA100, SA100 x DPL-7340-424, DPL-7340-424 x SA100, Laokra 5.5 x Stoneville 857, Stoneville 857 x Laokra 5.5, S14 x Stoneville 857, Stoneville x S14, B557 x AC134, AC134 x B557. Seeds were germinated in 20 cm plastic pots in the greenhouse and Genomic DNA was extracted from young expanding leaves using the Nucleon Plant DNA isolation and purification kit. The AFLP procedure (Vos et al. 1995) and as modified by Pillay and Myers (1999) was used to access the genetic diversity. DNA of 250 ng was extracted from all the 20 cultivars. The DNA was digested with *Eco*RIand *Mse*RI at 37°C for 2 hrs. A small aliquot of the digested DNA was run on a 1.5% (w/v) agarose gel to check if the DNA digestion was complete. The digested samples were incubated at 70°C for 15 min to inactivate the restriction endonucleases. *Eco*RI and *Mse*RI adapters were ligated to the digested DNA samples to generate template DNA for amplification. Preamplification was carried out with +1-primers each carrying one selective nucleotide (*Eco*RI + A, *Mse*RI + C) in a thermocycler for 20 cyclesset at 94°C denaturation (30 sec), 56°C annealing (60 sec), and 72°C extension (60 sec). The initial denaturation was done at 94°C for 30 sec and the final extension at 72°C for 8 min. The amplification products were diluted 20-fold in TE buffer and stored at -20°C. Selective AFLP amplification was carried out with *Eco*RI + 3 primers and *Mse*RI +3 primers and 5 μL of the diluted PCR products from the preamplification.Four primer pair combinations of *Eco*RI + 3 (E-plus three nucleotides) and *Mse*RI + 3 (M-plus 3 nucleotides) were tested and include: (i) E-AAG/M-CTC, (ii) E-AAG/M-CTG, (iii) E-ACC/M-CAC, and (iv)E-AAG/M-CAA. The PCR amplifications were carried out as follows: one cycle at 94°C for 30 sec, 65°C for 30 sec, and 72°C for 60 sec; followed by 12 cycles of touchdown PCR in which theannealing temperature was decreased by 0.7°C every cycleuntil a touchdown annealing temperature of 56°C was reached. Once reached, another 20 cycles were conducted as describedabove for preamplification. The reaction product (2 μL) was mixed with an equal volumeof formamide loading buffer (98% [v/v] formamide, 10 m*M* EDTA,0.005% [v/v] of each of xylene cyanol and bromophenol blue) denatured by incubating at 90°C for 5 min and quickly cooled on ice. The products were analyzed on 5% (w/v) denaturing polyacrylamidegels. The gel was run at constant power (50-55 W) until the xylene cyanol was about two-thirds down the length of thegel. The gel was silver stained. Bands that showed clear polymorphisms were scored visually as present (1) or absent (0). Cluster analysis was performed to provide a statistical basis to establish the number of cluster represented by the 20 genotypes. A clustering procedure (hierarchical cluster analysis) was performed using the unweighted pair group mean with arithmetical averages (UPGMA) method (Sneath and Sokal, 1973) by computer programme of SPSS. The output of this analysis was used to derive a dendrogram, which showed the phylogenetic relationships between all the cultivars.

Results and Discussion

Four primer-pair combinations were used to assay 20 cotton plants from each of the 20 accessions for AFLP analysis. An averageof 40 to 80 scorable bands was detected after selective PCR amplification with each primer combination. The bands rangedin size from 50 to 500 bp. The results of agglomeration schedule and the dendrogram of genetic relationshipsfrom UPGMA cluster analysis resulted in five major groups. The *G. hirsutum*geno types were clustered into four major groups depending upon their origins, while the *G. arboreum* formed one separate group. The AFLP dendrogram assigned the genotypesinto groups corresponding with their origin and pedigree relationships. This study showed that AFLP is a very sensitive technique for detecting markers for genetic studies in cotton. Banding patterns obtained with AFLP were highly reproducible when the same sample DNA is used in independent experiments (Pillay and Myers, 1999). We used silver staining, the silver stained AFLP gels are considered to produce a larger number of better-defined bands than ^{32}P-labeled gels (Cho et al. 1996). The cross Stoneville 857 x S14 (18) and cross S14 x Stoneville 857 (17) are reciprocal crosses of the parents Laokra 5.5 and SA100 and combined at the first level. Cultivar SA100 (6) joined this group at level three to form one group. The second group consisted of three sisters groups i.e. cross Stoneville 857 x Laokra 5.5 (16) and cross Laokra 5.5 x Stoneville 857(15) were reciprocal crosses, while cross B557 x AC134 (19) and cross AC134 x B557 (20) were also reciprocal crosses of parents Laokra 5.5 and Stoneville 857, while third sister group consisted of crosses SA100 x DPL-7340-424 (13) and DPL-7340-424 x SA100 (14), which were reciprocal crosses of parents SA100 and DPL-7340-424. These two groups comprised of all the genotypes of US origin; this could explain the formation of this cluster. The third cluster consisted of both US and Pakistan originated cultivars and crosses. The first subgroup consisted of crosses SA100 x Stoneville 857 (11) and Stoneville 857 x SA100 (12), while the second subgroup consisted of crosses S14 x SA100 (9) and SA100 x S14 (10), while cultivar (5) S14 combined with this cluster at stage 4. S14 cultivar was a selection from cultivar S12 which was a hybrid of Pakistan and US origin varieties (MNH93 x 7203-14-4 Arizona). The fourth cluster consisted of the crosses SA100 x Laokra 5.5 (8) and Laokra 5.5 x SA100 (7) formed the first subgroup and these were reciprocal crosses of cultivars SA100 and Laokra 5.5, this subgroup was combined with cultivar (3) B557, whose parent was (268F x L5). The cultivars AC134 (2) and FH87 (4) formed one group and these were the Pakistan local cultivars. The parentage of cultivar FH87 was (AC134 x Paymaster) while that of cultivar AC134 was (148F x 199F). The fifth group consisted of the only one cultivar Rohi (1) which originated from a cross (D9 x Local exotic) belongs to diploid spp. *G. arborium* and stands alone from the other cultivars of *G. hirsutum* spp. In the early 1970, high yielding tetraploid cotton varieties of US origin were introduced into Pakistan, and of these, the varieties that were better adapted were released directly for general cultivation. Those that were less adapted were crossed with local breeding lines. The same gene pool was used repeatedly and resulted in a narrow genetic base (Iqbal et al. 1997). A unique feature of the AFLP data is its ability to discriminate all the taxa used in this study making it a very promising marker system in cotton especially since modern cotton cultivars are closely related and have a high level of genetic uniformity (Van Esbroeck et al. 1998). AFLP data clearly differentiated the diploid and tetraploid species from each other. In conclusion this study showed that with the help of AFLP technique one can easily discriminate closely related taxa in cotton and provides sufficient evidence in the shape of numbers of polymorphic markers for variety identification.

PRODUCTION OF RHODOTORULA GLUTINIS

Rhodotorula glutinis is a yeast that secretes the enzyme á-L-arabinofuranosidase (E.C. 3.2.1.55) into the culture medium and thus has an interesting biotechnological potential. To determine improved culture conditions of this organism, different factors of the culture media were evaluated such as the use of peptone as nitrogen source, salts composition, pH and growth temperature. Likewise, beet molasses and beet cosette were tested as industrial carbon sources to induce the production of the enzyme and how they influence the yeast growth. Based on these studies a culture medium is proposed for growth of this yeast in a continuous system. By assaying different dilution rates an average specific activity for the enzyme of 82.4 U/mg of protein was obtained.

The study of the aromas of fruits has revealed an important source of volatile compounds that may enrich the aromatic profile of juices and fermented drinks. The chemical composition of these potential aromas is formed by volatile compounds such as monoterpenes, derived from shikimate or C13 nonsoprenoids, which are linked to â-D-glucosides or diglicosides (Williams et al. 1982; Gunata et al. 1985). These compounds linked to sugars are released in two steps: initially, an á-arabinofuranosidase (Abf), an á-rhamnosidase or a â-apiosidase participate, followed closely by the action of a â-D-glucosidase (Gunata et al. 1988). Many of these aromatic compounds are naturally liberated during the fruit ripening (Cordonnier et al. 1989); however, the enzymatic activities of the plants are unable to liberate them completely leaving an important source of potential aromas in the juice (Gunata et al. 1985; Cordonnier et al. 1989). Therefore, some studies have been carried out to obtain endogenous enzymes, mainly from fungi and yeasts, which release these aromas. In general, these studies have been centred on identifying microorganisms with â-glucosidase activities and very few microorganisms have been considered that secrete the enzymes that participate in the first step of the reactions of the release of aromatic compounds (Gunata et al. 1990; Dupin et al. 1992; Gueguen et al. 1995; Lounteri et al. 1995; Charoenchai et al. 1997; Le Clinche et al. 1997, Spagna et al. 1998; Fernández et al. 2000; Manzanares et al. 2000; Spagna et al. 2000; Gallego et al. 2001; Strauss et al. 2001; Belancic et al. 2003). Generally, the glycosylated compounds are formed by a non-reductor á-L-arabinofuranoside (Gunata et al. 1990); therefore it would be interesting to use enzymes that hydrolyze this bond and allow the liberation of the volatile compound through the action of a â-glucosidase. This sequence of enzymatic activities would permit the enrichment of the aromatic profile of the product. In grapes, the most abundant volatile compounds are monoterpenes, which can be free or linked to the disaccharides arabinofuranosilglucosides of geraniol, nerol and linalool (Williams et al. 1982; Gunata et al. 1988). The á-L-arabinofuranosidase activity (E.C. 3.2.1.55) has been mainly described in fungus (Rombouts et al. 1988; Gunata et al. 1990; Le Clinche et al. 1997; De Ioannes et al. 2000). However, due to the physicochemical characteristics of some products, such as wine, it is difficult to maintain the enzymatic activities stable during the elaboration process. Therefore, some authors have searched for enzymes from microorganisms that participate in the must fermentation process like yeasts, and these studies have been mainly focused on the â-glucosidase activity more than on the activities responsible for hydrolysis of the disaccharide bond (Gueguen et al. 1995; Manzanares et al. 1999; Charoenchai et al. 1997; Fernández et al. 2000; Strauss et al. 2001; Belancic et al. 2003). In light of the potential use that an Abf activity would have in the enological industry, in this work we studied the culture conditions of *R. glutinis*, a yeast that has been shown to produce Abf and are naturally present in fermentative processes. Furthermore, we evaluated the specific activity of this enzyme under continuous culture.

Microorganism

Rhodotorula glutinis strain L-1816 was isolated from Cabernet Sauvignon grapes and was maintained on YPD medium containing 2% (w/v) glucose, 2% (w/v) peptone and 1% (w/v) yeast extract.

Growth and Culture Assays

The yeast inoculums for batch and continuous culture with 1 x 10^6 cells/mL were obtained by growth in YPD. Duplicate batch cultures were carried out in 250-mL flasks with 125 mL of assayed medium under mechanical shaking at 150 rpm. During the culture period growth was monitored by measuring absorbance at 475 nm every 0.5 and 1 hr, depending on the growth phase in which the culture was found. The dry cell mass concentration was determined from the optical density reading by using the following equation: dry cell mass = 0.31 OD_{475}, 0.31 being the slope of a standard curve of dry cell mass (in g/L) versus OD_{475} (r^2 = 0.9931). The specific growth rates (μ) were calculated by least-squares fitting to the linear part of the semilog growth plot. The basal culture media used contained 0.5% (w/v) yeast extract and a salts solution composed of 0.3% (w/v) $(NH_4)_2SO_4$, 0.1% (w/v) KH_2PO_4 and 0.05% (w/v) $MgSO_4$ x $7H_2O$. Modifications to the basal media are described below. Similarly, different pH and temperature conditions were evaluated. As a way of defining an improved culture media for the growth of *R. glutinis*, several modifications to the basal media were evaluated. Growth assays of the yeast were carried out in basal media with and without peptone. Furthermore, assays were carried out with different types and concentration of salts denominated II (0.3% (w/v) $(NH_4)_2SO_4$, 0.1% (w/v) KH_2PO_4, 0.05% (w/v) $MgSO_4$ x $7H_2O$ and 0.005% (w/v) $FeSO_4$ x $7H_2O$), III (0.3% (w/v) $(NH_4)_2SO_4$, 0.1% (w/v) KH_2PO_4, 0.05% (w/v) $MgSO_4$ x $7H_2O$ and 0.001% (w/v) $MnCl_2$ x $4H_2O$) and IV (0.3% (w/v) $(NH_4)_2SO_4$, 0.1% (w/v) KH_2PO_4, 0.05% (w/v) $MgSO_4$ x $7H_2O$, 0.005% (w/v) $FeSO_4$ x $7H_2O$ and 0.001% (w/v) $MnCl_2$ x $4H_2O$). The salts composition of the basal culture media was denominated as salt composition I. Finally, as a means of determining the influence of the carbon source on the yeast growth, 2% (w/v) beet cosette and 2% (w/v) beet molasses were also evaluated.

For this, the beet cosette was weighed, grinded and mixed with 100 mL distilled water. This mix was vigorously agitated and kept at 80°C for 20 to 30 min. Subsequently, it was filtered using a Watman N°1 filter paper for use in the preparation of the culture media. The effect of the culture temperature on the growth of the yeast was also studied. The temperatures assayed were 20, 25, 28 and 37°C. Furthermore, the effect of the culture media pH on the growth of *R. glutinis* was determined. The cultures were initially adjusted to pH 4.0 or 5.2. The pH was adjusted using 0.5 M citric acid.

Enzymatic Assays

The á-L-arabinofuranosidase activity was qualitatively determined according to Ganga and Martínez (2004). In brief, Petri dishes with culture media containing 0.17% (w/v) yeast nitrogen base (YNB, Difco); 0.5% (w/v) ammonium sulphate, 0.004% (w/v) 4-methylumbelliferyl-á-L-arabinofuranoside (Sigma) and 2% (w/v) agar-agar were used. The carbon sources assayed were beet cosette (Industria Azucarera Nacional S.A (Iansa)-Chile) and beet molasses (Iansa-Chile) at 0.2, 0.5, 1 and 2% (w/v) concentrations as indicated. The glycosidase activity was observed by the presence of UV fluorescence around the colony. To quantify the Abf activity, the culture media was centrifuged at 8000 g for 15 min at 10°C. The supernatant was concentrated 20 times using a Minitan ultrafiltration system (Millipore Corp. Bedford, MA) with a 10,000 molecular weight cutoff polysulfone filter. The culture media without inoculum served as a control. The Abf quantification was done using 4 mM *p*-nitrophenyl-á-L-arabinofuranoside (*p*NPáAF) (Sigma) as substrate according to the methodology used by Le Clinche et al. (1997). Assays were performed by incubating a reaction mixture containing 250 ìL of 1 mM of substrate in 50 mM succinate buffer, pH 5.5 and 250 ìL of culture media at

40°C for 20 min. The reaction was stopped by addition of 1 mL of 2 M Na_2CO_3, and the liberation of *p*-nitrophenol was measured spectrophotomet-rically at 405 nm. One unit of enzyme activity was defined as the amount of enzyme necessary for the formation of 1 ìmol of *p*-nitrophenol per minute under the conditions of the assay. The protein quantification was carried out according to the equation $A_{205}/(27 + 120(A_{280}/A_{205}))$ with readings at both 205 nm and 280 nm wavelengths (Scopes, 1974).

Production of R. glutinis in a Continuous System

The growth of *R. glutinis* was carried out in a laboratory constructed fermentor under continuous operation. The fermentor was constructed with a 1 L glass vessel (with an internal diameter of 9.4 cm and 15.34 cm in height) submerged 14 cm in a controlled water bath. The system was agitated at 200 rpm with a magnetic stir plate (Heidolph, Germany), and fed with sterile culture media by a flow controlled peristaltic pump (Masterflex, USA). Furthermore, sterile air was injected by the use of a compressor and the flow regulated with a flowmeter (Gilmont Instruments, USA). The system was equipped with a pH probe and an acid/base flow controlled system (Cole Parmer Instruments Co, USA). Antifoam was added manually through a sterile syringe connected to the fermentor. The culture media was defined in the present study. The fermentation conditions were 1 L/min of air flow, pH 5.2 and 28°C.

Statistical Analyses

Statistical analyses were performed with Statgraphics Plus 4.0 software. Differences between treatment means were compared using the least significant differences (LSD) test with confidence level of 95%. As a way of estimating how the constituents of the culture media influence the growth of *R. glutinis* and the production of Abf, different culture assays were carried out varying the composition of our base medium as indicated above.

Effect of Peptone on Yeast Growth

The yeast *R. glutinis* L-1816 was tested for its capacity to grow, with or without 0.5% (w/v) peptone at 25°C, in the basal culture media supplemented with 2% (w/v) glucose as a carbon source. At 72 hrs of yeast growth, a basal value of 199 ± 0.007 h^{-1} was obtained, whilst for basal medium plus peptone the value was 0.191 ± 0.022 h^{-1}, both being statistically similar.Peptone is a broadly used component of yeast culture media because it is a rich source of nitrogen. However, our results showed that the specific growth rate is not dependent on the presence of peptone in the culture media. These suggest that the basal media used in our study contains an adequate amount of nitrogen salts that are easy assimilated by the yeast and consequently peptone would not be necessary for yeast growth, at least during the time that the assays were carried out.

Effects of the Media Salts Composition on Yeast Growth

Cho et al. (2001) have shown that the use of different nitrogen sources in culture media affects yeast growth. Therefore, a study was carried out to determine the most adequate salts composition in the culture media for optimum growth of the yeast strain used in our investigation. In these experiments, we evaluated the specific growth rates of *R. glutinis* L-1816 using the basal media without peptone and varying the type and concentration of salts as is described in Material and Methods. As before, growth was followed for 72 hrs at 25°C with 2% (w/v) glucose as a carbon. The salts composition I (0.3% (w/v) of $(NH_4)_2SO_4$; 0.1% (w/v) of KH_2PO_4 and 0.05% (w/v) of $MgSO_4$ x $7H_2O$) is an adaptation of that described for *Rhodotorula flava* by Uesaka et al. (1978) and our results show that it also is enough to support the growth of *R. glutinis* L-1816, being superior to the other salts compositions evaluated. The addition of Fe or Mn in the salts composition II, III or IV seems to not have important effects on yeast growth. The growth rate values showed by *R. glutinis* L-1816 in the presence of these minerals are lower than those obtained using salt composition I, which does not possess any of these metals. Likewise, it can be observed that the increase of KH_2PO_4 and $MgSO_4 \times 7H_20$ concentration could have a negative effect on yeast growth.

Study of Industrial Carbon Sources for R. glutinis L-1816 Growth and Abf Production

The industrial carbon sources such as beet molasses and beet cosette have been used in the production of this yeast (Roche et al. 1994; Luonteri et al. 1995; De Ioannes et al. 2000). Likewise, beet cosette has been studied as a cheap substrate source in Chile for some enzyme-producing microorganisms, especially fungi (Illanes et al. 1992; Chamy et al. 1994). Considering this information, we studied the effect of these industrial carbon sources on the growth of the yeast and the production of Abf. For this, the growth and Abf activity of *R. glutinis* L-1816 were evaluated in basal media at 25°C and an initial pH of the culture medium of 5.2 (see below). The media was supplemented with 2% (w/v) of the carbon sources as is indicated. The specific growth rates were determined from 72 hrs cultures showing that beet cosette support the lowest specific growth rate ($\mu = 0.151 \pm 0.012\ h^{-1}$) in comparison to glucose ($\mu = 0.205 \pm 0.010\ h^{-1}$) and beet molasses ($\mu = 0.219 \pm 0.007\ h^{-1}$), where these latter carbon sources did not show significant differences in this growth parameter ($p < 0.05$). Rubio et al. (2002) described that *R. glutinis* has a high invertase activity that would allow the use of media with a high sugar content such as beet molasses. On the other hand, beet cosette presents cellulose and hemicellulose content with only 3.7

g/L of reducing sugars (Illanes and Schaffeld, 1983). This fact could explain the low growth rate observed when the yeast is cultivated with beet cosette, since there would be little availability of easily assimilated carbon substrates when compared with the other two carbon sources assayed. Because the production of Abf in microorganisms is dependent on the substrate present in the culture media (De Ioannes et al. 2000) and considering the eventual applicability of beet molasses or beet cosette as industrial carbon sources for yeast growth, we study the effect of these two substrates on the production of Abf in qualitative assays. For this, *R. glutinis* L-1816 was grown in petri dishes with different concentrations of beet molasses or beet cosette. Our results show that an increase in beet molasses concentration has a negative effect on the Abf activity. This observation could be a consequence of an increase in the sucrose content present in beet molasses whichcan have an inhibitory effect on the production of Abf. For practical considerations, the greatest enzyme secretion was obtained at a concentration of 0.2% (w/v) of beet molasses. Also, beet molasses has approximately 62% (w/v) of carbohydrates and other residues that could induce the production of Abf by the yeast. On the other hand, the effect shown by the beet cosette on the production of Abf by *R. glutinis* L-1816 is independent of its concentration in the culture media. Illanes and Schaffeld (1983) by a hydrolysis experiment of this substrate indicated that its chemical composition includes 58.5% (w/v) of crude fiber. In our case, a hydrolysis was not carried out prior to its incorporation into the culture media, however, part of these components may have passed into solution and it is therefore possible that some induce the production of Abf. De Ioannes et al. (2000) showed that for the case of *Penicillium purpurognum*, beet cosette is a good inducer for the production of this enzyme.

Effects of Temperature and Initial pH of the Culture Media on Yeast Growth

The growth temperature conditions described for *R. glutinis* have been 22°C (Cho et al. 2001) and 30°C (Buzzini and Martin, 2000; Rubio et al. 2002). As a way of defining an adequate temperature for the growth of the yeast under our conditions, assays were carried out using culture temperatures of: 20, 25, 28 and 37°C. In these assays, we estimated the specific growth rates of *R. glutinis* L-1816 at the temperatures indicated using the basal media without peptone. As before, yeast growth was monitored for 72 hrs with 2% (w/v) glucose as a carbon source. Our results suggest that 28°C is the optimum growth temperature, with a specific growth rate value of 0.198 ± 0.006 h^{-1}, although previous reports have obtained yeast growth at 37°C (Kurtzman and Feel, 1999). On the other hand, we have carried out assays in Petri dishes of several native isolates to obtain yeasts with Abf activity (Ganga and Martínez, 2004). As a continuation of these studies, we found that *R. glutinis* L-1816 presents this activity at an acid pH (data not shown). As a way of evaluating the effects of the acid culture media on the growth of this yeast strain, assays were carried out in culture media with an initial pH of 4.0, 5.2 and 7.0. Cho et al. (2001) showed that this yeast showed an important biomass production at an initial pH of between 4.0 and 7.0. Our results that at an initial pH of 5.2, in unbuffered media, the yeast growth rate is greater. Under our culture conditions and pH 7.0, only a residual growth was observed. The study of pH evolution in unbuffered *R. glutinis* L-1816 72 hrs cultures showed an increase of this parameter reaching a value of 7.0, when basal media without peptone at 28°C and beet molasses as carbon source was used. Therefore, we analyzed the effects on the yeast growth of maintaining the pH stable during the whole growth period using phosphate citrate pH 5.2 as buffer. Our results showed that there are no statistical differences in the specific growth rate of the yeast using media at a constant pH of 5.2 or media without pH control but with an initial pH of 5.2. Furthermore, the biomass concentration values at the end of the growth period showed differences of less than 6%. Since growth of this yeast is affected by neutral pHs and these values are observed in our studies in batch cultures, it is therefore important to control this parameter in continuous cultures. Considering the assays above, we proposed that the best growth conditions for Abf production by *R. glutinis* L-1618 are 0.2% (w/v) beet molasses, 0.3% (w/v) $(NH_4)_2SO_4$, 0.1% (w/v) KH_2PO_4, 0.05% (w/v) $MgSO_4$ x $7H_2O$, 0.5% (w/v) yeast extract, pH 5.2 and 28°C.

Production of α-arabinofuranosidase in a Continuous System

Using the culture conditions described in the previous paragraphs, the growth of *R. glutinis* L-1816 was carried out in a continuous culture system for80 hrs to produce Abf. Two dilution rates were assayed. Under these conditions it was possible to obtain a positive correlation between dilution rate and Abf activity, where the latter increased almost five times. Furthermore, an increase in the production of total proteins is also observed, which allowed the specific activity of the enzyme under study be maintained constant. Uesaka et al. (1978) by growing *R. flava* in a medium with purified beet arabinan as carbon source obtained an á-arabinofuranosidase activity of 3.6 mU/mL, a lower value than that obtained in our study at the different flow velocities assayed. On the other hand, the specific activity described by these authors was 0.26 U/mg. In our case, the specific activity obtained for the *R. glutinis* strain L-1816, did not show significant differences between the flows velocities assayed, obtaining an average value of 82.4 U/mg, approximately 23 times greater than that described by

Uesaka et al. (1978). This is mainly because of the low amount of proteins secreted by the yeast, which could correspond to the enzyme under study and therefore our growth conditions for this yeast permit a greater increase in the Abf production.

PRODUCING PHARMACEUTICAL PROTEINS IN PLANTS

Protein-based pharmaceuticals traditionally used for the treatment of disease have been made through the expression of protein in bacterial, fungal, and mammalian cell cultures. Recently, the possibility to produce more diverse and complex pharmaceutical proteins in plants has reached the laboratory benches of scientists and companies worldwide. These pharmaceuticals are known as plant-made or plant-based pharmaceuticals. In this article, we will discuss pharmaceutical proteins, how genetic engineering makes it possible to produce proteins in plants, why plants are desirable for the production of pharmaceutical proteins, and which plant systems are being considered for their production. Additionally, we will discuss risk and regulatory issues associated with this new technology. Proteins are essential to all living organisms for function, structure, and regulation of the body. Protein development in a cell begins with DNA transcribing into RNA, and RNA translating into proteins. Proteins are made up of amino acids that are arranged in different combinations and lengths. The differences in arrangements and lengths of amino acids determine the function of the protein. Some examples of proteins include hormones, enzymes, and antibodies. Many people suffer from infectious, inflammatory, and cardiovascular diseases — and these numbers are growing. Protein-based drugs are the fastest growing class of drugs for the treatment of these diseases in humans and other diseases in animals. The reasons for this are because the numbers of people with diseases such as diabetes are growing and new technologies are making proteins easier to produce. The current methods of production of proteins for pharmaceutical application (mammalian, bacterial, and fungal cell cultures) are predicted to fall short of demand in the near future (Rogers 2003). Insulin was the first pharmaceutical protein produced using genetically engineered bacteria (Thomas et al. 2002). Insulin originally was isolated from cows and pigs that were slaughtered for food. This method was inefficient and caused some patients to develop allergies from the animal-derived insulin. Today it is made from the human gene that codes for the insulin protein and is expressed and cloned in the bacterium, *Escherichia coli.* Large quantities of *E. coli* are now grown in fermentation vats to make tons of human insulin available to the growing number of diabetic patients. Genetic engineering also has made it possible to use plants as factories for pharmaceutical protein production. Plant-made pharmaceuticals are made by inserting a segment of DNA that encodes the protein of choice into plant cells. The plants or plant cells are essentially factories used to produce the desired proteins and are only grown for the purpose of pharmaceutical applications. There are two common methods of transformation (the process by which DNA from one organism is incorporated into the DNA of another organism) that have been established through biotechnology to produce transgenic plants, which, in turn, could be used to create the plants used to make pharmaceutical proteins. The transformation techniques include the *Agrobacterium tumefaciens*-mediated transformation system and biolistics, also called particle bombardment. *Agrobacterium tumefaciens* is a bacterium that naturally infects plants and causes crown gall disease. It is very useful for the production of transgenic plants because it has the amazing ability to transfer a segment of its DNA, called T-DNA, into the nucleus of the plant cells.

The T-DNA from *A. tumefaciens* is then integrated into the plant and transcribed, causing crown gall disease. Scientists have used *A. tumefaciens* to their advantage by inserting their DNA of interest between the T-DNA to create a plant with qualities such as herbicide resistance, or pesticide resistance, as well as many others (Nester et al. 1984, Binns and Thomashow 1988). Crown gall disease does not occur in the plant after being transformed by *A. tumefaciens* because the plasmid has been constructed to disarm the tumor-inducing properties that cause the disease, and instead it expresses the DNA of interest. Biolistics, or the Particle Bombardment Transformation System, employs the use of metal particles either of gold or tungsten. The metal particles are coated with the DNA that is to be transferred into the plant cells. Using a pressurized system, a plastic bullet coated with metal and DNA particles is released from the biolistics machine when the pressure is released. The bullet is shot, and within seconds, stopped by a shield causing the metal coated DNA particles to be knocked off the bullet. The particles are then ultimately forced to be inserted into the plant cells below. Once the genes have been transferred into the cells, the cells expressing the gene of interest must be selected. In most cases, a selectable marker is included with the DNA construct, which will confer resistance to an antibiotic or herbicide. The plant cells that survive the antibiotic or herbicide application are the ones that have successfully received the gene of interest (Purdue Agricultural Biotechnology 2004).

Plant Systems vs. Mammalian and Bacterial Cell Cultures

Plants and plant cells offer several advantages in the production of proteins for pharmaceutical purposes. Unlike mammalian cells and bacterial cells, plants are capable of post-translational modification and other assembly steps that are needed for biological activity in complex multi-component proteins such as antibodies. This in turn allows for more diversity and possibilities of drugs that could be conceived from the proteins produced in plants (Rogers 2003, Goldstein and Thomas 2004). When a protein is glycosylated, this means a certain sugar molecule is added to its structure, causing it to fold in a specific and unique orientation. The way the protein is folded determines its function and activity. Plants are capable of producing more complex proteins with no assistance because they are capable of glycosylation on their own, whereas mammalian cells need assistance to glycosylate complex proteins. The system needed to maintain and create complex proteins in mammalian cells is expensive and difficult to maintain, which makes plant systems a more attractive source for protein production. (Fischer et al. 2003). Mammalian cells are difficult and expensive to grow; therefore, bacterial cells are used to produce proteins when glycosylation is not required. Bacterial cells still have the potential of being contaminated, and require facilities to be built to keep up with the growing demand of proteins needed for drug production. This is why plants are an excellent alternative to mammalian and bacterial cell cultures; they have to ability to glycosylate complex proteins and are inexpensive to grow in large quantities.

Plant Options

Plant-made pharmaceutical production has the potential to provide large amounts of protein for the pharmaceutical industry. The types of plants used for pharmaceutical protein production depend largely on their final application. To date, the plants that have successfully been transformed include tobacco, potato, tomato, corn, soybeans, alfalfa, rice, and wheat. However, it is important to emphasize that no commercially available pharmaceutical products are currently produced in plants (Ma et al. 2003). Tobacco was the first plant to be genetically engineered and has the advantage of being used as a plant biopharmaceutical for exactly that reason; the methods for gene transfer and expression are well established for this plant. Tobacco can also be cropped multiple times per year, giving it an edge over other plants in producing a large biomass (Fischer et al. 2003). The protein of interest can also be targeted to the seed. In tobacco, up to one million seeds can be made on a single plant (Daniell et al. 2001). One concern associated with using tobacco as a protein factory is that it has toxic alkaloids associated with it, which could be present in the final drug that is administered to the patient. Another concern is that if the protein is targeted for the leaf tissue, it must be frozen or dried and then processed immediately, making it difficult to harvest and store for preservation of the protein (Ma et al. 2003). Legumes, such as alfalfa and soybean, and cereal crops, such as corn and rice, have been considered as ideal candidates for plant biopharmaceuticals because the protein can be targeted to accumulate in the seed and the seed can be harvested and stored for an extended amount of time. Legumes are good candidates because they naturally produce large amounts of protein in their seeds, making the final protein recovery much larger. When considering a cereal crop as a protein factory, yield is the main quality of importance, as well as ease of transformation and speed of production scale-up (Ma et al. 2003).

Protein Application

The application of the proteins made in plants include, antibodies, vaccines, hormones, enzymes, interleukins, interferons, and human serum albumins. Monoclonal antibodies have the potential to be among the first protein pharmaceuticals commercially produced in plants (Rogers 2003). Antibodies are produced in vertebrate immune systems to recognize and bind to antigens with amazing specificity. Because antibodies possess this specificity they can be used as diagnostic tools as well as prevention and treatment of diseases (Fischer et al. 2003). There are at least six types of plant-derived recombinant antibodies that have moved to the preclinical stage of testing, and one more advanced antibody in phase II clinical trial (Ma et al. 2003). A possible use for monoclonal antibodies is to one day attach a chemotherapeutic agent onto the antibody and allow it to specifically bind to a tumor cell and eventually the chemotherapeutic agent will destroy the tumor cell (Rogers 2003). Another application for plant-made pharmaceuticals is the production of vaccines. Subunit vaccines are made up of specific macromolecules that induce a protective immune response against a pathogen. Subunit vaccine technology has increased the safety of administering vaccines because it does not involve the use of live or weakened viruses. Currently, it is very expensive to produce subunit vaccines as well as to store them because they are not heat-stable. Because the vaccines are not heat-stable, this limits where they can be sent for use and unfortunately makes them unavailable in the developing countries where vaccines are needed the most. Producing the vaccines in plants eliminates the heat-stability issue because the vaccinogenic plant tissue can be administered raw, dried, or in an encapsulated form; all of these forms can be stored and shipped at room temperature (Sala et al. 2003). The risk of contamination with animal pathogens during production is also eliminated (Walmsley et al. 2000). Oral delivery of the vaccine is another reason that vaccines produced in plants are an attractive possibility because they can eliminate injection-related risks. Overall, the fact that the vaccines can be stored as seeds are advantageous because large amounts of vaccines can be produced in limited time and storage is less of an issue because the seed is a stable form that will not degrade the protein over time. The choice of the crop will determine the way the vaccine is finally administered because only some plants can be consumed raw whereas others must be processed. With processing there is the potential that heat or pressure treatments could destroy the protein. Cereal crops are an attractive species for expressing subunit vaccines because they can produce proteins in their seeds, which are stable for long storage periods. For animal vaccines the plant choice could be chosen based on what is eaten as a major part of its diet, therefore eliminating the need to process the protein and the risk of destroying it as well (Daniell et al. 2001).

Regulation

In the U.S., a three-agency coordinated framework including the Food and Drug Administration (FDA), the United States Department of Agriculture (USDA), and the Environmental Protection Agency (EPA) is responsible for regulating all products made from biotechnology. Currently, the FDA regulates pharmaceuticals in the U.S., but with the introduction of plant-made pharmaceuticals the USDA plays a key role. Each agency has its own regulatory scope. For example, the FDA is responsible for overseeing the production of pharmaceuticals for their safety to humans and animals. The USDA evaluates genetically engineered plants and animals to assess whether they will pose unacceptable risks to U.S. agriculture and the environment. For plant-based pharmaceuticals, EPA will play a lesser role, but will help ensure safety to the environment. The activities of the FDA and USDA include not only products that are registered, but also experimental products grown in laboratory, field, and greenhouse environments. Specific regulations are currently evolving, but at this time the specific responsibilities and activities of the two agencies remain unclear (Peterson and Arntzen 2004). The production of proteins in plants to be used in the pharmaceutical industry will largely follow the same regulatory requirements that have already been established for non-plant produced pharmaceuticals. However, there are key challenges for the regulation of plant-based pharmaceuticals. These challenges primarily are associated with the fact that some production systems will include manufacturing pharmaceutical proteins in the open environment. Further, many production systems will involve food. These are unique aspects of pharmaceutical manufacturing — aspects that will present novel risks that must be considered. As Peterson and Arntzen (2004) stated, "Because of this, questions of intra- and inter-species gene flow, allergen exposure to the public and non-target organism exposure come into play."

Potential Risks

The potential risks associated with plant-based pharmaceuticals include: pollen transfer to related species, contamination of non-transgenic crops intended for the consumption by humans, allergic reactions to the drugs produced from the genetically engineered plant, and persistence of genetically engineered material to persist in the environment and accumulate in non-target organisms (Daniell et al. 2001). Risk assessment of plant-made pharmaceuticals should be reviewed on a case-by-case basis because the plants used to produce proteins each have different risks associated with them (Peterson and Arntzen 2004). To address the out-crossing potential of transgenic crops to a receptive crop species or weedy relative, physical isolation distances have been considered. This can mean containment in a greenhouse setting or buffer zones between fields of the same species. Some species have enclosed flower structures, reducing the distance needed in between fields and therefore are being evaluated as good candidates for producing plant-made pharmaceuticals. In the case of corn — a wind pollinated crop — because it has many benefits for being a plant biopharmaceutical, the tassels can be manually removed and male-sterile varieties could be used to contain the pollen. The transgenic plants can also be planted at different times from food crops to make sure they flower at different times, which decreases the potential for pollen transfer (Thomas et al. 2002). According to Goldstein and Thomas (2004), "virtually every pharmaceutical product currently on the market can cause allergic reactions in some people." The FDA approved the drugs because their benefits outweighed their allergenic potential. This will be the same approach taken on plant-made pharmaceuticals; the FDA will be concerned if, and only if, the plant-made pharmaceuticals are more allergenic than pharmaceuticals not derived from plants (Rogers 2003). However, there is a question of the allergic risk for people not taking the drug but happen to inhale or topically receive pollen from the genetically engineered plant. Will the contact from the genetically engineered plant cause a reaction or immunity? Because these proteins are in the environment does not necessarily make them environmental contaminants or even human health hazards. The specificity of the proteins produced in plants potentially makes the risk negligible. Non-target organisms are organisms not intended to be affected by the plant-produced protein. These organisms include insects, mammals, birds, fish, plants, and other wildlife in and around the area where the genetically engineered plant is growing. Animals potentially could be affected by genetically engineered plants, by eating or landing on the plant or plants nearby that have the pollen from the genetically engineered plants on them. There are ways to prevent or reduce the risk of these non-target organisms from being affected by the genetically engineered plant. Planting border crops that are not genetically engineered near the engineered crops, or containing the plants in greenhouse facilities are a couple preventative ways to keep non-target organisms unharmed. Fortunately, many of the plant-made pharmaceutical proteins currently produced or being considered are species-specific (such as antibodies) which reduces their effects (Goldstein and Thomas 2004).

Risk Assessment

Uncertainties in the evolving regulatory environment and the need to evaluate the human-health and environmental risks of plant-based pharmaceuticals on a case-by-case basis necessitate using a robust, transparent science-based methodology. Therefore, Peterson and Arntzen (2004) recommended using the established paradigm of environmental risk assessment. Additionally, Wolt and Peterson (2000) argued that the risk assessment framework was sufficiently robust to evaluate risks from most applications of biotechnology. Environmental risk assessment is a formalized basis for the objective evaluation of risk in a manner in which assumptions and uncertainties are clearly considered and presented. Risk assessment proceeds in a systematic, stepwise fashion that includes the following five steps: (1) problem formulation; (2) hazard identification; (3) dose-response relationships; (4) exposure assessment; and (5) risk characterization. Hazard and dose are considered in relation to exposure to determine risk or what additional information is needed to calculate or refine risk estimates (NRC 1983).

Plants used as protein factories to assist the pharmaceutical industry in drug manufacturing have the advantage of producing proteins which could not be made using other systems, reducing the cost of production, and increasing the amount of proteins available to be used to make drugs. With this increased availability and potentially lower cost, more patients will be able to receive the drugs they need. Plant systems are capable of producing large quantities of protein and have an advantage over mammalian and bacterial cell cultures because of the ease of scale-up that is possible with the equipment and land already in existence for these plants. These systems should be assessed for risk using the risk assessment paradigm. Risk analysis (which includes risk assessment, risk management, and risk communication) is a flexible and robust framework, making it ideal for addressing the myriad issues associated with this new technology.

Genetically Engineered Virus-Resistant Squash Approved For Sale

On December 13, 1994, the Animal and Plant Health Inspection Service (APHIS) of the USDA finally deregulated the genetically engineered virus-resistant yellow crookneck squash line designated ZW-20 (Federal Register, pages 64187-64189). The controversial virus-resistant squash, developed by the Asgrow Seed Co., had been regulated under the Plant Pest Act in part because it contains DNA sequences derived from plant pathogens. ZW-20 squash resists infection by zucchini yellow mosaic and watermelon mosaic viruses because the coat proteins of those viruses were inserted into the line. It was field tested under 14 APHIS permits at 46 sites in 10 states. Following submission of a petition for deregulation by Upjohn, Asgrow's parent company, APHIS sought public comment on the ZW-20 squash petition and the agency's preliminary finding of no significant environmental impact on three different occasions. Opponents of deregulation argued that the use of two viral coat proteins could lead to the creation of new plant viruses and perhaps cause the squash to become a weed, and that the virus resistance genes could move to wild squash relatives with detrimental impact on these wild plants. Based upon an analysis of the data submitted by Upjohn, a review of scientific literature and comments received from the public, APHIS concluded that the ZW-20 squash is as safe to grow as traditionally bred virus-resistant squash and therefore no longer needs to be regulated. Opponent organizations such as the Union of Concerned Scientists have expressed disappointment over APHIS' determination. In November 1994, a U.S. Food and Drug Administration (FDA) Public Advisory Committee, after reviewing data provided by Upjohn, found that as food, ZW-20 squash appeared to be as safe as its non-engineered counterpart. This spring, Asgrow Seed will begin marketing the genetically engineered squash seeds under the name "Freedom II." The seeds will bear a label stating that they are the product of genetic engineering.

3

Bioengineered Food and Stem Cells: Ethical and Safety Issues

BIOENGINEERED FOODS: SAFETY ISSUES

Since 1994, a growing number of foods developed using the tools of the science of biotechnology have come onto both the domestic and international markets. With these products has come controversy, primarily in Europe where some question whether these foods are as safe as foods that have been developed using the more conventional approach of hybridization. Ever since the latter part of the 19th century, when Gregor Mendel discovered that characteristics in pea plants could be inherited, scientists have been improving plants by changing their genetic makeup. Typically, this was done through hybridization in which two related plants were cross-fertilized and the resulting offspring had characteristics of both parent plants. Breeders then selected and reproduced the offspring that had the desired traits. Today, to change a plant's traits, scientists are able to use the tools of modern biotechnology to insert a single gene—or, often, two or three genes—into the crop to give it new, advantageous characteristics. Most genetic modifications make it easier to grow the crop. About half of the American soybean crop planted in 1999, for example, carries a gene that makes it resistant to an herbicide used to control weeds. About a quarter of U.S. corn planted in 1999 contains a gene that produces a protein toxic to certain caterpillars, eliminating the need for certain conventional pesticides. In 1992, the Food and Drug Administration published a policy explaining how existing legal requirements for food safety apply to products developed using the tools of biotechnology. It is the agency's responsibility to ensure the safety of all foods on the market that come from crops, including bioengineered plants, through a science-based decision-making process. This process often includes public comment from consumers, outside experts and industry. FDA established, in 1994, a consultation process that helps ensure that foods developed using biotechnology methods meet the applicable safety standards. Over the last five years, companies have used the consultation process more than 40 times as they moved to introduce genetically altered plants into the U.S. market.

Although the agency has no evidence that the policy and procedure do not adequately protect the public health, there have been concerns voiced regarding FDA's policy on these foods. When most people talk about bioengineered foods, they are referring to crops produced by utilizing the modern techniques of biotechnology. But really, if you think about it, all crops have been genetically modified through traditional plant breeding for more than a hundred years. Since Mendel, plant breeders have modified the genetic material of crops by selecting plants that arise through natural or, sometimes, induced changes. Gardeners and farmers and, at times, industrial plant breeders have crossbred plants with the intention of creating a prettier flower, a hardier or more productive crop. These conventional techniques are often imprecise because they shuffle thousands of genes in the offspring, causing them to have some of the characteristics of each parent plant. Gardeners or breeders then look for the plants with the most desirable new trait.

With the tools developed from biotechnology, a gene can be inserted into a plant to give it a specific new characteristic instead of mixing all of the genes from two plants and seeing what comes out. Once in the plant, the new gene does what all genes do: It directs the production of a specific protein that makes the plant uniquely different. This technology provides much more control over, and precision to, what characteristic breeders give to a new plant. It also allows the changes to be made much faster than ever before. No matter how a new crop is created—using traditional methods or biotechnology tools—breeders are required by our colleagues at the U.S. Department of Agriculture to conduct field testing for several seasons to make sure only desirable changes have been made. They must check to make sure the plant looks right, grows right, and produces food that tastes right. They also must perform analytical tests to see whether the levels of nutrients have changed and whether the food is still safe to eat. As we have evaluated the results of the seeds or crops created using biotechnology techniques, we have seen no evidence that the bioengineered foods now on the market pose any human health concerns or that they are in any way less safe than crops produced through traditional breeding.

Plant researchers look for genes that will benefit the farmer, the food processor, or the consumer. So far, most of the changes have helped the farmer. For example, scientists have inserted into corn a gene from the bacterium Bacillus thurigiensis, usually referred to as BT. The gene makes a protein lethal to certain caterpillars that destroy corn plants. This form of insect control has two advantages: It reduces the need for chemical pesticides, and the BT protein, which is present in the plant in very low concentrations, has no effect on humans. Another common strategy is inserting a gene that makes the plant resistant to a particular herbicide.

The herbicide normally poisons an enzyme essential for plant survival. Other forms of this normal plant enzyme have been identified that are unaffected by the herbicide. Putting the gene for this resistant form of the enzyme into the plant protects it from the herbicide. That allows farmers to treat a field with the herbicide to kill the weeds without harming the crop. The new form of the enzyme poses no food safety issues because it is virtually identical to nontoxic enzymes naturally present in the plant. In addition, the resistant enzyme is present at very low levels and it is as easily digested as the normal plant enzyme. Modifications have also been made to canola and soybean plants to produce oils with a different fatty acid composition so they can be used in new food processing systems. Researchers are working diligently to develop crops with enhanced nutritional properties.

All of the proteins that have been placed into foods through the tools of biotechnology that are on the market are nontoxic, rapidly digestible, and do not have the characteristics of proteins known to cause allergies. As for the genes, the chemical that encodes genetic information is called DNA. DNA is present in all foods and its ingestion is not associated with human illness. Some have noted that sticking a new piece of DNA into the plant's chromosome can disrupt the function of other genes, crippling the plant's growth or altering the level of nutrients or toxins. These kinds of effects can happen with any type of plant breeding—traditional or biotech. That's why breeders do extensive field-testing. If the plant looks normal and grows normally, if the food tastes right and has the expected levels of nutrients and toxins, and if the new protein put into food has been shown to be safe, then there are no safety issues. If one is allergic to a food, it needs to be rigorously avoided. Further, we don't want to create new allergy problems with food developed from either traditional or biotech means. It is important to know that bioengineering does not make a food inherently different from conventionally produced food. And the technology doesn't make the food more likely to cause allergies. Fortunately, we know a lot about the foods that do trigger allergic reactions. About 90 percent of all food allergies in the United States are caused by cow's milk, eggs, fish and shellfish, tree nuts, wheat, and legumes, especially peanuts and soybeans. To be cautious, FDA has specifically focused on allergy issues. Under the law and FDA's biotech food policy, companies must tell consumers on the food label when a product includes a gene from one of the common allergy-causing foods unless it can show that the protein produced by the added gene does not make the food cause allergies. We recommend that companies analyze the proteins they introduce to see if these proteins possess properties indicating that the proteins might be allergens. So far, none of the new proteins in foods evaluated through the FDA consultation process have caused allergies. Because proteins resulting from biotechnology and now on the market are sensitive to heat, acid and enzymatic digestion, are present in very low levels in the food, and do not have structural similarities to known allergens, we have no scientific evidence to indicate that any of the new proteins introduced into food by biotechnology will cause allergies.

Antibiotic resistance is a serious public health issue, but that problem is currently and primarily caused by the overuse or misuse of antibiotics. We have carefully considered whether the use of antibiotic resistance marker genes in crops could pose a public health concern and have found no evidence that it does. First, there is little if any transfer of genes from plants to bacteria. Bacteria pick up resistance genes from other bacteria, and they do it easily and often. The potential risk of transfer from plants to bacteria is substantially less than the risk of normal transfer between bacteria. Nevertheless, to be on the safe side, FDA has advised food developers to avoid using marker genes that encode resistance to clinically important antibiotics.

Bioengineered foods actually are regulated by three federal agencies: FDA, the Environmental Protection Agency, and the U.S. Department of Agriculture. FDA is responsible for the safety and labeling of all foods and animal feeds derived from crops, including biotech plants. EPA regulates pesticides, so the BT used to keep caterpillars from eating the corn would fall under its jurisdiction. USDA's Animal and Plant Health Inspection Service oversees the agricultural environmental safety of planting and field testing genetically engineered plants. Let me talk about FDA's role. Under the federal Food, Drug, and Cosmetic Act, companies have a legal obligation to ensure that any food they sell meets the safety standards of the law. This applies equally to conventional food and bioengineered food. If a food does not meet the safety standard, FDA has the authority to take it off the market. In the specific case of foods developed utilizing the tools of biotechnology, FDA set up a consultation process to help companies meet the requirements. While consultation is voluntary, the legal requirements that the foods have to meet are not. To the best of our knowledge, all bioengineered foods on the market have gone through FDA's process before they have been marketed.

Here's how it works. Companies send us documents summarizing the information and data they have generated to demonstrate that a bioengineered food is as safe as the conventional food. The documents describe the genes they use: whether they are from a commonly allergenic plant, the characteristics of the proteins made by the genes, their biological function, and how much of them will be found in the food. They tell us whether the new food contains the expected levels of nutrients or toxins and any other information about the safety and use of the product. FDA scientists review the information and generally raise questions. It takes several months to complete the consultation, which is why companies usually start a dialog with the agency scientists nearly a year or more before they submit the data. At the conclusion of the consultation, if we are satisfied with what we have learned about the food, we provide the company with a letter stating that they have completed the consultation process and we have no further questions at that time.

The food additive provision of the law ensures that a substance with an unknown safety profile is not added to food without the manufacturer proving to the government that the additive is safe. This intense review, however, is not required under the law when a substance is generally recognized as safe (GRAS) by qualified experts. A substance's safety can be established by long history of use in food or when the nature of the substance and the information generally available to scientists about it is such that it doesn't raise significant safety issues. In the case of bioengineered foods, we are talking about adding some DNA to the plant that directs the production of a specific protein. DNA already is present in all foods and is presumed to be GRAS. As I described before, adding an extra bit of DNA does not raise any food safety issues. As for the resulting proteins, they too are generally digested and metabolized and don't raise the kinds of food safety questions as are raised by novel chemicals in the diet. The proteins introduced into plants so far either have been pesticides or enzymes. The pesticide proteins, such as BT, would actually be regulated by EPA and go through its approval process before going on the market. The enzymes have been considered to be GRAS, so they have not gone through the food additive petition process. FDA's consultation process aids companies in determining whether the protein they want to add to a food is generally recognized as safe. If FDA has concerns about the safety of the food, the product would have to go through the full food additive premarket approval process.

Traditional and bioengineered foods are all subject to the same labeling requirements. All labeling for a food product must be truthful and not misleading. If a bioengineered food is significantly different from its conventional counterpart—if the nutritional value changes or it causes allergies—it must be labeled to indicate that difference. For example, genetic modifications in varieties of soybeans and canola changed the fatty acid composition in the oils of those plants. Foods using those oils must be labeled, including using a new standard name that indicates the bioengineered oil's difference from conventional soy and canola oils. If a food had a new allergy-causing protein introduced into it, the label would have to state that it contained the allergen. We are not aware of any information that foods developed through genetic engineering differ as a class in quality, safety, or any other attribute from foods developed through conventional means. That's why there has been no requirement to add a special label saying that they are bioengineered. Companies are free to include in the labeling of a bioengineered product any statement as long as the labeling is truthful and not misleading. Obviously, a label that implies that a food is better than another because it was, or was not, bioengineered, would be misleading.

Dr. Henney: Yes, I am convinced that the health of the American public is well protected by the current laws and procedures. I also recognize that this is a rapidly changing field, so FDA must stay on top of the science as biotechnology evolves and is used to make new kinds of modifications to foods. In addition, the agency is seeking public input about our policies and will continue to reach out to the public to help consumers understand the scientific issues and the agency's policies. Not only must the food that Americans eat be safe, but consumers must have confidence in its safety, and confidence in the government's role in ensuring that safety. Policies that are grounded in science, that are developed through open and transparent processes, and that are implemented rigorously and communicated effectively are what have assured the consumers' confidence in an agency that has served this nation for nearly 100 years.

ETHICAL AND POLICY DEBATES REGARDING STEM CELL RESEARCH

The announcement of the Bush administration's human embryonic stem cell research funding policy in the summer of 2001 certainly did not end the debates surrounding the issue. The policy offered a particular target to which participants in the debate could react, but the basic questions involved in assessing how the federal government should approach embryonic stem cell research remained just as relevant, and just as controversial, as they had been before. In this chapter, we offer an overview of that still continuing debate as it has developed in the past two years. Without attempting to provide anything like a full account of different positions and arguments, we hope, rather, to point to the major items under argument— to the issues that any interested citizen might wish to ponder. First, we will outline the general form of the moral argument as it has developed over time. Second, we will discuss specific questions and critiques regarding the current policy, as those have emerged in public discussion. Third, we will review the various positions on the moral standing of human embryos, seeking again to outline the chief fault lines in that continuing debate. And finally, we will highlight some critical ethical concerns that do not arise directly out of the debate over the moral standing of human embryos but that may be no less important to the larger question confronting the country.

This array of subjects includes both some that are clearly ethical questions and some that may fall closer to questions of policy. We take up both together because we believe both are essential to a full understanding of the issues involved and because even the policy debates—as understood and engaged in by participants on all sides—are clearly directed to a set of underlying moral issues and informed by ethical beliefs and opinions. Critiques (and defenses) of the present policy, and proposals of alternatives, are almost without exception based on moral grounds.

This chapter will, of course, revisit several of the themes raised in the previous chapter. There, our aim was to present some basic facts regarding the current policy, its context, and its execution. Here, we take up arguments on all sides of the issue—including those that dispute the understanding of the policy put forward by its authors and those that raise other issues or alternative courses of action.

While we will raise these arguments and counterarguments, examining problems, questions, and concerns, our purpose is not finally to assess the validity of the competing claims or to arrive at a conclusion, but—in line with the Council's charge to monitor developments in this area—to present them more or less as they have appeared in the public debates of the past several years. This way of proceeding suffers from one especially prominent drawback: it tends to present all arguments as equal in importance or prevalence. We will seek to avoid this whenever possible, by offering some sense of which arguments have been most crucial for the public debate.

I. The Nature of the Moral Argument

Before entering upon a detailed review of the debates, we take a moment to consider the *character* of the moral reasoning and argumentation we will confront. Different participants in the stem cell debates tend to hold different views not only regarding individual substantive judgments, but also regarding the kind of moral question, in the most general terms, we are facing in deciding about stem cell research policy. At first glance, people seem to be disagreeing about whether a balancing of competing interests and goods is called for, or whether some one overriding moral duty ought to shape our judgment, though of course that dichotomy is not in every case quite so stark.

In casual conversation, and sometimes in more theoretical reasoning, moral questions are often analyzed in the language of "weighing" and "balancing," or else in terms of overriding concerns, inviolable principles, or fundamental "rights." These two sets of terms and metaphors point to two distinct ways of making difficult moral judgments. In some circumstances there need be no irresolvable conflict between the two approaches.

Those who seek to respect fundamental rights and adhere to inviolable principles need not ignore the complexities of moral situations or the consequences of our actions when they form their judgments. Likewise, those who seek to weigh or balance competing goods may think of those goods as involving not only benefits to be realized but also principles to be upheld.

There may also be circumstances, however, in which those differences that do exist between these two approaches constitute a fork in the road, constraining our decision. Thus, to take an example from outside the domain of bioethics, the principle that civilians should be safeguarded from direct, intended attack in time of war may be understood to trump all other competing goods (without denying the importance of those goods), or it may be understood as one good to be balanced against others. Which fork in the road of moral reasoning one takes at such a point will have a decisive influence on the character of the arguments employed and the conclusions reached.

This has often also been the case in the public debate over federal funding of human embryonic stem cell research. Many observers have agreed that federal policy must seek a certain balance between two competing goods or interests: the progress of medical research and therapy, and respect for nascent human life. Indeed, President Bush himself framed the issue in these terms, saying a few weeks before his decision was announced that his policy would "need to balance value and respect for life with the promise of science and the hope of saving life." But not all participants in the debate have had the same idea of what such balance should entail and, therefore, how weight should be assigned to the competing demands.

For some, the degree of medical promise should profoundly affect the degree of government support for embryonic stem cell research. For them, the critical element (though of course not the exclusive one) in establishing policy must be scientific data about what might be achieved with human embryonic stem cells. The greater the promise of the research, the more support it should receive and the more it should outweigh reasons offered for opposing the techniques involved. On this view, the concern given greatest prominence and weight in reaching a judgment ought to be the very great good of medical progress toward the relief of suffering. Most of the arguments in favor of increased taxpayer funding of embryonic stem cell research have begun from this premise—explicitly or implicitly—and have proceeded by laying out the possible medical benefits of the research or the possible harms (to patients or to American science) of withholding support. We shall review a number of these lines of argument in more detail below. But it is worth noting at the start that most of them tacitly assume that the policy decision at hand ought to be based on a reasoned balancing of crucial concerns—all of which matter but none of which simply overrides the others.

Others, however, have suggested that at least a substantial portion of the opposition to the research rests upon the belief that human embryos should not be violated and therefore—if this claim is valid—that the threat to their life and worth cannot be justified by the promise of research. It follows, on this view, that the federal government should do nothing to encourage or support the future destruction of human embryos, regardless of the promise of research. What remains then to be considered is the extent to which the government might advance the additional aim of progress in medical research *within* the bounds of the principle. In this case, the moral reasoning is understood to be decisively affected by an unbreachable boundary, and only the extent of some particular provisions of the policy are left to be settled by a weighing and balancing of other priorities. Proponents of the various forms of this position generally argue that the claim of human embryos to our protection presents us with a fundamental duty, to be overridden, if at all, only in extreme circumstances, rather than with just one good to be balanced off against others. In presenting the matter this way, adherents of this view consciously appeal to the ethics governing research with human subjects, which obliges those engaged in efforts to advance knowledge and seek cures to keep from trespassing upon human safety, freedom, and dignity. The decades-old and nearly universal adherence of researchers to rules protecting human subjects, these commentators suggest, demonstrates that the needs of research are not always treated as paramount and that the scientific community itself joins the general public in recognizing instances in which research—however important—must be limited for ethical reasons. Researchers do not weigh the interests of human subjects against the importance of their work; rather they respect a principled boundary—that human subjects are not to be harmed or put at risk without their informed consent— the importance of which trumps even the most promising experiment. For some defenders of human embryos, the prospect of embryo research raises precisely these concerns; accordingly, they argue that this issue too should be decided on the basis of a moral rule, not by a shiftable tally on a balance sheet of benefits. But this assertion about the proper form of moral argument depends on the truth of the claim that human embryos are indeed human subjects of research. Therefore, one's position in the debate about the basic character of the moral issue may depend, in many cases, on one's understanding of the moral standing of human embryos. As we shall see, the question of the moral standing of embryos is by no means the only relevant question. But in the actual public debate, as it has developed, this question seems to have been most central and prominent and probably most responsible for shaping the different basic approaches pursued. It is this question that very often informs the differing views regarding which aims or goods are more weighty or which should not be compromised at all.

We turn next to arguments regarding that very issue: Which moral aims or which concerns should be given priority in shaping government policy toward human embryonic stem cell research?

II. The Moral Aims of Policy

A significant part of the public debate surrounding the policy governing funding of embryonic stem cell research has involved differing views of just which purposes or ideals should most directly guide policymakers in this arena. The current funding policy—while it appears to strike some balance between protecting human embryos and advancing biomedical research—seems to take as its overriding concern the insistence that the federal government not encourage or support the deliberate violation or destruction of human embryos. But a number of commentators in recent years—and, of course, particularly those who ascribe lesser moral status to human embryos—have proposed alternative principles to govern policy.

A. The Importance of Relieving Suffering

Many observers argue that the proper governing principle should be the duty to relieve the pain and suffering of others— the purpose that ultimately motivates the work of biomedical science. This aim is broadly, perhaps universally, shared.

Indeed, the current policy, as outlined by its advocates, while it seeks to protect nascent human life, explicitly seeks to advance medical research as far as its authors believe is morally permissible. Some commentators argue, however, that the administration has chosen the wrong one of these aims as the governing principle of its approach.

The cause of curing disease has a human face, the face of a loved one or neighbor, bent under the suffering of an incompletely understood or treated disease. As a result, the aspiration to know is linked to a desire to relieve. How, wonder many commentators, could anyone think of withholding support for research that might yield therapies for devastating diseases and conditions such as spinal cord injury, diabetes, and Parkinson disease? Surely, they argue, the pain and suffering of those in need should outweigh concerns for human embryos frozen in a laboratory. Indeed, for many this is an especially critical issue in light of the likely ultimate fate of these embryos. Will they be frozen indefinitely? If not, then will they be thawed out and discarded and destroyed, or used to potentially benefit mankind? One form of this argument, heard increasingly over the past few years, begins with data about disease prevalence and suggests that anyone who obstructs public funding of research that might someday help patients suffering from such diseases must bear some of the responsibility for their future suffering and (perhaps) death. Some opponents have countered that any assertion that makes relief of human suffering the highest moral principle to this extent might logically impugn any and all deflection of resources into less ultimate concerns such as recreation, beautification, or social ceremony. Others respond more directly that an unwillingness to violate one's moral principles in order to help relieve the sick does not make one responsible for their sickness. In most cases, however, the arguments for grounding federal funding policy in the importance of biomedical research do not blame opponents for the suffering of the sick. Rather, they focus on the promise of bringing relief to those who most need it. They point to the immense benefits already delivered to us by modern medicine and argue that the federal government should advance this cause in whatever ways it reasonably can. Many advocates of this view agree that nascent human life should receive respectful treatment, but they argue that the claims of our duties to human embryos— whether in general or in particular circumstances, like those stored in fertility clinic freezers—cannot simply trump the claims of promising medical research and our duties to suffering humanity. The obligation to aid the sick, they contend, and the fact that the research in question might relieve the pain and terrible suffering of countless patients and their families, should lead us to do all that can reasonably be done to find treatments and cures, and to offer help. This does not mean simply ignoring the significance of human embryos, or taking lightly the decision to destroy them in research, but, they suggest, it should mean taking seriously the moral calling to help the suffering and deciding how to proceed based on more than one sort of obligation. In response, one commentator has argued in broad terms against the underlying assumption that the demands of biomedical research should somehow be seen as "imperative." Such work, he contends, should not be seen as inherently and always obligatory, and claims to support it may be overridden even by a level of respect for nascent human life that does *not* suppose that embryos possess full human moral standing. He suggests that it is not at all obvious that individuals or the government have a definite responsibility to support such research or that such a responsibility would override other moral duties. Others point out that the duty to find cures for disease cannot be an unqualified or absolute imperative. Pointing to the present rules governing the treatment of human subjects in research, they argue that the case for embryonic stem cell research cannot rest on an alleged and overriding imperative to pursue that research. These rules prohibit certain sorts of procedures on human subjects of research, and the same, they suggest, should be required in stem cell research. Yet those who argue that the importance of medical research and treatment should override the aim of protecting human embryos presumably would not propose to override protections for human subjects in research on children or adults. Rather, they approach the present matter differently because they do not consider human embryos the developmental, anthropological, or moral equivalent of children or adults, or worthy of the same protection. The difference, therefore, has to do not so much with a dispute over the imperative importance of research, but rather (at least to a significant extent) with the status of nascent human life, which again turns out to be the fundamental point at issue. Nevertheless, the moral claims of medical research and treatment are extremely powerful in the debate over human embryonic stem cell policy, and they are acknowledged as profoundly important even by those who do not finally take them to be decisive. Most arguments in opposition to the present funding policy and in support of expanded embryonicstem cell research are grounded in these claims.

B. Freedom to Conduct Research

Other opponents of the present policy argue not from the value of medical benefits but on the basis of freedom to conduct research, which they believe is the principle by which federal policy ought to be governed. They regard government restraints on scientific research as inherently offensive and generally unjustifiable. The cherished ideals of freedom of thought, freedom of conscience, and—specifically in this context—freedom of inquiry, trump concerns over the moral status of human embryos, they contend. The most common claim advanced for protecting research as a basic right (employed, among others, by the American Bar Association) involves some form of an appeal to the First Amendment's protection of free speech, interpreted through the years by the Supreme Court to encompass free expression and perhaps freedom of inquiry and thought. Some argue that research is a form of expression, particularly when it is politically or socially controversial, and when restraints upon it are imposed for moral reasons. "One could make the case that research is expressive activity and that the search for knowledge is intrinsically within the First Amendment's protection for freedom of thought," says one ethicist. Others, however, contend that this claim, never tested in the courts, seems far-fetched. Most currently controversial biological research involves experimental manipulation of living matter, rather than theoretical exploration or mere observation of natural objects. It is therefore as much action as expression, as much creation as inquiry. It is difficult to see, they argue, how such activity (as opposed to the reporting of the results of such activity) could be classified as a form of expression. "Scientists may have the right to pursue knowledge in any way they want cognitively, intellectually," argues one observer, "but when it comes to concrete action in the lab, that becomes conduct and the First Amendment protection for that is far, far weaker."

Moreover, argues at least one commentator, even if one did stipulate that research activity is to be protected from governmental proscription or restriction, it is far from clear that failure to provide federal funding would constitute such a restriction. Indeed, legislative and judicial precedents suggest it would not. The government routinely refrains from funding activities it otherwise permits or even guards as constitutionally protected. A line of Supreme Court decisions stretching from 1977 to 1991, dealing with abortion and government funding, established the principle that the Constitution does not require the government to fund even those activities that the Constitution protects. Because the only issue in the present debate is one of federal funding, the protected status of scientific activity seems not to be a determining factor. Finally, some critics of the case for a paramount right to research point again to the fact that scientific research— conducted both with private and (especially) with government funding—is already subject to certain restrictions, particularly with regard to protecting human subjects. The proposition that embryo research should not be subject to the same restrictions hinges on an argument about the standing of human embryos, rather than about the unrestrictable standing of research as such. Once more, an important part of the question turns on the status of extra-uterine human embryos.

C. The Moral Standing of Human Embryos

However they approach the matter, then, many people engaged in the debate over federal funding policy find they must consider the fundamental question of the moral standing of human embryos: What *are* early human embryos, and how should we regard them morally? Approaches to the question of federal funding of embryonic stem cell research that propose some other guiding principle—relief of suffering, freedom of research—seem almost by necessity to assume that human embryos do not possess the same human moral standing as persons already born. Conversely, if human embryos ought rightly to be treated as inviolable—as some have argued— then questions of balancing other goods or giving priority to other principles are largely rendered moot. Thus, to many observers, some of the central questions in this arena would appear to be those that surround human embryos: How ought we to think about and act toward human embryos? Should all ex vivo human embryos be treated the same, or are some, because of their circumstances, origins, or prospects, to be treated differently from others? Or are embryos of sufficiently little moral significance that we should simply decide the funding question solely on the basis of the merits and promise of the proposed biomedical research? We shall, in due course, review the recent arguments on these critical questions. But before doing so, we examine a series of other more specific objections to the present policy.

These arguments recognize that the current policy rests on the conviction that federal funds should not support or encourage the violation or destruction of human embryos.

Rather than disputing this premise, a number of commentators—including both supporters and critics—have assessed the policy on its own grounds and judged it against its own claims and terms. As a result, several general categories of criticism of the policy itself have emerged.

II. The Character of the Policy

In addition to debating which aims ought to guide federal policy, many observers in the past two years have also assessed the *particulars* of the present funding policy, considering them in scientific, political, and moral terms.

Critics have generally found fault with the policy through one or more of three general lines of argument: that it is arbitrary, that it is unsustainable, and that it is inconsistent. Defenders of the policy, meanwhile, have usually sought to counter these critics on these terms and to rebut these assertions and criticisms.

A. Arbitrary

One quite common line of argument criticizes the present funding policy as essentially arbitrary, because it relies on what is deemed a capricious cutoff date. Cells derived from embryos destroyed on August 9, 2001 are eligible for federal funding, but those obtained from embryos destroyed the next day are not.

The only difference is the date of embryo destruction, argue some critics, and what moral difference could that possibly make? If the policy of funding human embryonic stem cell research serves a genuine good, these commentators suggest, would it not be equally good regardless of when the cell lines were derived? Would it not, therefore, make sense to permit funding for *all* cell lines derived on either side of the date, provided they are otherwise eligible? If, on the contrary, federal funding of embryo research is unacceptable, then it should simply not be allowed at all, regardless of when cell lines were first derived. "It is difficult to see," writes one critic, "what ethical reasoning would commend a policy that takes as its central distinction the time chosen for political convenience to deliver a presidential address."

In response, some supporters of the policy contend that while the cut-off date (August 9, 2001) certainly has no inherent moral significance, it acquires moral meaning by the simple fact that it was the operative date of a newly announced policy that turned on a crucial distinction between the "up-until-now" and the "from-now-on," between past (irrevocable) deeds and future (preventable) ones. That date of announcement was the line between past embryo destruction, which could no longer be undone, and future embryo destruction, which could still be influenced by the federal government's funding rules. If the policy sought to avoid encouraging or offering incentives for any future destruction of human embryos, they argue, then drawing a hard line between past and future would be indispensable. That line could only reasonably be drawn at the moment of the decision's announcement (or before it), since drawing it at some point in the future would create a powerful incentive to quicken the pace of work until the cutoff date arrived. The date, they say, is therefore not a morally arbitrary marker in the context of the policy, but is rather a crucial and unavoidable element of the policy's logic.

B. Unsustainable

A further, and more common, critique of the current policy suggests that its approach cannot be expected to hold over time and that it will fairly quickly prove unsustainable. One form of this argument suggests that the policy has created a situation in which scientists may make some progress using existing stem cell lines but would then be prohibited from capitalizing on what they have learned and making further progress using stem cell lines not now eligible for federal funds.

As the editors of the *Washington Post* put it: "Mr. Bush's compromise policy will be a reasonable one only as long as the existing lines are capable of supporting the research scientists need to perform." Indeed, some have argued that by explicitly encouraging and speaking of the potential medical value of human embryonic stem cell research, the President himself created the circumstances that will make the constraints of the policy unsustainable. "Bush's decision was at its core an endorsement of the promise of human embryonic stem cells and their importance to the fledgling field of regenerative medicine," wrote one critic, and if that is the core message of the decision, then the resulting policy seems insufficient.

Others, arguing on more practical grounds, claim that, regardless of the reasonableness of the principle behind the policy, its effects will prove unbearable for American scientists, who will then force a reconsideration. The limits placed on funding in the current policy, several observers have predicted, will seriously hamper and hold back embryonic stem cell research work in the United States, perhaps causing prominent scientists to leave the country in search of greater support abroad. If that were to occur, it is argued, the policy would prove genuinely damaging to American science, and therefore to the national interest, and would need to be changed.

In response to this specific point, some defenders of the

policy have noted that for the time being there has not been news of any notable migration of prominent stem cell researchers to foreign countries, that federal funding *is* now available with no ceiling on its amount, and that American researchers can continue to work with private funds. But even apart from worries about a "brain-drain" in the field, some have argued that both the lack of funding, and particularly the complexity of the set of conditions under which research using such funding may be conducted, is preventing progress in research and discouraging even private funding in the field, and that the lines made available simply will not be enough, or indeed that they have already proved insufficient.

Some argue that the very low number of applications submitted to the NIH for postdoctoral and training projects using the approved stem cell lines provides striking evidence for the chilling effect of the current "in limbo" situation. Some have also suggested that safety issues connected with the way the eligible lines have been derived and developed may make them less suitable for use in human trials and treatments, thus making other cell lines necessary (although presentations before this Council by NIH Director Elias Zerhouni and FDA Commissioner Mark McClellan have contradicted some of these claims). Others, meanwhile, worry that the eligible lines do not offer sufficient genetic diversity to be adequate for research needs or for eventual therapies. As scientists make their case that important work is being hampered, it is argued, the policy will prove unsustainable politically and practically. A similar argument has also been made in nearly the opposite terms. That is, some have said that if or when ongoing embryonic stem cell research produces a spectacular breakthrough in understanding or treating disease, the pressure to alter the policy would prove unstoppable.

This way, whether the future brings announcements of great progress, or whether it brings no news of advances, the result will be pressure for a policy that funds research more broadly. Those defenders of the policy who have addressed these claims of unsustainability have pointed out that the present policy does not limit the *amount* of federal funds available to the kind of research that may be performed with the approved cell lines. They also point out that much of the pioneering work in mouse stem cell research was done using very few (approximately five) cell lines (though of course the challenge of working with human cell lines is more complex and daunting). But they have also generally pointed to the policy's stated grounding in principle—a principle that would not change in light of scientific advances or delays. In August of 2001, for instance, Health and Human Services Secretary Tommy Thompson told reporters that "neither unexpected scientific breakthroughs nor unanticipated research problems would cause Bush to reconsider" the approach drawn by the policy, because it is based on "a high moral line that this president is not going to cross." As another observer has put it: "The general question is, well, will these cell lines be enough . . . and a non-complicity argument [like the one implied by the policy] will only work if the answer to that question is well, I guess they'll have to be enough." Or, put differently, if the policy is founded primarily in a determination to prevent government funds from encouraging the destruction of human embryos, and only secondarily in a judgment about the value of embryonic stem cell research, then advances in research alone (or the absence of advances alone) would not be sufficient to overturn it. If it is sound before such advances, some argue, it would still be valid after —though again, of course, whether it is right to begin with is itself a point of great contention.

C. Inconsistent

In responding to critiques like those just discussed, defenders of the administration's policy generally point to the principles that define the approach of the policy, as partially laid out in the previous chapter. But some criticism of the policy, directing itself precisely to the claim of consistent adherence to principle, has charged that the policy is morally contradictory, or at least inconsistent, in its own terms.

One common form of the charge of inconsistency concerns the distinction the policy tacitly draws between public and private funding. The current policy addresses itself only to federal funding of embryo research and is silent on the conduct of such research in the private sector. But the source of funding, this line of criticism suggests, could have no bearing on the question of the moral status of human embryos or the propriety of using them in research. If federal funding for research that destroys human embryos is so troublesome, then why should such research be allowed to proceed when privately funded? Acting to restrict one but not the other may be prudent, but it seems inconsistent. Indeed, by implicitly excluding such research from federal guidelines, it may actually encourage more reckless practices and may simply transfer the problem of complicity to the private sphere, where it is even more difficult to monitor and moderate the uses to which human embryos are put. Though these critics understand that the President cannot simply ban embryo research by himself, they argue that he could attempt to convince the Congress to do so, and he could have made such an attempt as an element of his funding policy decision. But he did not—thus bringing into question (for these critics) not only his commitment to the principle articulated by the policy, but also his own view of the moral standing of human embryos, which the policy itself does not make simply apparent.

Moreover, critics argue, some prominent defenders of the policy, by making the fact of ongoing private research an element of their defense, might be said to contribute to these doubts about its grounding in consistent principle. There may be some political or structural reasons for drawing a distinction in federal policy between what is funded and what is permitted. Questions of federalism and other legal realities no doubt enter the picture, and indeed those who oppose the destruction of human embryos are, in many cases, actively seeking prohibitions on all embryo research in individual states. But, critics point out, they generally say little on the larger question of permissibility at the federal level. By making funding the center of concern, these critics argue, the policy puts into question the importance of preventing embryo destruction more generally, casting some uncertainty over the relation of that policy to one or another position regarding the moral standing of early human embryos.

A related criticism contends that the distinction drawn between research practices in which human embryos are destroyed and research practices that use the products of previous embryo destruction is itself inconsistent—a distinction without a difference, drawn for political cover. "Pretending that the scientists who do stem cell research are in no way complicit in the destruction of embryos is just wrong, a smoke and mirrors game," writes one critic. "It would be much better to take the issue on directly by making the argument that destroying embryos in this way is morally justified—is, in effect, a just sacrifice to make."

Similar objections have also been raised by critics on the other side of the embryo question, who believe that embryo destruction is morally unjustified and that the present policy does not sufficiently distance the federal government from such destruction. "The federal government, for the first time in history, will support research that relies on the destruction of some defenseless human beings for the possible benefit to others," one critic contended in the immediate wake of the August 9, 2001 announcement. "However such a decision is hedged about with qualifications, it allows our nation's research enterprise to cultivate a disrespect for human life."

A further critique of the policy on grounds of inconsistency focuses more particularly on specific elements of the implicit claim to non-complicity, discussed in the previous chapter. If, as many of its advocates argue, the policy takes embryo destruction to be essentially a morally unjustifiable act, and if its provisions aim to make use of the irreversible consequences of that act without in any way encouraging or abetting the act itself, then, critics contend, it is curious that the policy would insist on requiring (in addition) that the eligible stem cell lines must have been obtained from embryos originally intended for reproduction and used with donor consent and without financial inducements.

If embryo destruction is in principle a wrong, and if the policy's provisions seek only to keep the federal government from complicity in that wrong, then why should it matter how precisely the wrong was originally committed? The presence of these conditions, it is argued, suggests that the policy is not in fact based in a consistent and principled adherence to the proposition that human embryos should not be destroyed.

Indeed, some have argued that this character of the policy suggests that its authors, including the President, may not hold the view that human embryos deserve the same protections as human children or adults. These critics suggest not so much that the current policy is necessarily inconsistent, but that it may only be consistent with a view of human embryos as possessed of intermediate or indeterminate moral standing, rather than a view that holds that human embryos ought simply not to be destroyed for the benefit of others.

In response to these last arguments, some have suggested that the qualifying conditions included in the policy reflect a secondary commitment to long-standing principles of humansubject and embryo research and a recognition of pre-existing standards in such research, rather than a contradiction of the fundamental commitment to avoiding any support for the destruction of nascent human life. The government, they argue, has multiple aims in this area, and these need not undercut each other.

In addition to discouraging the creation and use of embryos for purposes other than producing children, one commentator argues, the government also seeks to support the requirement for informed consent to all procedures involving human subjects and to discourage commercial trafficking in human material. Another observer has suggested that the additional conditions are an expression of the fact that some standards for stem cell derivation did exist before August 9, 2001, including those reflected in the Clinton administration's funding guidelines.

Even in rejecting the legitimacy of the act of embryo destruction and seeking to discourage it in the future, it is still reasonable to recognize the value of those earlier standards. The policy, it is argued, while establishing a new standard, still takes account of previous standards. In response to the more general complaints of inconsistency, defenders of the policy, within and outside the administration, have described the present policy as both principled and prudent.

The policy, as articulated by these defenders, aims (at

least minimally) to uphold and advance the principled conviction that the federal government should not offer support or incentives for the destruction of nascent human life for research. At the same time, they say, it seeks, as much as reasonably possible within the bounds of the principle, to benefit from the results of embryo destruction that has already occurred and can no longer be undone. As President Bush put it in announcing the policy, "This allows us to explore the promise and potential of stem cell research without crossing a fundamental moral line, by providing taxpayer funding that would sanction or encourage further destruction of human embryos that have at least the potential for life."

The policy, argue some of its advocates, aims to put into practice the moral principle of not destroying nascent human life, even if it does not do so on every possible front, or to the greatest possible extent.

Regarding the alleged inconsistency of withholding federal funding but not calling for a ban on all private embryo research, some have pointed out that the Dickey Amendment, under which the President was acting, is itself a "don't fund, don't ban" law. Moreover, they argue that neither statesmanship nor prudence requires that the President do battle with what is settled practice (the free use of embryos in private-sector research) or push zealously against everything to which he is morally opposed, especially in a pluralistic society that is deeply divided on the moral issue. An analogous case may be found in the administration's approach to abortion, a practice that the President says he opposes deeply on moral grounds: the administration supports the legislative ban on federal funding, but has not called for a constitutional amendment that would ban abortion.

As President Bush told the pro-life "March for Life"

participants in January 2002: "Abortion is an issue that deeply divides our country. And we need to treat those with whom we disagree with respect and civility. We must overcome bitterness and rancor where we find it and seek common ground where we can. But we will continue to speak out on behalf of the most vulnerable members of our society."

In a similar way, its defenders contend that the current administration policy on stem cell research funding keeps the public ethical conversation open, may be acceptable to some individuals who hold that human embryos possess an intermediate or unknowable moral standing, and, at the same time, also advances the cause of those who contend that human embryos should be protected from destruction altogether.

The present funding policy has also been defended from the charge of inconsistency on rather different grounds, which, for their advocates, carry different consequences for future federal funding. This defense contends that, if the early embryo is morally equivalent to a child, then the proper moral response would be to ban all future embryo destruction and all stem cell research (public and private) on embryos destroyed after August 9, 2001, and not merely deny it federal funding.

Confronted with a practice that involved killing children so that their organs could be used to save the lives of others, advocates of this view contend, no one would simply deny it federal funding while allowing the gruesome practice to continue. But, they point out, there is no reason to attribute to the current funding policy the assumption that the early embryo is morally equivalent to a child. In fact, they contend, the President has never said that early embryos are inviolable, or are persons, or morally equivalent to children. While President Bush explained his funding policy by arguing that "it is unethical to end life in medical research," he has not sought to prohibit privately-funded embryonic stem cell research.

This leads some to conclude that implicit in the President's policy is either the view that the embryo has an intermediate moral status (worthy of serious moral consideration as a developing form of human life) or uncertainty about its moral status. Those who interpret the President's policy in this way point out that, in his address to the nation on stem cell research, he spoke in terms of a human embryo's "potential for life": Research on embryonic stem cells raises profound ethical questions, because extracting the stem cell destroys the embryo, and thus destroys its potential for life. Like a snowflake, each of these embryos is unique, with the unique genetic potential of an individual human being.

This, they contend, does not constitute an argument for treating human embryos as possessed of fully human moral standing. If the present policy is seen to reflect either the intermediate or uncertain view of the moral standing of human embryos, these advocates argue, it is not inconsistent to withhold federal funding, at least for now, when the medical benefits of stem cell research are still speculative, while permitting privately funded embryo research to proceed. They argue that restricting or limiting federal funding is a reasonable way of registering either doubt about the moral status of the embryo, or the moral unease felt by someone who takes nascent human life seriously and does not want it used wantonly, and who therefore wants scientists to prove the promise of this research before permitting them to go further with the support of federal funding. Indeed, they argue, this interpretation is consistent with the President's words in his August 9 address: [W]hile we're all hopeful about the potential of this research, no one can be certain that the science will live up to the hope it has generated. . . . Embryonic stem cell research offers both great promise and great peril. So I have decided we must proceed with great care." Viewing the administration's policy as based on an intermediate or uncertain view of the moral standing of human embryos also makes plausible, in the view of these observers, the fact that the President has neither called for a ban on privately funded embryo research, nor called upon scientists to desist from research on stem cell lines created after August 9, 2001. They contend that it also makes sense of the requirements, discussed above, that stem cell lines created before that date must, in order to qualify for federal funding, be derived from excess embryos created for reproduction, with donor consent, and without financial inducements.

Those who interpret the policy as reflecting an intermediate or uncertain view of the moral status of human embryos argue further that, if embryonic stem cell research vindicates its promise, there would be no categorical reason to prevent a reconsideration of federal funding in the light of medical advances. A further implication is that people may reasonably draw different conclusions about whether this principle justifies federal funding of stem cell lines derived after August 9, 2001 provided they are derived from embryos left over from IVF procedures, donated with consent, and without financial inducement. Although the President has declared that he regards destructive embryo research as unethical without additional qualifications, and although HHS Secretary Tommy Thompson has said that scientific advances would not cause he President to reconsider his policy, those who interpret the President's policy as reflecting an intermediate or uncertain view of the embryo argue that the moral logic of this principle admits the possibility that significant medical breakthroughs could justify a reconsideration.

III. The Moral Standing of Human Embroys

Many elements (though, as we shall make clear, not all elements) of the ongoing debate about federal funding of human embryonic stem cell research seem, as we have reviewed them, to turn on a basic disagreement about the nature, character, and moral standing of human embryos.

Public debate over the moral standing and appropriate treatment of human embryos has been quite contentious and divisive in recent years. In part, this had to do with its almost inevitable entanglement with the abortion debate, itself a deep and thorny controversy in America. In part, too, this has been connected to the fact that the question of the moral standing of human embryos touches many other fundamental moral and existential questions involving human origins, human dignity, the moral significance of our biology, and its relation to numerous traditional and widely shared moral teachings. Differences of opinion on the moral standing of human embryos often suggest differences on these larger questions of overall worldview. Nonetheless, the question of the moral standing of human embryos itself has been taken by nearly all commentators to be amenable to human reason and argument, and a lively debate has raged despite (or perhaps precisely because of) these widely diverging starting assumptions.

In the public arena, the question of the moral standing of human embryos has often been summed up in the question, "When does (a) human life begin?" This question suggests something of the quandary, although the academic and intellectual debate generally takes a somewhat more nuanced question as its starting point. That question has as its unstated premise the fact that under normal circumstances we regard all born human beings (from newborns through adults) as possessing equal moral worth and meriting equal legal protection. It then reflects upon the ways in which human embryos are similar and different from live-born human individuals, the moral significance of those similarities and differences, and therefore whether embryos should or should not be afforded protections. The first and most common recourse in seeking an answer to such questions has been human biology, and particularly human embryology. Nearly all participants in the dispute make some reference to biological findings, whether to claim that they teach us about an embryo's essential continuity with and similarity to human beings at other stages of life, or to argue that they reveal profound and morally meaningful discontinuities between embryos and live-born persons.

While we examine these differing contentions, it is crucial to remember—as several commentators in recent years have noted—that the biological findings, however relevant, are not themselves necessarily decisive morally. They may serve better to challenge moral positions founded on erroneous assumptions than to ground some positive moral affirmation or conclusion. For example, a recognition of biological continuity might in some measure undermine the argument that embryo destruction is permissible when certain biological markers or states of development are absent. But it would not by itself show indisputably that embryos are to be treated as simply inviolable. Meanwhile, recognizing the biological significance of some particular point, marker, characteristic, or capacity would not, in itself, imply some decisive moral significance. A description of early embryonic development is necessary though not sufficient to an understanding of the nature and worth of an early embryo. It is not sufficient because any purely biological description requires some interpretation of its anthropological and moral significance before it can function as a guide to action. With these provisions in mind, we offer the following brief review of developments in the debate over the moral standing of human embryos in the past several years. Readers may find it helpful to consult Notes on Early Human Development.

A Continuity and Discontinuity

Many participants in the debate take the question of the biological continuity or discontinuity between nascent and later human life to be crucially significant. Some argue that the fundamental organismal continuity from the moment of fertilization until natural death means that no lines can be drawn between embryos and adults. Others argue, on the contrary, that some particular point of discontinuity (or the sum of several such points) marks a morally significant distinction between stages, which difference should guide our treatment of human embryos.

1. The Case for Continuity.

Many of those who seek to defend human embryos base their case on some form of the argument for biological continuity and sameness through time. For example, they argue that a human embryo is an organic whole, a living member of the human species in the earliest stage of natural development, and that, given the appropriate environment, it will, by selfdirected integral organic functioning, develop progressively to the next more mature stage and become first a human fetus and then a human infant. Every adult human being around us, they argue, is the same individual who, at an earlier stage of life, was a human embryo. We all were then, as we still are now, distinct and complete human organisms, not mere parts of other organisms. This view holds that only the very beginning of a new (embryonic) life can serve as a reasonable boundary line in according moral worth to a human organism, because it is the moment marked out by nature for the first visible appearance in the world of a new individual. Before fertilization, no new individual exists. After it, sperm and egg cells are gone—subsumed and transformed into a new, third entity capable of its own internally self-directed development.

By itself, no sperm or egg has the potential to become an adult, but zygotes by their very nature do. Many authors therefore regard the activation of the oocyte (by the penetration of the sperm) or the completion of syngamy (the combining of paternally- and maternallycontributed haploid pro-nuclei to result in a unique diploid nucleus of a developing zygote) as a meaningful marker of the beginning of a new human life worthy of protection. After this point, there is a new genome, in a new individual organism, and there is a zygote (single-celled embryo) already beginning its first cleavage and embarking on its continuous developmental path toward birth. All further stages and events in embryological development, they argue, are discrete labels applied to an organism that is persistently itself even as it continuously changes in its dimensions, scope, degree of differentiation, and so on. We can learn names for the various stages as if they were static and discrete, but the living and developing embryo is continuously dynamic.

More to the point, in the view of these commentators no discrete point in time or development would seem to give any justification for assuming that the embryo in question was one thing at one point and then suddenly became something different (turning, for example, from non-human to human or from non-person to person). None of the biological events (or "points" in processes), they contend, is sufficient to tell us what we are morally permitted or obligated to do to human embryos, in the absence of one or another *additional* premises that shape one's view of these biological events. And if one's guiding premise is that all human persons possess equal moral standing—regardless of their particular powers, size, or appearance—then there are no grounds for denying the earliest human embryo full moral standing as a person.

Some critics of this position argue that it makes too much of mere genetic identity and (uncertain) potential or that it does not make enough of present condition and the significance of development itself. There is more to being human, some observers argue, than possessing a human genome or spontaneous cell division, and it matters that the early human embryo is but a ball of cells, without sentience or sensation and without human form.

It matters, too, they argue, that an ex vivo human embryo does not have the potential to develop independently, without further technical intervention. Indeed, some argue that a human embryo in its earliest stages is essentially no different from any human issue culture in the laboratory, or that, because the ex vivo embryo cannot develop if left to itself, it cannot be thought of as truly continuous with more developed human organisms.

It may be, in the description of one observer, not much different from a pile of building materials stored in a warehouse. Nonetheless, advocates of the argument from continuity suggest that it is dangerous to begin to assign moral worth on the basis of the presence or absence of particular capacities and features, and that instead we must recognize each member of our species from his or her earliest days as a human being deserving of dignified treatment. They contend that a human embryo already has the biological potential needed to enable the exercise, at a later stage of development, of certain functions. Sentience and sensation come in later in the process of development, but their seeds are there right from the beginning. And the fact that an embryo cannot develop outside the body is not an argument for leaving it outside the body.

There is, they argue, no clear place to draw a line after the earliest formation of the organism, and so there can be no stark division between the moral standing of nascent human life and that of more mature individuals. *2. The Case for Meaningful Discontinuity and Developing Moral Status.*

Many other observers, however, argue that some biologically and morally significant discontinuities do in fact present themselves in the course of early human development. These arguments generally do not simply hinge on biological descriptions—which are, in the absence of analysis, largely devoid of obvious moral significance—but instead begin from some implicit or explicit claim regarding the importance of a particular feature, capacity, form, or function (or the progressive accumulation of these) in defining a developing organism as meaningfully a member of the human race. Not simply grounded in biology, they appeal also to a moral or even metaphysical claim about the meaning of humanity. They * Also, several traditional religious views of the embryo (among some Jews and some Muslims, for instance) have attributed humanity to the embryo only after a particular point in its development, for example the 40th day.

The developing human organism might become (at once or progressively) deserving of protection as it becomes able to feel pain, or to exhibit neural activity, or rudimentary features of consciousness, or some elements of the human form, or the capacity to function independently—or as it progressively exhibits more and more of these or other criteria.

Until that time, many argue, a developing human deserves some respect because of what it might become, but not protection on par (or nearly so) with that afforded to fully human subjects. They suggest that genetic identity and organismic continuity are not sufficient; what matters is present form and function, more than mere potential. Several particular putative discontinuities (and combinations of them) have been proposed as candidates for the division between early stages, when a human embryo may be disaggregated for research, and later stages, when it deserves some greater level of protection.

(a) Primitive streak: The most popular candidate for a meaningful point of discontinuity is the appearance of the *primitive streak*, the earliest visible "structure" that defines the region of the embryo along which the vertebral column will form. The primitive streak generally appears around the 14 day after first cell division. It is taken to indicate the anterior-posterior axis of an embryo (in vertebrates), although recent studies suggest that polarity may be established much earlier, and in fact may be indicated by the point at which the sperm enters the egg. A principal reason for the importance placed on the primitive streak has to do with the biology of twinning. Prior to the appearance of the primitive streak, an embryo may (rarely, and for unknown reasons) divide completely to form identical twins. Some conclude that individuality must not yet be established, since the embryo might yet become two embryos. Since individuality is essential to human personhood and capacity for moral status, since individuality presumes a definitive single individual, and since the singularity of the embryo is not irrevocably settled prior to the appearance of the primitive streak, they argue that the entity prior to the primitive streak stage lacks finitive individuality and hence also moral status. Critics of this line of reasoning point to the

low statistical probability of monozygotic twinning: one in 240 live births (though rates clearly vary among populations in different regions, and precise figures probably cannot be known because some zygotes that split likely later fuse into one, and some singleton births may conceal a twin who died early in gestation). Critics also point to evidence that twinning results, not from an intrinsic drive within the embryo, but from a disruption of the fragile cell dynamics of embryogenesis. Evidence for this, they suggest, may be seen in the increased incidence of monozygotic twinning (up to tenfold in blastocyst transfer) associated with IVF.

This suggests, in their view, that twinning is neither a proof of the absence of an integrated individual organism with a drive in the direction of development nor a demonstration ex post facto of the absence of moral worth of the embryo before twinning. Nonetheless, for this reason, and for others (discussed below) having to do with the formation of the nervous system, the primitive streak has often been taken to be a highly significant marker of embryological development, and many commentators suggest it as a reasonable candidate for a meaningful point of discontinuity.

For this reason, many supporters of embryo research regularly propose the 14 day of development as a logical stopping point for permissible embryo research. *(b) Nervous system:* A second argument for discontinuity focuses on the developing nervous system. Many observers regard the nervous system as an especially important marker of humanity, both because the human brain is critical for all "higher" human activities, and because the nervous system is the seat of sensation and, especially relevant to this case, the sensation of pain. Proponents of this view hold that before an embryo has developed the capacity for feeling pain (or, in some forms of the argument, before sentience), we cross no crucial moral boundary in subjecting it to destructive research. For some, this is taken to mean that the primitive streak, as the first marker of a future nervous system, is a crucial feature of developing life.

For others, only later points of neural development (where pain might plausibly be experienced) are held to be decisive. Critics meanwhile contend that neural development as well as development of other systems (such as the cardiovascular system) are the natural outcome of the genetic program in action, and should be explained by reference to the previous stage and as leading to the subsequent stage, rather than marking a significant discontinuity. They maintain that the human being is, from the start, an inseparable psycho-physical unity, rather than a pure rationality or consciousness that exists with no meaningful ties to our bodies. From a scientific perspective, such critics hold, there is no meaningful moment when one can definitively designate the biological origins of a human characteristic such as consciousness, because our mind works in and through our body, and the roots of consciousness lie deep in our development.

The earliest stages of human development serve as the indispensable and enduring foundations for the powers of freedom and self-awareness that reach their fullest expression in the adult form. Some of those who believe that neural development is crucial, however, argue that the fact of nonsentience and of an inability to experience pain possess great moral significance, quite apart from the question of probable potential.

(b) Human form: Some observers also argue that certain rudimentary features of the human form must be apparent before we can consider a human embryo deserving of protection. In this view, the human form truly signals the

presence of a human life in the making and calls upon our moral sentiments to treat the being in question as "one of us." Different versions of this argument appeal to different particular elements (or combinations of elements) of the human form as decisive, but all suggest that a "ball of cells" is not recognizably human and therefore ought not to be treated as *simply* one of us. Some critics of this view argue that humans have different external forms or shapes throughout their lives, and that an organism, particularly in its early stages, should not be judged by its external shape, but rather by its biological constitution, and especially its genetic identity. But adherents of the argument that human form matters contend that genetic identity cannot simply be decisive of moral worth.

These various particular cases for discontinuity (and these are not the only ones that have been propounded over the years) are not mutually exclusive. Indeed, many of them point to more than one particular element of early human development as finally decisive of moral standing. But they share the belief that moral status accrues only at some later stage of the developing human organism. Their claim, in the broadest terms, is that in its earliest stages a human embryo is not yet simply a human being or a human person, and that it need not be treated as though it were.

Human development, they contend, is an essential element in any understanding of human life, and an organism at the earliest stages of that process is not to be treated the same as one much farther along. There are developmental differences, and these differences matter, in ways to be determined by human choice and understanding, as well as by a grasp of the biological facts. Critics of this view contend that while it is certainly true that human beings at different stages of development are not to be treated the same (as children are not given the responsibilities of adults), the crucial treatment here at issue is destructive treatment.

No human being, at any stage, they argue, should simply be destroyed for research, and the "use" of an embryo for research, no matter how valuable one deems the research to be, could not amount to treatment of that embryo as "deserving some degree of respect." The degree of respect granted in destroying the embryo would be zero, they contend. Nonetheless, the case for developing moral status, as articulated by a great number of participants in the policy debates of the past several years, often results in an expression of what has sometimes been termed the "special respect" approach to human embryos: an embryo in its earliest stages is not accorded the full moral standing of a human person, but it is nonetheless regarded as deserving some degree of respect and is treated as more than a mere object or collection of somatic cells in tissue culture.

In practice, adherents of this view tend to accept the use of early human embryos in medically valuable research under some circumstances, but they seek to apply some scrutiny to the reasons for which embryos will be used, the circumstances under which those embryos are obtained, and other relevant factors. Several bodies advising the federal government on human embryo research over the years have expressed this view, to varying degrees.

The Ethics Advisory Board to the Department of Health, Education and Welfare concluded in 1979 that the early human embryo deserves "profound respect" as a form of developing human life (though not necessarily "the full legal and moral rights attributed to persons"). The NIH Human Embryo Research Panel agreed in 1994 that "the preimplantation human embryo warrants serious moral consideration as a developing form of human life," though the panel argued that this did not mean that research should be prohibited. In 1999, the National Bioethics Advisory Commission (NBAC) cited broad agreement in society that "human embryos deserve respect as a form of human life," but, like its predecessors, did not recognize the embryo as having the full rights of a human person. The special respect position has been held by its advocates to be consistent with a range of possible particular policies on embryo research, including fairly restrictive ones, and indeed could be held consistent even with an outright restriction on the destruction of human embryos. To consider the embryo "inviolable" (and therefore not a mere utility to be instrumentally used), it is not necessary to presuppose its moral equality with a child, an adult or even a later stage gestating fetus. There may be increasing moral obligations (and natural sentiments) associated with a deepening relationality that extend moral duty without in any way implicitly eroding an imperative of protection at earlier stages of developing life. Most of those who have articulated the special respect position in the public debate have, however, tended to then argue that some research * This is partly due to the fact that "*special* respect," and "*intermediate* moral status," are rather vague terms, and embrace a very wide range of degrees of "specialness" and "intermediacy."

B. Special Cases and Exceptions

Some arguments in favor of permitting and funding embryo research, grounded in the "special respect" approach, do not in fact explicitly (or exclusively) rely on arguments about discontinuity or a biologically grounded view of developing moral status. Instead, or in addition, they rely upon questions of embryo viability and potential, and they are aimed at exploring unique circumstances to address and perhaps resolve questions of the moral standing of *certain particular* human embryos.

1. IVF "Spares

" Much of the debate surrounding embryonic stem cell research has focused on the use of cryogenically preserved IVF embryos, left over from assisted reproduction procedures and stored, perhaps indefinitely, in the freezers of IVF clinics.

One recent study suggests there are hundreds of thousands of such embryos in the United States alone, though only a very small percentage of them (less than 3 percent, approximately 3,000 or more) has ever been donated for research. Although all were produced with reproductive intent and were stored for further reproductive efforts should the first attempt fail, most of these frozen embryos may never be claimed by the original egg and sperm donors for use in assisted reproduction procedures. They are almost certain to remain frozen and, eventually, to die without developing further.

Although there have been some efforts to build interest in adopting such embryos, such adoption, some commentators argue, is very unlikely to become a large-scale phenomenon or to affect the fate of most of these stored embryos. Under the present funding policy, if these frozen embryos were donated for research and embryonic stem cells were derived from them, research on the resulting cells would not be eligible for federal funding.

Many observers argue that it should be: Since *these* particular embryos are almost certainly destined to die without ever developing, it would be appropriate to at least redeem some possible good from their existence and unavoidable demise. Some people have pushed the point further.

Since the vast majority of the (huge number of)

cryopreserved embryos will almost certainly not be adopted, and since many may not be viable even if they were to be transferred to a woman's uterus, a few observers have argued that, practically speaking, the frozen embryos are virtually all already lost.

To be sure, they are not already dead, but they are in a so-called "terminal situation" from which no rescue is practically possible. In view of this situation, one commentator proposes extending to these embryos the principle that sometimes, he argues, permits the killing of innocents. That is, killing may be morally permissible in cases where the person will soon die for other unavoidable reasons and where there is another person who can somehow be rescued through or as a result of such a normally impermissible act of killing (thus, as he puts it, "nothing more is lost").

He admits that the case of cryopreserved embryos stretches the application of the "nothing is lost" principle beyond its previous uses, because the embryos in question are alive and at risk of death *only* because of human choices and designs specifically directed toward them. The principle is also stretched because the lives that might someday be saved through today's embryo deaths are quite remote.

The potential lives saved are those of unspecified future persons with diseases that might be treated by therapies that as yet do not exist and may or may not exist in the future. However, against the weight of all these *ifs*, which some find formidable, there is the present fact that (like the embryos used to create stem cell lines derived before August 9 of 2001) the cryopreserved embryos are already here, with little or no prospect of rescue—they are, in this observer's description, already lost. Presumably, if destruction of "spare embryos" for human embryonic stem cell research were generally agreed to be permissible through this "nothing is lost" principle, it could be federally funded, subject to such routine secondary considerations as the need for free and informed consent by donors. Yet this argument, not surprisingly, has met with opposition. Some critics have claimed that it employs circular moral reasoning. The embryos, they argue, are in a "terminal situation" because of human choice and design; thus to then decide that, since they are going to die anyway, they may as well be put to good use is to ignore the moral implications of the original decision to create and freeze them.

Critics argue, moreover, that when thinking about our responsibilities to those who are soon to die, we would normally say that it makes a considerable moral difference whether we simply accept their dying or whether we positively embrace it as our aim. Yet some proponents of using IVF spares argue that the present situation is best understood as a forced choice between two regrettable alternatives for the final disposition of stored embryos (whether donated for research or abandoned). One choice may then be justified as the lesser evil.

Even if one deems the original decisions leading to the creation and storage of these embryos questionable, the embryos exist, and the earlier decisions cannot be undone. Some have also worried about the possibility of a "slippery slope," by which the uses of "spare" IVF embryos under this justification might open the door to their wider use in experiments in natural embryogenesis, toxicological studies or chimerizations, or perhaps their development in an artificial (or natural) endometrium, (though the reasonableness of "slippery slope" arguments is often disputed). Other critics point out that the "nothing is lost" principle is not permitted to govern decisions regarding lethal experiments on the terminally ill, on death-row inmates, or even on fetuses slated for abortion.

A further issue involves the question of whether accepting the "nothing is lost" principle for already existing embryos condones in principle the use of future excess embryos, or whether the principle actually requires efforts to prevent the creation or storage of "excess" embryos in the future.

Further, this application of the principle relates only to embryos originally created for the purpose of reproduction but not transferred to initiate a pregnancy. Should their use in research be accepted, however, it is not clear that it would be possible to differentiate between embryos created originally for reproduction and extra embryos created with an eye to research uses, since the process of producing them would be identical (though consideration of the extra risks involved for the woman egg donor could act as a counter against any largescale embryo-creation-for-research). Other observers, however, begin from the presence of cryogenically preserved embryos but extend further the argument justifying their use in research.

They argue that there is good reason to use embryos for research, not only because a situation some judge tragic already exists but because donating embryos is an act of beneficence and using them is a social obligation incurred by their gift. This approach would have us start by recognizing that, in the current situation, there is a set of embryos (in IVF clinics) none of which will ever enter a uterus, or even a (still hypothetical) artificial uterus.

These embryos, in one commentator's term, are "unenabled" and have no potential for full development. Since there is no possible way for such embryos to develop, there is no "possible person" to whom any "unenabled" embryo corresponds; therefore using them in research involves no loss of possible life. Critics of this approach argue that in effect it allows the moral standing of any given embryo to be decided simply by those responsible for it. Thus, whether a given embryo has moral standing depends only on whether it has a practical prospect of developing, as evidenced by whether it will be transferred to a uterus. But whether it enters a uterus depends on human choices, so the moral standing of a given embryo depends on human choices. If we choose to withhold essential enabling conditions for an embryo's development, these critics argue, then that embryo will lack not moral standing but merely the opportunity to develop.

Its intrinsic nature, including its *own* potential to develop (given needed conditions), has not changed. Nonetheless, in the view of a number of commentators, the fact that so many frozen embryos already exist (even if only a small percentage of them are donated for research) changes the balance of duties and respect owed to any single ex vivo embryo. Several observers have argued that the presence of these frozen embryos, with little or no chance of attaining birth, creates special circumstances in which the use of embryos in research (whether destroying them in the course of research or allowing them to die and subsequently using them) is independent of any final judgment regarding the moral standing or worth of the ordinary human embryo, as such.

2. Natural Embryo Loss

Some authors tie their moral arguments regarding the use of embryos in research to the fact of the high rate of embryo loss under natural conditions of sexual intercourse and unassisted reproduction. They argue that directed destruction of ex vivo embryos for the purpose of research would not result in greater embryonic loss than occurs in this natural process and would result in far greater benefits for humanity.

The rate of natural embryo loss after conception in unassisted human reproduction (taking in losses both before and after implantation), though not accurately known, is thought to be high, some suggest as high as 80 percent. Moreover, the fact of natural loss is now fairly well known, so that persons who engage in unprotected intercourse, whether seeking to reproduce or not, are knowingly bringing about the conception of many embryos that will die. We generally do not regard this embryo loss as unacceptably tragic, and we do not engage in great efforts to avert it or to find ways to diminish it (beyond research to prevent miscarriage, for instance).

For this reason, these commentators argue, using artificially created embryos for purposes of research would not destroy a greater portion of those embryos than ordinarily die in natural unassisted reproduction. Moreover, they suggest, the high rate of natural embryo loss should call into question the views of those who believe that early-stage human embryos merit equal treatment with human children and adults. If so many die in the natural course of things, why do we not treat natural procreation as a great fountain of tragedy and carnage?

The natural rate of embryo loss, and most people's failure to mourn its consequences, they suggest, should teach us something about the limited significance of human embryos in the earliest stages. One observer adds that the same logic should diminish our concerns about creating extra human embryos for research, as long as sufficient embryos are created for implantation to keep the chances of survival for any given embryo as good as the chances in natural reproduction. Another argues further that human embryonic stem cell research might actually raise the probability of longer survival for all humans, including embryonic ones, and is therefore a case of permissible taking of life, even on the assumption that the embryos are persons.

Opponents of this view, however, have argued that natural deaths of embryos and the deaths caused by intentional efforts to destroy ex vivo embryos for research are not morally equivalent. There are many things that happen naturally that we are not therefore justified in doing deliberately. Indeed, the rate of natural loss of live-born human beings is 100 percent, but that does not justify their killing.

And, they argue, even if one were permitted to analogize the deaths of frozen embryos in vitro to the embryonic wastage in vivo, in neither case were the embryos lost destined or created for anything other than their procreative end. In contrast, they argue, using embryos for research bears no relation to their natural direction or trajectory. Critics also argue that the character of our reaction to the natural embryonic death does not justify our practice of destructive embryo research.

For they believe that a creature's moral worth is not dependent on the emotional reaction of others to its death. The absence of moral sentiment does not imply an absence of moral obligation (nor a right of adverse intervention in a naturally developing human life). Moreover, critics contend, it is not clear how many of these "natural losses" were in fact failures of the fertilization process, so that there was never a unified, integrated organism in the first place, and thus never the loss of a human embryo. It is also unclear, they argue, how much of the supposedly "natural" loss rate is actually due to contingent and changeable factors, such as environmental pollution, pesticides, or endometrial problems, and so is not simply an unavoidable fact of embryonic existence.

3. Prediction of Non-Viability of Embryos

Some people, hoping to get around the moral dilemma of destroying even "unenabled" embryos, seek to identify a subset of embryos that might reasonably be regarded in advance as *non-viable*. One proposal has involved the possibility that cloned human embryos, created by somatic cell nuclear transfer, may prove to be non-viable or unable to develop beyond a certain point (biological evidence that this may be the case is presented by Rudolph Jaenisch in Appendix N) or may even, by their nature and origins, simply not constitute the equivalent of human embryos. If this turns out to be true, it is further argued, it might be possible to use them without arousing some of the ethical dilemmas that accompany the use of otherwise potentially viable human embryos. Others point to a possible subgroup of those embryos currently frozen in storage as potentially non-viable.

Although those embryos are not yet dead and, if thawed, would still exhibit some cellular function, some would be unlikely to survive even were transfer attempted. Since IVF procedures usually produce more embryos than can be transferred at one time, goes the argument, the clinicians choose for transfer those among the available embryos that look "the best" and seem most likely to survive and develop—so that those that are frozen are those deemed less likely to develop. Moreover, by applying similar judgment to the unimplanted embryos, we might identify those that would be least likely to survive even under the most favorable circumstances. These embryos might then reasonably be regarded as non-viable and therefore available for research since their use will not disrupt a potential life.

There has not been much direct reaction to this view in the ongoing ethical debates. Yet some observers have noted, in other contexts, that the techniques used to identify which

IVF embryos are more or less likely to develop successfully—estimates based usually on visual assessment of the embryos—have never been proven effective or even tested to ascertain their validity. Moreover, some argue, the true viability of cloned human embryos or of cryogenically stored embryos could not be determined in advance without attempting to implant them.

4. Creation of Non-Viable Embryo-Like Artifacts.

Others, seeking to bypass altogether the issue of viability, propose the possibility of creating a biological entity that cannot rightly be called a living organism, yet that has the generic organic powers necessary to produce embryonic stem cells. They suggest that somatic cell nuclear transfer, or a similar technique, could be used to create an entity that lacks, by design, the qualities and capabilities essential to be designated a human life in process. By intentional alteration of the somatic cell nuclear components or the cytoplasm of the oocyte into which they are transferred, researchers may be able to construct an "artifact" that is biologically (and morally) more akin to cells in tissue culture, but could still provide a source of functional human embryonic stem cells.

Proponents of this innovation aim to shift the ethical debate from the question of whether or when a human embryo should be considered a human being to the question of which organized structures and potentials constitute the minimal criteria for considering an entity *to be* a human embryo. Absent all the essential elements (including a full complement of chromosomes, proper genetic sequence and chromatin configuration, and cytoplasmic structures and transcription factors), advocates of this proposal argue, there can be no integrated whole, no organism, and hence no human embryo.

By technically constructing biological entities lacking these essential elements yet bearing the partial organic potential often found in failures of fertilization, they suggest it may be possible to procure embryonic stem cells without producing an organismal or embryonic entity that can meaningfully be designated a being with moral standing. Proponents argue that there is a natural biological precedent for such an entity lacking the qualities and characteristics of an organism yet capable of generating cells with the character of embryonic stem cells. Teratomas are germ cell tumors that generate all three germ layers as well as more advanced cells, tissues, and partial limb and organ primordia.

Yet these chaotic, disorganized, and nonfunctional masses lack entirely the structure and dynamic character of an organism.

Likewise, failures of fertilization due to abnormal complements or chromatin configurations (imprinting) of the chromosomes may still proceed along partial trajectories of organic growth without being meaningfully designated as organismal entities.

These natural examples of "partial generative potential" (described by some as 'pseudo-embryos'), together with other observations of early embryonic process, have led to a diverse array of suggestions for ways that embryonic stem cells may be produced without raising the moral issues involved in the creation and destruction of human embryos. These suggestions include the use of aneuploidies, polyploidies, viable cells from embryos in arrested development, parthenotes, and chimeras of human nuclear material and animal oocytes. Each presents its own particular technical challenges and raises unique and unfamiliar moral considerations. The scientific prospects for such projects remain largely unexplored in humans, though some animal work has shown promise, and proponents argue that they are within the reach of current technology. The crucial principle in all such efforts, proponents argue, is the preemptive nature of the intervention: undertaken at a stage before the transition to organismal status. They contend that just as we have learned that neither genes, nor cells, nor even whole organs define the locus of human moral standing, in this era of developmental biology we will come to recognize that cells and tissues with "partial generative potential" may be used for medical benefit without a violation of human life or dignity. Moreover, they argue, the moral distinctions essential to discern and define the categories of organism, embryo, and human being will be critical to progress in scientific research involving embryonic stem cells, chimeras, and laboratory studies of fertilization and early embryogenesis.

These advances in developmental biology, they contend, will depend on clarifying these categories and defining the moral boundaries in a way that at once defends human dignity while clearing the path for scientific progress. This proposal has drawn criticism on several fronts. First, critics suggest, it would require significant research to ensure that the procedure reliably produced the desired sort of "nonembryonic" entity yet also still yielded normal human embryonic stem cells, and such research might itself be morally problematic. Second, this proposal raises a series of further scientific and ethical questions, including those regarding the minimal degree of "partial generative potential" for an entity to be considered an organism, and for an entity to be considered a human embryo. They point further to the risk of creating entities that are so ambiguous as to leave their moral standing in serious doubt, at least for those people who believe that the early stages of human life have at least some moral worth. Finally, proposals to use human oocytes raise moral concern regarding the source of supply, in this case as in the larger arena of in vitro fertilization and experimentation. Although this approach has never been tested in humans, animal experiments suggest it has potential, and it has begun to play a part in the debates over the moral standing of human embryos and the permissibility of embryo research more generally.

V. Societal Sifnificance and Public Responsibility

While the bulk of the public debate surrounding embryonic stem cell research has been directed to the question of the moral standing of human embryos, some commentators have raised a number of other crucial and serious concerns. They have argued that the debate suffers from focusing too narrowly on questions of the standing of human embryos, when other issues—including the duties and responsibilities of those who engage in embryonic stem cell research, the implications of such uses of nascent life for our society (rather than just for the embryos themselves), the significance of the public debate, and a series of other issues—also bear heavily on the subject, and may illuminate it in ways at least as significant.

Some authors, including some who do *not* believe that human embryos should simply be treated as inviolable persons, have argued that the instrumentalization of human embryos—the seeds of the next generation—might tend to coarsen the sensibilities of our society toward future generations, and toward human life in general, quite apart from the effects on the embryos themselves. Others also argue that by setting down the path laid out by human embryonic stem cell research, we open the way for other, and more troubling, techniques and developments. Since human suffering and disease will never come to an end, they suggest, the resort to extreme and potentially exploitative methods is unlikely to find a logical stopping point.

Today, they argue, scientists want to use only the earliest embryos; but what will happen when it turns out that later-stage embryos are even more valuable in developing treatments for disease? Critics of this view have generally argued that it fails to offer a sufficient ground for impeding the promise and potential of medical treatments that might result from embryonic stem cell work. These critics see medical research as a central moral duty, and they argue that a society that prevents such research undermines not only medical progress, but the moral progress of the community as a whole. While instrumentalization and moral coarsening are real worries, these critics argue, longterm fears of a "slippery slope" do not justify renouncing the potential of today's research. Future difficulties, they say, can be faced if and when they arrive in earnest.

Other observers have raised concerns related to the ethical and policy debate itself, rather than to the specifics of one technique or another, or of one funding policy or another. Some, for instance, have argued that what is needed in the human embryonic stem cell research debate is not only an exchange of views about the substantive issues (though that is surely crucial) but also some sense of the appropriate democratic process for deliberation and for establishing appropriate public policy on such a profoundly contentious matter. The embryonic stem cell debate, it is argued, offers a valuable opportunity to think through the ways in which the American polity debates the most contentious moral issues.

Some even suggest that such matters should be removed from the political process altogether, and left in the hands of a regulatory body specifically charged with monitoring and decision-making authority. Other observers worry that the promise of embryonic stem cell research to bring swift or immediate cures to those who are now ailing has been oversold. They point out that, two decades ago, similar claims of rapid cures were made on behalf of fetal tissue transplantation research, but have not as yet been realized (though, of course, the danger of unfulfilled hope always looms over medical research).

Such talk, some observers have argued, tends to raise false hopes, and thus does a genuine disservice to the sick and disabled. Worse, some regard it as cruel and immoral to exploit the hopes and fears of the desperately ill and their families, especially when— as several scientists in the field have remarked—it is not very likely that stem cell based remedies will be available for most people now suffering from the potentially targeted diseases.

This moral concern is tied directly to the longstanding bioethical principle of truth-telling, which obliges physicians to inform their patients honestly about their condition and prognosis and encourages researchers to be truthful in their assessments of the potential for new treatments and cures, whether or not what they have to say is what patients and their loved ones want to hear. "It is misleading to suggest that stem cells will bring cures," one writer observes, "particularly cures for patients now coping with the serious diseases the research targets."

A related concern, raised by some of the same commentators, involves what has been termed "the disproportionate emphasis on stem cell research in contemporary health politics." The prominence of this debate in American politics, they argue, may tend to distract us from the fact that many Americans, and even more people elsewhere, lack very basic healthcare and have no access to those medical tools and techniques that already exist and that raise no profound controversy.

The concern for justice, and for the proper setting of priorities, they argue, requires us to see this line of research in its proper perspective. Because federal resources for research are limited, decisions must be made about which areas should receive high (and low) priority, and decisions must be made about how much to devote to research and how much to devote to programs that provide proven health care to patients. These commentators suggest that this view does not mean that stem cell research should not be funded, but only that we must keep in mind that funds are also needed for many other approaches to fighting suffering and disease. Critics of this view, however, respond that an excessive preoccupation with *existing* health care needs can jeopardize new medical research and medical progress, and that today's "basic medicine" was once experimental research. Meanwhile, others have argued that the debate has been too narrow in another way.

Any federal policy, they suggest, must take note not only of the potential promise of embryonic stem cell science, but also possible alternatives to such research, alternatives less morally troubling to many Americans. Many opponents of public funding for human embryonic stem cell research, for instance, have argued that more attention should be paid, and more resources devoted, to *adult* stem cell research, which raises few of the moral difficulties present in the embryonic stem cell debates (though, for some, it still does raise a number of ethical difficulties). Such work, they contend, might even make embryonic stem cell research (or, at the very least, publicly funded embryonic stem cell research) unnecessary, if it proves sufficiently useful. In response, however, others point out that adult stem cell research already receives about ten times the amount of federal funding apportioned to human embryonic stem cell research.

Critics also argue that embryonic stem cells may possess unique advantages over adult stem cells, just as (in some circumstances) the opposite may be the case, and that therefore both avenues, as well as research using stem cells derived from fetal tissue, should be pursued simultaneously. And they contend that opponents of embryonic stem cell research have oversold the promise of adult stem cells so that the public might come to see embryonic stem cell research as unnecessary. In the next chapter, we examine some of the scientific facts regarding adult and embryonic stem cells, but in the context of the ethical and political debates, the distinctions between them have been quite important and prominent. In these ways, the controversial possibility of scientific alternatives, as well as concerns about the health of American culture and democracy, the honesty of a political debate that touches on the hopes and fears of many who are suffering, and the bigger picture of health-care politics all impinge upon the question of federal funding of human embryonic stem cell research.

In 1999, the National Bioethics Advisory Commission stated that, "In our judgment, the derivation of stem cells from embryos remaining following infertility treatments is justifiable only if no less morally problematic alternatives are available for advancing the research," though the commission did *not* conclude that adult stem cells were sufficiently shown to offer such an alternative. (National Bioethics Advisory Commission, *Ethical Issues in Human Stem Cell Research*, Washington, D.C.: Government Printing Office, 1999, p. 53.)

Participants in the public debate surrounding human embryonic stem cell research and the administration's funding policy have addressed themselves to many complicated and difficult ethical matters: the character of the moral question at issue; the nature, object, ethical assumptions, and premises of the policy itself; the vexing question of what is owed to the early human embryo; and a number of other related concerns.

As we have seen, strong and powerfully argued views have been presented on various sides of each of these questions.

For now, neither side to the debate seems close to fully persuading the other of the truth it thinks it sees. But the rich and growing ethical debates do suggest the possibility of progress toward greater understanding of the issues, and toward more informed public decisionmaking, as all parties to the deliberation appreciate better just what is at stake, not only for them or their opponents, but indeed for all of us.

Bio-Fuels: A Case Study

With the spike in oil prices in 2005, much attention has turned to the utilization of alternative fuels. A popular alternative fuel source is bio-fuel. Bio-fuel is a broad term that encompasses both bio-diesel and ethanol. It is a fuel not derived from fossils, but is instead derived from one of two sources: agricultural crops such as corn, soybean, and sugar cane, or biomass resources such as agricultural, wood, animal, and municipal wastes and residues. Bio-fuel is a renewable source of fuel used as liquid fuels for transportation, but it also can be used for direct combustion for electricity production. Bio-diesel is different from ethanol because it is made from the oils of plants, mainly soybean, sunflower and waste vegetable oil. It contains no petroleum, is free of sulfur and aromatics, and can be blended at any level with petroleum diesel, usually called bio-diesel blend. The chemical process of turning cellulose and starch into dimethyl ether (ethanol) first requires breaking the chemicals into single sugar molecules. Both cellulose and starch are a polysaccharide or string of many individual sugar molecules (monomers) attached together in a plant. The sugars, once they are broken down, are fermented into ethanol. The ethanol then needs to be distilled before it is ready for automobiles (Moreira 2005). Currently, researchers are working on engineering an organism that will break down the cellulose and ferment the sugars in one step. This will reduce the cost of producing ethanol and make the process feasible for quicker scale-up. After the ethanol is produced, it is blended with petroleum-based fuel that can be pumped directly into the gas tank of our current vehicle models depending on the ethanol/petroleum blend. All cars can run on E10, which is 10 percent ethanol and 90 percent petroleum, but cars need to be altered to run efficiently on a blend any higher than E10 (for example E20, E85). Cars cannot tolerate high concentrations of ethanol because ethanol has higher oxygen content than petroleum-based fuel and cars need to be able to detect this with a fuel sensor. Many of the other car parts exposed to ethanol also need to be modified because it is an alcohol and it can disrupt the parts. To make a vehicle that can tolerate the high ethanol concentrations, it may cost the manufacturer about 100 dollars more than making a non-flexible fuel vehicle (Des Garennes 2005). The popularity of bio-fuels is increasing because of the many benefits, especially in a world that is becoming more environmentally conscious and pressured by the instability of oil supplies and prices. Crops used for the production of bio-fuel take in carbon dioxide from the atmosphere and some argue that this offsets the greenhouse gases released when the fuel is burned. Replacing petroleum with bio-fuel has the potential of reducing air pollution, including emissions of fine particulates and carbon monoxide. Greenhouse gas emissions from vehicles are reduced when vehicles run on any blend of ethanol or bio-diesel. Powering vehicles with a blend of 10% ethanol can potentially reduce greenhouse gas emissions by 10 grams of carbon dioxide for every kilometer driven (Iogen Corporation 2006). Another benefit is that rural economies may have the chance to sustain themselves and possibly grow because the process of making bio-fuels creates jobs and may raise farm incomes. Bio-fuel can be produced locally and at the same time is a renewable fuel, giving opportunities to diversify energy sources and lower the dependence on foreign oil. The benefits are numerous, but will only make the biggest difference in the environment if bio-fuels become a main energy source. The largest obstacle to this is land availability, therefore land efficiency or maximizing energy yield per acre is an essential aspect when considering bio-fuels as a main energy source. The impact of biotechnology is making this latter point less of a challenge with advances in crop yield productivity. Plant efficiency is important when considering the input/output ratios of energy. Corn for example is one of the least efficient sources of ethanol. Sugar beets and sugarcane produce double the ethanol yield per acre compared to corn. The energy input to make ethanol from corn (growing, transporting, and distilling) uses almost as much energy contained in the ethanol itself. Sugarcane yields eight times as much energy that is needed to produce ethanol compared to corn. Unfortunately, with growing fuel demands in tropical countries like Brazil, fuel demand translates into increased sugarcane production, meaning a demand for more fields, resulting in reductions in rainforest area (Murray 2005).

Some would argue that ethanol production from biomass requires the consumption of more fossil fuel-derived energy than it saves. David Pimentel from Cornell University says that ethanol production from corn consumes 29 percent more energy than it returns as fuel (Pimentel and Patzek 2005). When farming corn there is the use of plows, combines, and other farm machinery and petroleum-based fuels power them all. There are alternative arguments to this such as using the bio-fuels as a source of energy for powering the plants producing bio-fuels, which will reduce the use of fossil fuels. The balancing of energy consumption, meaning the growing, the harvesting and the production of fuel, is just one debate of the pros and cons of bio-fuels. Others have argued that energy balance is not the main concern for energy security, but supplementing the capacity needed to support growing fuel demands is more important. The oil fields are not running dry yet, but the oil is increasingly more difficult to reach and pump out and the demand is growing every year. If the oil suppliers can keep up with the demand, the world can remain dependent on oil, but if the demand is not met, the world needs an alternative. Another debate is the amount of land use and fertilizer and pesticide consumption to support the development of crops for bio-fuel production. Replacing the U.S. fuel supply with corn ethanol would require at least 60 percent of the nation's available cropland. Using plant waste or cellulosic biomass would decrease the use of crops such as corn and decrease the amount of cropland needed to produce enough bio-fuel (Moreira 2005). There are locations in the U.S. more suited for producing crops for fuel, but these same locations also support food crops. An alternative for corn production to produce bio-fuels is the production of sugar beets. They have a higher energy output than input and could reduce the amount of land that is needed to produce fuel. The use of bio-fuels and constructing cars that are compatible with the fuel is a topic that has continued for more than a century. In 1900, Rudolf Diesel showed an engine at the World Exhibition in Paris that ran on peanut oil and since the 1930's bio-diesel has been in small-scale use in Paris.

In the 1920's Henry Ford was an enthusiast for crop-based ethanol. In 1973, Brazil built cars adapted to burn pure ethanol until the 1980's when oil prices began to plummet and sugar prices soared. Because of this, many of the cars used for ethanol use were no longer being built (The Economist 2005). The drop in oil prices in the 1980's not only made it unnecessary for biomass-derived ethanol production, but it increased the price of producing bio-fuels. Perhaps, beyond the oil price/bio-fuel price competition the largest reason why this technology has not caught on is the lack of a focused national effort to make it happen. Research on bio-fuels ceased, or at least slowed down, and the consequence of the hiatus devastated the progress because knowledge was inherently lost (Lee 2004). The guarantee from car manufacturers to the purchaser is an issue if that guarantee is invalidated when the owner decides to fill up with bio-fuel. A few car companies are setting limitations on the percentage of bio-fuel they will guarantee on your car. For example, Volkswagen has extended its guarantee on their diesel-engine cars, which are now available in the U.S. On January 8th 2006, Volkswagen, Shell, and Iogen (Bio-fuel company in Canada), signed an agreement to conduct a study into the economic feasibility of producing cellulose ethanol in Germany. This is the first time an automotive manufacturer, an oil company, and a technology company have collaborated to advance the possibility of using clean fuel (Iogen Company 2005). One positive aspect that might increase bio-fuel use is that by June 2006, diesel is going to be required to eliminate sulfur. Sulfur in the fuel makes the fuel "slippery", but by adding bio-diesel, the "slipperiness" can be regained.

Opportunities in Nano-Enabled Drug Delivery Systems

Nanomedicine is widely expected to become a multi-billion dollar business over the next decade. Although some of the applications for nanomedicine are quite futuristic, others are on the verge of generating significant revenues. One of these is nano-enabled drug delivery systems which promise to increase the bioavailability of drugs and reduce the likelihood of toxicity. Researches pinpoint several areas where nano-engineering of drug delivery systems is leading to greater control over active compounds, resulting in the physician's ability to send the smallest dose possible in order to achieve the desired result in the patient. This chapter reviews the main opportunities that are emerging for nano-enabled drug delivery systems. In most cases, these are based on delivering drugs in nanoparticulate form. Most drugs perform better as nanoparticles, because they can be targeted better and there are fewer side effects. In addition, by using smaller amounts of drugs, treatment costs may be reduced. For example, according to researches, patients show a strong preference for nanoparticle inhalers as an alternative to the widely used injectable methods, which may permit far lower doses of expensive protein-based drugs like insulin. It is expected that the dosing benefits of nano-enabled drug delivery systems will be extended to compounds used in treating both infectious disease and cancer, and has identified six types of drug delivery systems in which nanotechnology is likely to have an impact. Although injectable delivery systems have some inherent discomfort for the patient and other types of delivery may be preferred by both the patient and the physician, nanotechnology may be applied to produce improvements and additional revenue streams for the drug company. A case in point is Johnson & Johnson, which, at the beginning of 2005, announced that its Élan NanoCrystal technology would be used in a Phase III clinical trial for an injectable formulation of paliperidone palmitate, an anti-schizophrenia drug. This is a new "nano formulation" of an older drug which overcomes the original's insolubility, by reducing the particle size to under 200 nm. This new formulation enables the product life cycle to be extended by a significant amount. Implantable drug delivery systems are often preferable to the use of injectable drugs, because the latter frequently display first-order kinetics (e.g. initial concentration is elevated, which then drops exponentially over time). This may cause difficulties with toxicity, if and when the peak concentration remains above the therapeutic range. Conversely, drug efficacy often diminishes as the drug concentration falls below the targeted range. By contrast, implantable "time release" systems may help minimize peak plasma levels and reduce the risk of adverse reactions; allow for more predictable and extended duration of action; reduce the frequency of re-dosing; and improve patient acceptance and compliance. To these advantages nanotechnology can add the benefits listed at the beginning of this White Paper. Implantable drug delivery systems are expected to be used for the delivery of proteins, hormones, pain medications, and other pharmaceutical compounds. An example of how nanotechnology is already making its impact felt in this part of the drug delivery business is provided by pSivida's BioSilicon product. BioSilicon is a novel nanostructured material that effectively stores an active compound in nanosized pockets that controllably release minute amounts of drug as the silicon dissolves. pSivida is currently exploring biodegradable implantable methods for tissue engineering and ophthalmic delivery. Nano-implants will also be used in the not-too-distant future for treating cancer. Among the first nanoscale devices to show promise in anti-cancer therapeutics and drug delivery are structures called "nanoshells," which it is believed may afford a degree of control never before seen in implantable drug delivery products. Nanoshells typically have a silicon core that is sealed in an outer metallic core. By manipulating the ratio of wall to core, the shells can be precisely tuned to scatter or absorb very specific wavelengths of light. For example, Gold encased nanoshells have been used to convert light into heat, enabling the destruction of tumors by selective binding to malignant cells. A physician can use infrared rays to pass harmlessly through soft tissue, while initiating a lethal application of heat when the nanoshells are excited. Some researchers are experimenting with temperature-sensitive drug delivery control methods, using nanoshells that release their payload only when illuminated with the proper infrared wavelength. The vast majority of consumers prefer an oral drug delivery system to implantables or injectables. With this in mind, various development groups are working to enhance traditional oral delivery systems with nanoengineered improvements. There are some areas where nano-enhanced drugs could make a big difference in increasing oral bioavailability and reducing undesirable side effects. By increasing bioavailability, nanoparticles can increase the yield in drug development and more importantly may help treat previously untreatable conditions. Because of the blood brain barrier (BBB) many new chemical entities aimed at treating brain disorders have proved not to be clinically useful. By contrast, nanoparticles have been demonstrated to cross the BBB with little difficulty. Companies such as Germany's NanoPharm have developed systems capable of reaching the brain for anesthesia (Dalargin, an analgesic), cancer drugs, and various therapeutics. The company claims several advantages over existing systems, including:

1. no requirement to open the BBB,
2. the ability to use potentially any drug, whether hydrophilic or hydrophobic, and
3. the drug does not need to be modified.

Meanwhile, researchers at the University of Texas at

Austin have described a means of using nanospheres for oral drug delivery. These nanosphere carriers are derived from hydrogels, which are highly stable organic compounds that swell when their environment becomes more acidic. They have been successfully formulated into controlled-release tablets and capsules, which release active compounds when the hydrogel body swells. NanoMarkets' research indicates that nanomaterials provide a unique opportunity for rapid topical delivery of active compounds. Given their very small size, nanoparticles are able to enter human tissues and cells quickly. Companies such as Novavax have already developed regulated topical systems that take advantage of the unique properties of micellar nanoparticles.

It has two hormone replacement therapies dubbed Estrasorb (which received FDA approval in October 2003) and Androsorb (which successfully completed Phase I human trials in 2003). The number of FDA-approved polymers available for use on-skin is increasing rapidly. With this in mind, the industry will be presented with opportunities to create new transdermal platform designs that improve on-skin properties and diffusion of active molecules from patches. This interesting trend is expected to result in smaller and less invasive patches that increase the universe of available drug candidates. In some cases, electronics are even being integrated into patch-like platforms involving wound care, monitoring, and diagnostic methods.

As such, patch-like platforms will play an important role in healthcare to treat, measure, diagnose, and generally improve quality of life. Colloidal dispersions have been demonstrated to remove potentially lethal compounds from the bloodstream, including high concentrations of lipophilic therapeutics, illegal drugs, and chemical and biological agents. A team of scientists at the University of Florida and Clarkson University in Potsdam, N.Y., has demonstrated favorable results to this end, using biocompatible microemulsions. These oil-in-water systems have a rapid and efficient absorption capacity for many target molecules that are frequently overdosed, whether this be intentional or accidental. The microemulsions use a polymeric surfactant, in combination with an ionic co-surfactant. Other oil compositions have been made with varying absorption characteristics for different toxins, in all cases avoiding hemolysis and unwanted blood coagulation. The mechanism by which nanoparticles trap toxins involves aromatic or cyclodextrin receptors with electron deficiencies, which form complexes with selected toxins, sometimes referred to as "benzenoid moieties. The analysis above establishes that the impact of nanotechnology on the drug delivery business is likely to be very broad in three senses:

- Nanotechnological improvements promise to impact almost every common mode of drug delivery oral, implantable, injectable, etc.
- Such improvements will themselves cover a lot of ground, including lower drug toxicity, lowering cost of treatments, improved bioavailability and extension of the economic life of proprietary drugs.
- Nano enabled drug delivery will provide improvements in the treatment of some of the most widespread diseases, such as cancer and diabetes.

This is an impressive list. Also impressive is the fact that many of the categories of nano-enabled drug delivery systems are already close to or at the point of marketing. It is believed that not only will the nano-enabled drug delivery market be one of the first true nanomedicine markets to evolve, but as it does so, the revenues from nano-enabled drug delivery systems will be quite large. The pharmaceutical industry has to discover and develop innovative medicines for a wide range of diseases in a marketplace that is (1) likely to experience growing regulatory and pricing pressures and (2) that is increasingly targeted towards diseases that have been traditionally resistant to pharmacotherapy (e.g., solid tumors). This chapter profiles a number of tools that are emerging from nanotechnology that are believed will be important aids in the process of drug discovery in this environment. Today, nearly all pharmaceutical companies follow common technology processes for discovering drugs. These include cloning and expressing human receptors and enzymes in formats that allow high-throughput, automated screening and the application of combinatorial chemistry. Thus, random screening can now be achieved with libraries sufficiently large and diverse to have a relatively high probability of finding a novel molecule. These libraries are possible because they can be generated by the techniques of combinatorial chemistry (combichem). Backing this are important developments in the application of genetics and genomics to understand associations between diseases and gene products. Importantly, bioinformatics are beginning to identify putative targets for a number of diseases. An important consequence of today's approach is that more lead molecules are being discovered for diverse targets, giving the medicinal chemist more scope to find a candidate molecule. Yet the probability of success of launching a candidate molecule into the market remains basically unchanged at around 8 percent, and the perception is that the time to market is not reducing as might be expected with greater automation. Numerous problem areas remain:

- Current methodologies for compound synthesis.
- Storage and retrieval are inefficient and inadequate.
- Better information is needed to improve target selection and validation.

- More predictive screens are essential.
- More emphasis must be placed on acquiring good ADMET data earlier in the discovery process.
- Novel screening methodologies are needed that dramatically increase throughputs and reduce reagent consumption.

It is becoming clear that many of the important solutions will be nanotechnological in nature. This is because the size range that holds the most interest in drug discovery is more or less the same as that which defines nanotechnology from 100 nm down to the atomic level (approximately 0.2 nm). Nanotechnology cannot provide the ultimate solutions to all these problems. However, it is becoming clear that many of the tools developed to pursue nanotechnology and nanoscience will have important roles in drug discovery. While AFM microscopes are invaluable for imaging objects at the nanoscale, until recently they haven't been able to see how components of a cell react in biological processes, such as their response to a specific chemical or compound. New imaging techniques involve attaching antibodies specific to individual proteins to the tip of an atomic force microscopes' probe. When an antibody reacts with the protein to which it is targeted, it creates a variance in the microscope's reading compared to a reading with a bare tip, showing the presence of a protein or other specific material in the region being scanned. This technique leads to a greater understanding of the chemical dynamics involved in how cells react to stimuli, and could prove particularly significant for drug discovery. However, although NanoMarkets believes that AFM is a useful tool to improve the understanding of molecular interactions, our research also indicates that the widespread use of this technology in bioanalytical applications has been hindered by the limited throughput of these techniques and the high experimental burden imposed by complicated and expensive instrumentation. Highly parallel micrometer and submicrometer cantilever arrays, which are currently being developed, might increase the throughput of AFM-based force spectroscopy. NSOMs allow the study of optical properties of the sample surface with a resolution better than the wavelength of the light. By scanning the optical probe at very small distances from the sample (a few nanometers) "evanescent waves" from the surface are detected by the probe. The use of evanescent waves allows bypassing of the wavelength limitation of traditional optical techniques (the traditional limit of resolution being half the wavelength in use). NSOM can be used to image biological samples and could ultimately be a significant contributor to drug discovery. However, there is an obstacle to such deployment at the present time manufacturing the probes reliably, the requirement for a very small hole through which the light passes being problematic. SPR is a phenomenon that occurs when light is reflected off thin metal films and a small amount interacts with electrons in the film, reducing the light intensity. The refractive index of the materials sandwiching the film dictates the angle at which the light reduction (essentially a shadow) occurs. Using an SPR-based approach, the interaction of biomolecules can be detected in real time, offering applications largely for observing biological systems in action on a very small scale, but also with potential for biosensors. Surface plasmons were the subject of some interesting general research in late 2002 and early 2003. There is still a lot to be learned in this field, but NanoMarkets believes that there will be important improvements for imaging systems (and thus for drug discovery) as this learning process proceeds. Current technologies used for proteomic studies are based on a variety of separation techniques followed by identification of the separated proteins and proteolytic peptides using mass spectrometry (MS). One popular technique is high-resolution two-dimensional (2D) gel electrophoresis, which is capable of resolving 2500 or more distinct protein spots from complex samples. The in-gel protein spots are then identified using sensitive MS and sequence database searching. An alternative approach to 2D gel electrophoresis is chromatographic separation of peptides with electrospray ionization (ESI)-MS or tandem MS (MS/MS) detection. The need for relatively large sample volumes is a major challenge for conventional ESI-MS analysis. There are now systems that address this challenge by applying nanotechnology to the electrospray nozzles. Thus, Advion's ESI Chip contains an array of nanoelectrospray nozzles, each one-fifth the diameter of a human hair, etched in a silicon wafer. Nanolithography is the art and science of etching, writing, or printing at the nanoscopic level. DPN is a scanning probe nanopatterning technique in which an AFM tip is used to deliver molecules to a surface via a solvent meniscus, which naturally forms in the ambient atmosphere. This direct-write technique offers high-resolution patterning capabilities for a number of molecular and biomolecular "inks" on a variety of substrates, such as metals, semiconductors, and monolayer functionalized surfaces. DPN is becoming a significant tool for the scientist interested in fabricating and studying soft- and hard-matter on the nanoscale. DPN enables precise multiple patterns with near-perfect registration. It's both a fabrication and imaging tool, as the patterned areas can be imaged with clean or ink-coated tips. The ability to achieve precise alignment of multiple patterns is an additional advantage earned by using an AFM tip to write, as well as read, nanoscopic features on a surface. NanoMarkets believes that together, all these attributes make DPN a valuable tool for studying fundamental issues on colloid chemistry, surface science, and nanobiotechnology. The central paradigm in proteomics studies has been to identify differential protein levels in healthy and diseased cells, characterize these proteins and determine the protein's role in biochemical pathways. These proteins can then serve as diagnostic markers and potential drug targets. Traditionally, 2D gel electrophoresis has been the workhorse in proteomics on the front end of mass spectroscopy. This technology, however, has been described as a bottleneck in high-throughput proteomic studies. As a result there has been a significant push to develop alternative technologies that serve to alleviate this rate failing step in protein separation prior to further analysis. At the forefront of these emerging and growing technologies are protein and DNA microarrays that allow the highly specific capture and analysis of a large number of proteins expressed in various cell types exposed to given perturbations in a high throughput manner. Microarrays are generally defined as a substrate and surface chemistry onto which a biomolecule or capture agent has been immobilized for the purpose of expression analysis and functional characteristic.

The potential to decrease the time required for the critical steps or protein separation and characterization are serving as a considerable driver in the protein microarray market. Microarray technologies can be considered platforms for nanoscale bioanalysis, and these products have already proven their value in the marketplace. However, currently available microarray technologies suffer from certain limitations that prohibit the exploitation of the full range of drug discovery applications. These limitations are already being addressed at the nano level with "nanoarrays," which are ultra-miniaturized versions of the traditional microarray that can measure interactions between individual molecules down to resolutions of as little as one nanometer. Nanoarrays are being touted as the next evolutionary step in the miniaturization of bioaffinity tests for proteins, nucleic acids, and receptor-ligand pairs. It is believed that nanometer-scale resolution capabilities of nanoarray technology offer many advantages in the emerging field of functional proteomics. Unlike nucleic acids, which can easily be multiplied by amplification methods, individual proteins cannot be easily increased in quantity. Using nanoarray technology, very small quantities of individual proteins can be effectively screened against a large set of drug targets. In addition, nanoarrays can be incorporated as sensors in ways that would be impossible with larger microarrays. In addition, unlike traditional microarrays, a nanoarray can be used "in solution." Microarrays, once exposed to the target protein, must be removed from solution and rinsed before they are scanned to see whether or not there have been any "hits." Not only does this take time, but the rinsing process can also easily result in the degradation of the array itself.

QDots are nanometer-sized semiconductor crystals, or electrostatically confined electrons. While other bio-imaging tools such as fluorescent organic dyes have been available for many years. QDots hold the promise of a true revolution in bio-imaging quality and sensitivity. Since 1914, researchers studying everything from blood tests to the effects of cancer drugs on the workings of a cell have used fluorescent dyes to tag cells. The dyes, however, can be problematic. Each dye molecule requires a laser of the same wavelength to cause it to illuminate. The dyes are also imprecise and have a tendency to bleed together. They can only be lit up for very short periods of time, typically just a few seconds after a light source is applied. QDots take advantage of the quantum confinement effect predicted by quantum mechanical theory to fluoresce extremely brightly when excited by a light source such as a laser. And they don't have any of the disadvantages of conventional technologies. By varying the size of the crystals one can cause a rainbow of colors to fluoresce. In addition, QDots stay lit for much longer periods of time than conventional dyes often hours or days. QDots enable the tagging of a variety of different biological components like proteins or different strands of DNA with specific colors. QDots are designed to bond with and illuminate individual biological targets of choice whether genes, nucleic acids, proteins, small molecules, cancer cells, or even entire blood vessels. It may be noted that some of the world's largest pharmaceutical and biotech companies, such as GlaxoSmithKline, Pfizer, and AstraZeneca, and leading biotech firm Genentech are applying QDots in high-content drug screening and have completed initial drug screens using QDots as the biological read-out. Genentech is applying QDots to the detection of breast cancer. This chapter demonstrates how nanotechnology offers several improvements in drug discovery technology. These include:

- Improved imaging (including real-time imaging) that enables researchers to better understand how biological processes are affected by a new compound.
- The use of dip pen technology to improve fundamental research techniques for drug discovery applications.
- Major improvements in today's microarray and fluorescent dye technologies.

As the drug industry strives to meet the increasingly difficult task of producing new drugs and especially new blockbuster drugs, it is increasingly seeking new drug discovery technologies that can improve R&D success rates and time to market. It is therefore believed that these improvements are likely to lead to substantial new business revenues over the next few years.

Opportunities for Clusters and Nanocrystalline Materials

Clusters are groups of atoms or molecules that display

properties different from both the smaller atoms or molecules and the larger bulk materials. Many techniques have been developed to produce clusters, beams of clusters, and clusters in a bottle for use in many different applications including thin film manufacture for advanced electronic or optical devices, production of nanoporous structures as thermal barrier coatings, and fabrication of thin membranes of nanoporous materials for filtration and separation. An apparatus developed at the University of Göteborg to measure cluster reactivity and sticking probability as a function of the number of metal atoms in the cluster. The unique properties of nanoparticles make them of interest. For example, nanocrystalline materials composed of crystallites in the 1-10 nm size range possess very high surface to volume ratios because of the fine grain size. These materials are characterized by a very high number of low coordination number atoms at edge and corner sites which can provide a large number of catalytically active sites. Such materials exhibit chemical and physical properties characteristic of neither the isolated atoms nor of the bulk material. One of the key issues in applying such materials to industrial problems involves discovery of techniques to stabilize these small crystallites in the shape and size desired. This is an area of active fundamental research, and if successful on industrially interesting scales, is expected to lead to materials with novel properties, specific to the size or number of atoms in the crystallite. Schematic drawing of the experimental setup used in Göteborg for studies of chemical reactivity and/or sticking probability of various molecules with the clusters. The production of clusters is via laser vaporization of metal substrates and detection via photoionization time-of-flight mass spectrometry (A. Rosen, University of Göteborg, Sweden). A typical objective of nanoscale catalyst research is to produce a material with exceedingly high selectivity at high yield in the reaction product or product state, i.e., chemicals by design, with the option of altering the product or product state simply by changing the surface functionality, elemental composition, or number of atoms in the catalyst particle. For instance, new catalysts with increasing specificity are now being fabricated in which the stoichiometry may be altered due to size restrictions or in which only one or two spatial dimensions are of nanometer size. Five recent examples where nanocrystalline metallic and ceramic materials have been successfully investigated for catalytic applications are discussed below (Trudeau and Ying 1996).

4

Regulatory Oversight in Biotechnology: A US Case Study

UNITED STATES REGULATORY OVERSIGHT IN BIOTECHNOLOGY RESPONSIBLE AGENCIES—OVERVIEW

The Agencies primarily responsible for regulating biotechnology in the United States are the US Department of Agriculture (USDA), Environmental Protection Agency (EPA), and the Food and Drug Administration (FDA). Products are regulated according to their intended use, with some products being regulated under more than one agency.

Agency	*Products Regulated*
U.S. Department of Agriculture	plant pests, plants, veterinary biologics
Environmental Protection Agency	microbial/plant pesticides, new uses of existing pesticides, novel microorganisms
Food and Drug Administration	food, feed, food additives, veterinary drugs, human drugs and medical devices

Before commercialization, genetically engineered plants/organisms must conform with standards set by State and Federal marketing statutes such as State seed certification laws, the Federal Food, Drug, and Cosmetic Act (FFDCA), the Federal Insecticide, Fungicide, and Rodenticide Act (FIFRA), the Toxic Substances Control Act (TSCA), and the Federal Plant Pest Act. There are no national requirements for varietal registration of new crops.

Examples:

New Trait / Organism	*Regulatory Review Conducted by:*	*Reviewed for:*
Viral Resistancein food crop	USDA EPA FDA	Safe to grow Safe for the environment Safe to eat
Herbicide Tolerance in food crop	USDA EPA FDA	Safe to grow New use of companion herbicide Safe to eat
Herbicide Tolerancein ornamental crop	USDA EPA	Safe to grow New use of companion herbicide
Modified Oil content in food crop	USDA FDA	Safe to grow Safe to eat
Modified flower color ornamental crop	USDA	Safe to grow
Modified soil bacteria degrades pollutants	EPA	Safe for the environment

Frost-resistant Strawberries: A Risk/Benefit Analysis of Food Biotechnology

Ice Minus Version

Believe it or not, bacteria are found on all plants. Bacteria thrive on plants because they feed on plant material (leaves, stems and fruit). A particular bacteria, Pseudomonas syringae (soo-du-mone-us sir-in-gay) is commonly found on plants. Pseudomonas has a protein in its cell membrane that promotes ice crystal formation. So when the Pseudomonas is sitting on the leaves or fruit of a strawberry plant and the temperature dips, this protein will result in ice crystals forming on the strawberry plant. Once the ice forms, the plant is damaged and the Pseudomonas can have a feast on the weakened plant. Not such a dumb microbe, huh? Well, scientists have isolated the gene in Pseudomonas that codes for the ice crystal forming protein. They can remove the gene, grow a new version of Pseudomonas without the gene called "ice-minus" Pseudomonas, and spray the strawberry plants with the ice-minus Pseudomonas. These plants can tolerate temperatures down to 27° F without freezing. The end result is reduced loss to the farmer and more undamaged strawberries for you!

Artic Flounder Antifreeze Version

Another way that scientists are working to keep strawberries from freezing is by using the help of a fish called the Arctic flounder. The Arctic flounder makes an "antifreeze" protein to protect itself against the chilly waters in which it lives. Scientists have isolated the gene that codes for this antifreeze protein and are now attempting to insert this gene into the DNA of the strawberry plant. If this insertion is successful, the strawberry plant should be able to make this antifreeze protein and therefore protect itself when the mercury drops!

Potato Plant Pesticide

Many different types of bacteria find their homes on the leaves, stems and fruit of plants. These microbes must often compete for their nutrients (food) with other plant pests such as insects or fungi. How do they compete? They produce a substance called a toxin which is harmful to their opponents, the insects and fungi. As scientists observed this competitive relationship between the plant pests, some came up with the idea to allow the plant to defend itself by producing this toxin all on its own. How did they do it? Let's explore the background in a little more detail. There is a specific bacteria known as Bacillus thuringiensis or Bt for short. Bt produces a substance which is toxic to many insects. Scientists identified the Bt genes responsible for the production for this toxin and transferred these genes into certain crop plants such as potatoes, corn and cotton. Now these plants which have been genetically engineered are able to produce the toxin on their own and protect themselves against the damaging insects. The toxin produced directly by the plant is called a "plant pesticide". Many people who support this research feel that by enabling plants to protect themselves through producing plant pesticides, the use of conventional or chemical pesticides will be reduced. The U.S. Environmental Protection Agency has approved some limited use of the Bt plant pesticide. Also, they have determined that the use of the Bt plant pesticide will not pose an unreasonable risk to the health of people or other organisms which are not targeted by the plant pesticide.

Recombinant Bovine Somatrotropin

Bovine somatotropin is a protein hormone which is naturally produced in dairy cows. It is also known as BST. BST plays a role in some vital functions of the cow such as growth and milk production. In the early 1980's scientists at a biotechnology company called Genetech isolated the genes that code for the production of BST in cows. By inserting these genes into bacteria, scientists were able to produce large quantities of BST in the laboratory. This form of BST which is produced through genetic engineering is called recombinant BST or rBST. The next step was to see how the rBST affected the cows. It was found that when rBST is given (via injections) to lactating cows, milk production is increased by about 10%. Since this discovery, two companies (Monsanto and Eli Lilly) have developed a commercially available form of rBST to be used by dairy farmers, The U.S. Food and Drug Administration (FDA) has approved the use of rBST in dairy cows. The FDA reported that rBST does not change the composition of milk and poses no health threats to individuals who consume the milk. According to research conducted on rBST and cows supplemented with rBST: (i) The concentration of BST in the milk of cows treated with usual doses of rBST is not higher than the concentration in untreated cows (ii) When people ingest BST orally or receive an injection of BST, BST has no biological activity in these people. (iii) BST is a protein and is digested like other proteins in the human digestive tract.

Virus-resistant Squash and Sweet Potatos

Viruses are ultramicroscopic infectious agents. Scientists call viruses "infectious agents" for two reasons. First, viruses have both living and nonliving features, so it is difficult to call a virus an organism. Second, viruses must live inside the cells of a living host in order to survive. Viruses infect their living hosts (mainly bacteria, plants, or animals) and make the hosts sick. Hence, viruses are infectious agents. In plants, many viruses are transmitted by aphids (little insects that feed on plants). Viruses can be detrimental to the development of a plant and to the success of a farmer's crop. To engineer a virus resistant plant, scientists take a gene out of a virus and then insert that gene into the plant of choice. Once the virus gene is inside the plant the gene becomes part of the plant's DNA and acts as a vaccine. Virus resistant squash and virus resistant sweet potatoes are two examples of plants which have been genetically modified to combat deadly plant viruses In 1992, the Asgrow Seed Company of Michigan developed a yellow crookneck squash that was resistant to two different viruses. These two viruses can wipe out up to 80 percent of an annual squash crop. Disease symptoms include fruit discoloration and a distorted shape. Because of the effects of the virus, squash producers cannot sell infected fruit. Thus virusresistant squash plants could greatly impact how much of the squash the farmer sells. (Note: Scientists use the Agrobacterium tumefaciens method of gene transfer to produce the new squash. See Chocolate Flavored Cherry activity.) In Africa, sweet potatoes are one of the staple crops. Unfortunately, a virus called feathery mottle virus (FMV) kills two-thirds of the typical sweet potato crop every year. Many African farmers cannot afford chemical pesticides so the development of a virus-resistant sweet potato could have tremendous value by reducing hunger and enhancing nutritional status.

Herbicide-resistant Soybeans

How do modern farmers deal with weed problems? One solution is to use chemical herbicides. Herbicides are chemical substances used to destroy plants or limit their growth. One such herbicide is called Roundup®. Roundup® has a compound called glyphosate in it. Glyphosate is called a broad spectrum herbicide because it negatively impacts many different types of plants (for example, broad leaf plants and grasses).

Therefore, Roundup® will not only harm the pesky weeds, it may also harm the desired crop plant. So, scientists from a company called Monsanto identified a gene which enables a plant to tolerate Roundup®. They transferred this gene into a soybean plant and then, through traditional plant breeding methods, created many of these Roundup®-resistant soybean plants.

The name given to the plants are Roundup® Ready™ soybeans. Now, farmers are able to apply Roundup® to their fields to get rid of the weeds yet do not have to worry about harming their soybean crop. Those who advocate the use of this application of biotechnology note that Roundup® is an herbicide that is easily degraded in the environment and that by making the crop plants resistant to Roundup®, the end result will be less overall volume of herbicides used. Individuals opposed to this technology fear that the genes for herbicide-resistance will be somehow passed to the weeds.

Peanut Protein in Corn

Peanuts are high in protein, but are also high in fat. In order to utilize the protein in a peanut and avoid the fat, scientists and nutritionists have suggested putting the genes that code for peanut protein into corn. Corn that contains the peanut protein will have a higher protein content than normal corn. A high protein corn has tremendous potential in our country and in third world countries as well. In our country, corn is used in processed food like cereals, breads, and chips Increasing the protein content in corn would therefore increase the nutritional value of these processed foods. In third world countries, malnutrition is a big problem. Because corn is a staple crop in most of these countries, a highprotein corn could help combat protein calorie malnutrition world-wide The condition of protein calorie malnutrition in people is called kwashiorkor (kwash-ee-or-kor). Now for the controversy! Yes, it's true that peanuts are high in protein, yet this peanut protein causes an allergic reaction in some people. So if the gene coding for the peanut protein is transferred into another food, such a corn, how is that person to know that he/she should avoid eating the corn? Other biotechnologists argue that genetic engineering techniques can actually be used to reduce the presence of allergy causing proteins in food since scientists can isolate the gene coding for the allergen and reverse it or cut it out so that protein will no longer be made.

The Stakeholder Concept

The stakeholder concept is one of the most attractive conceptual devices in business ethics. This concept has its origins in a theory of management, but has been seized upon by scholars in business ethics as a way of expressing the idea that businesses have obligations to a wide range of parties, beyond the stockholders to whom corporate heads were traditionally thought to be beholden. According to Freeman, the author responsible for popularizing the concept within the field of business ethics, stakeholders simply "are those groups who have a stake in or claim on the firm." Stakeholder theory has served as part of a reconciliation between forward-thinking business leaders, on one hand, and public interest groups and consumer advocates, on the other.

It involves a reinterpretation of the social role of business, and a move away from the view, famously advocated by economist Milton Friedman, that the only proper function of corporate leaders is to increase the wealth of stockholders. The stakeholder concept, whatever its weaknesses, gives due credit to the fact that the motives of agents involved in business are relatively complex. The conflict between those varied motives has been a central theme in the business ethics literature. Freeman includes in his list of stakeholders suppliers, customers, employees, stockholders, and the firm's local community. This list, though typical of the lists given by stakeholder theorists, is not uncontroversial. Indeed, the stakeholder concept itself has its critics. Those critics charge that the stakeholder approach is incapable of guiding necessary improvements in corporate governance, that the multiple lines of accountability implied by acknowledging a multiplicity of stakeholders reduces efficiency, and that indeed the very idea of stakeholders as morally significant undermines the morally significant relationship between corporate executives and stockholders. Nonetheless, the stakeholder concept can be a useful one. In particular, the process known as "stakeholder analysis" can provide biotechnology companies with a lens through which to pay attention to the full range of interested parties. Stakeholder theory suggests that we should pay attention to the interests of any group or individual who is affected by, or who may affect, a decision or policy. A rich body of literature exists on the extent to which the interests of various stakeholders should be integrated into corporate decision-making, and ways in which that can be accomplished. I will not venture to take a position on just how long, or short, a list of relevant stakeholders would be. Nor will I stake a claim on the critical question of whether those stakeholders deemed relevant should merely have their wishes or needs accounted for, or whether they should instead be consulted directly. I will simply suggest that the concept of a stakeholder, and the understanding that a very wide range of individuals and groups have a stake in the workings of a given company, can serve as a focal point for discussing what obligations a company has, and to whom. Stakeholder analysis, in practice, is a relatively complex process, aimed at "identifying and understanding multiple (often competing) political, social, legal, economic, and moral claims of many constituencies."

A simplified stakeholder analysis for a biotech firm, conducted in relation to its efforts at determining appropriate modes of benefit sharing, would proceed in approximately the following manner. The first, descriptive phase of the analysis would begin with listing the range of parties having a stake in the issue. These might include: employees, stockholders (if these exist), providers of biological resources (i.e., human research subjects), local communities, competing firms, firms in related fields (such as traditional pharmaceutical firms), government agencies (at home and abroad), and university-based researchers. All of these parties, and perhaps others, can be said to have a stake in the benefit sharing practices of a particular corporation. The next step in this descriptive process would be to assess the nature of each stakeholder's interest in this issue, perhaps categorizing such interests as ethical, political, economic, legal, and so on. The second, normative phase of the stakeholder analysis would include an assessment of the kinds and degrees of obligation that the corporation has to each stakeholder. With regard to some stakeholders, for example, the obligations will be written, contractual obligations. With regard to other stakeholders, they will be what are known as "fiduciary," or trust-based, obligations. Other stakeholder obligations might be grounded in theories of what good neighbours owe each other. In other cases, the conclusion may be that a particular stakeholder is owed no obligations at all. There is no straightforward, uncontroversial algorithm for determining the nature and extent of obligations to various stakeholders. The point here, however, is not to settle upon a canonical rank-ordering of the corporation's obligations to various stakeholders, but rather to accurately situate the corporation as enmeshed in a range of ethically significant relationships, and to begin the complex task of meeting the demands of those various relationships.

The stakeholder concept has, of course, already played a role in discussions related to biotech benefit sharing. For example, both the World Bank and the World Intellectual Property Organization have made use of the concept in discussion documents. But the use of the stakeholder concept in such discussions has occurred in relative isolation from the rich literature that exists concerning the plausibility and application of that concept. A more well-informed application of the concept is required.

AGENCY INFORMATION

U.S. Department of Agriculture – USDA

Within USDA, the Animal and Plant Health Inspection

Service (APHIS) is responsible for protecting US agriculture from pests and diseases. Under the authority of the Federal Plant Pest Act, APHIS regulations provide procedures for obtaining a permit or for providing notification, prior to "introducing" a regulated article in the United States. Regulated articles are considered to be organisms and products altered or produced through genetic engineering that are plant pests of that there is reason to believe are plant pests.

The act of introducing includes any movement into (import) or through (interstate) the United States, or release into the environment outside an area of physical confinement. The regulations also provide for a petition process for the determination of nonregulated status. Once a determination of nonregulated status has been made, the product (and its offspring) no longer requires APHIS review for movement or release in the US.

Environmental Protection Agency – EPA

EPA ensures the safety of pesticides, both chemical and those that are produced biologically. The BioPesticides and Pollution Prevention Division of the Office of Pesticide Programs (OPP) uses the authority of the Federal Insecticide, Fungicide, and Rodenticide Act (FIFRA) to regulate the distribution, sale, use and testing of plants and microbes producing pesticidal substances. Under the Federal Food, Drug and Cosmetic Act (FFDCA) EPA sets tolerance limits for substances used as pesticides on and in food and feed, or establishes an exemption from the requirement of a tolerance.

EPA also establishes tolerances for residues of herbicides used on novel herbicide-tolerant crops.

Under the authority of the Toxic Substances Control Act (TSCA), EPA's TSCA Biotechnology Program regulates microorganisms intended for commercial use that contain or express new combinations of traits. This includes "intergeneric microorganisms" formed by deliberate combinations of genetic material from different taxonomic genera.

Food and Drug Administration - FDA

As a part of the Department of Health and Human Services, FDA regulates foods and feed derived from new plant varieties under the authority of the Federal Food, Drug, and Cosmetic Act. FDA policy is based on existing food law, and requires that genetically engineered foods meet the same rigorous safety standards as is required of all other foods. FDA's biotechnology policy treats substances intentionally added to food through genetic engineering as food additives if they are significantly different in structure, function, or amount than substances currently found in food. Many of the food crops currently being developed using biotechnology do not contain substances that are significantly different from those already in the diet and thus do not require pre-market approval. Consistent with its 1992 policy, FDA expects developers to consult with the agency on safety and regulatory questions.

Announcements

2006

- Notice of Availability: Guidance: Recommendations for the Early Food Safety Evaluation of New Non-Pesticidal Proteins Produced by New Plant Varieties Intended for Food Use June 21, 2006
- Guidance: Recommendations for the Early Food Safety Evaluation of New Non-Pesticidal Proteins Produced by New Plant Varieties Intended for Food Use. June 20, 2006

2005

- FDA Statement on Bt 10 Corn April 27, 2005
  - o EPA Statement on Bt 10 Corn April 27, 2005

2004

- FDA Proposes Draft Guidance for Industry for New Plant Varieties Intended for Food Use November 19, 2004
  - o Notice of Availability: Draft Guidance: Recommendations for the Early Food Safety Evaluation of New Non-Pesticidal Proteins Produced by New Plant Varieties Intended for Food Use November 24, 2004
  - o DRAFT Guidance: Recommendations for the Early Food Safety Evaluation of New Non-Pesticidal Proteins Produced by New Plant Varieties Intended for Food Use. November 24, 2004
- National Research Council Report: Safety of Genetically Engineered Foods: Approaches to Assessing Unintended Health Effects (available in PDF)

2003

- Notice of Meeting. Food Advisory Committee: Food Biotechnology Subcommittee Meeting, September 24, 2003. September 5, 2003
  - o Transcript

2002

- FDA Action on Corn Bioengineered to Produce Pharmaceutical Material November 19, 2002
- Notice of Meeting. Food Advisory Committee: Food Biotechnology Subcommittee Meeting, August 13-14, 2002. July 25, 2002
  - o Transcript

- Genetically Modified Foods: Experts View Regimen of Safety Tests as Adequate, but FDA's Evaluation Process Could Be Enhanced GAO-02-566, May 23, 2002

2001

- FDA and CDC Reports to EPA on Cry9C in StarLink™ Corn
  - o CDC: Investigation of Human Health Effects Associated with Potential Exposure to Genetically Modified Corn
  - o FDA Documents:
    - — Food and Drug Administration cover letter regarding their findings concerning StarLink™ (available in PDF) June 12, 2001
    - — FDA Evaluation of Consumer Complaints Linked to Foods Allegedly Containing Containing StarLink™ Corn (available in PDF) June 13, 2001
    - — Development and Use of a Method for Detection of IgE Antibodies to Cry9C (available in PDF, 6.26 Mb) June 13, 2001
  - o Additional FDA letters to EPA regarding StarLink™ Corn
- FIFRA Scientific Advisory Panel Meeting on July 17-19, 2001 on StarLink™
- How to Facilitate a Traceback Investigation: Overall Program Evaluation May 2001
- FDA 2002 Performance Plan: Biotechnology Strategies April 2001
- Second Joint Symposium on Food Safety and Nutrition, July 11-13, 2001: Current Issues in Food Biotechnology

- Letter About Updated Internet Site Regarding Completed Consultations Between FDA and Developers of Foods Derived Through Biotechnology March 14, 2001
- FDA Announces Proposal and Draft Guidance for Food Developed Through Biotechnology January 17, 2001

2000

- U.S. District Court Dismisses Genetically Engineered Food Law Suit Against FDA October 6, 2000
- FDA to Strengthen Pre-Market Review of Bioengineered Foods May 3, 2000
- Clinton Administration Agencies Announce Food and Agricultural Biotechnology Initiative: Strengthening Science-Based Regulation and Consumer Access to Information May 3, 2000

1999

- FDA Announces Meetings on Bioengineered Foods October 18, 1999

o More information on Public Meetings

1992-1998

- Announcement Archives

FDA Presentations and Testimony about Bioengineered Foods

- Statement by CFSAN Director Joseph A. Levitt before the Senate Committee on Health, Education, Labor, and Pensions September 26, 2000
- Association for Food and Drug Officials (AFDO) Millenium Conference June 19, 2000 Presentation — FDA's Policy on Genetically Modified Food

- Testimony Before the Senate Committee on Agriculture, Nutrition and Forestry October 7, 1999
- Presentation Archives

Information for Consumers

- Genetic Engineering: The Future of Foods? FDA Consumer, November-December 2003
- Cloning: Revolution or Evolution in Animal Production? FDA Consumer, May-June 2003
- Proposed Rules Issued for Bioengineered Foods FDA Consumer, March-April 2001
- Are Bioengineered Foods Safe? FDA Consumer, January-February 2000
- Bioengineered Foods: Will They Cause Allergic Reactions? from *Food Allergy News*, October-November 1997

Regulations and Guidance on Safety Assessments

- Recommendations for the Early Food Safety Evaluation of New Non-Pesticidal Proteins Produced by New Plant Varieties Intended for Food Use June 2006
- Statement of Policy: Foods Derived From New Plant Varieties (available in PDF, 2 MB) Federal Register, May 29, 1992
- Proposed Rule: Premarket Notice Concerning Bioengineered Foods January 18, 2001
- Draft Guidance for Industry: Use of Antibiotic Resistance Marker Genes in Transgenic Plants - September 1998
- Consultation Procedures under FDA's 1992 Statement of Policy: Foods Derived from New Plant Varieties - October 1997

- Summary: Conference on Scientific Issues Related to Potential Allergenicity in Transgenic Food Crops April 18-19, 1994

Products

- List of Completed Consultations on Bioengineered Foods

Food Labeling

- Draft Guidance for Industry: Voluntary Labeling Indicating Whether Foods Have or Have Not Been Developed Using Bioengineering January 17, 2001
- Report on Consumer Focus Groups on Biotechnology and Labeling October 20, 2000

Compliance

- Guidance for Industry: FDA Recommendations for Sampling and Testing Yellow Corn and Dry-Milled Yellow Corn Shipments Intended for Human Food Use for Cry9C Protein Residues January 19, 2001

International

- Codex Alimentarius Commission Guidelines
  - o Principles for the Risk Analysis of Foods Derived from Modern Biotechnology, adopted 2003
  - o Guideline for the Conduct of Food Safety Assessment of Foods Derived from Recombinant-DNA Plants, adopted 2003
  - o Guideline for the Conduct of Food Safety Assessment of Foods Produced Using Recombinant-DNA Microorganisms, adopted 2003
- Codex Ad Hoc Intergovernmental Task Force on Food Derived from Biotechnology
  - o Elaboration of Standards, Guidelines or Other

Principles for Foods Derived from Biotechnology December 27, 1999

- Organisation for Economic Co-operation and Development (OECD)
  - o Consensus Documents for the work on the Safety of Novel Foods and Feeds
- International Activities and Codex

Additional Information

- Information from FDA's Center for Veterinary Medicine
  - o Biotechnology in Animals and Feeds
  - o A New Kind of Fish Story: The Coming of Biotech Animals FDA Consumer Magazine - January/ February 2001
- Information from Other Federal Government Agencies
  - o United States Regulatory Agencies Unified Biotechnology Website
  - o U.S. Department of Agriculture
    - — Biotechnology Regulatory Services of the Animal & Plant Health Inspection Service
  - o U.S. Environmental Protection Agency
    - — Office of Pesticide Programs

Information from Non-Government Sources

- o Food and Agricultural Organization of the United Nations
  - — Food and Nutrition Division's Biotechnology Home Page

FDA-Approved Biopharmaceutical Drugs and Vaccines

The following biopharmaceutical agents have been approved by the Food and Drug Administration for marketing in the United States. The trademarked name is followed by the generic name of the drug in parentheses.

Acctimmune (gamma interferon)

Genentech, Inc.

Approved for use in the management of chronic granulomatous disease (December, 1990).

Activase (recombinant alteplase)

Genentech, Inc.

Approved for use in the treatment of myocardial infarction (November, 1987) and acute pulmonary embolism (June, 1990).

Adagen (adenosine deaminase)

Enzon, Inc.

Approved for use in the treatment of infants and children with severe immunodeficiency (March, 1990).

Alferon N

Interferon Sciences, Inc.

Approved for use in treating genital warts (October, 1989).

Betaseron (recombinant interferon beta 1-B)

Berlex Laboratories/Chiron Corp.

Approved for use in the management of relapsing, remitting multiple sclerosis (August, 1993).

Ceredase (alglucerase)

Genzyme Corp.

Approved for use in treating Type 1 Gaucher's disease (April, 1991).

Cerezyme (imiglucerase)

Genzyme Corp.

Approved for use in treating Type 1 Gaucher's disease (June, 1994).

Engerix-B

SmithKline Beecham

Approved for use as a hepatitis B vaccine (September, 1989).

EPOGEN (epoetin alfa)

Amgen Ltd.

Approved for use in treating anemia associated with chronic renal failure and anemia in Retrovir-treated, HIV-infected patients (June, 1989).

Humatrope (somatropin)

Eli Lilly & Co.

Approved for treating human growth hormone deficiency in children (March, 1987).

Humulin (recombinant human insulin)

Eli Lilly & Co.

Approved for the treatment of diabetes (October, 1982).

Intron A (alpha-interferon)

Schering-Plough Corp.

Approved for the treatment of hairy cell leukemia (June, 1986), genital warts (June, 1988), AIDS-related Kaposi's sarcoma (November, 1988), non-A, non-B hepatitis (February, 1991), and hepatitis B (July, 1992).

KoGENate (antihemophiliac factor)

Miles, Inc.

Approved for use in the treatment of hemophilia A (February, 1993).

Leukine (yeast-derived GM-CSF)

Immunex Corp.

Approved for use in autologous bone marrow transplantation (March, 1991).

Neupogen

Amgen Ltd.

Approved for use in treating cheomtherapy-induced neutropenia (February, 1991) and bone marrow transplant-associated neutropenia (June, 1994).

Oncaspar (pegaspargase)

Enzone/Rhone-Poulenc Rorer

Approved for use in treating acute lymphoblastic leukemia (February, 1994).

Orthoclone OKT 3

Ortho Biotech

Approved for use in reversal of acute kidney transplant rejection (June, 1986).

Procrit (epoetin alfa)

Ortho Biotech

Approved for use in the treatment of anemia associated with chronic renal failure (December, 1990) and anemia in Retrovir-treated, HIV-infected patients and chemotherapy-associated anemia (April, 1993).

Proleukin, IL-2

Chiron Corp.

Approved for the treatment of kidney (renal) carcinoma (May, 1992).

Protropin (somatrem)

Genentech, Inc.

Approved for treating human growth hormone deficiency in children (May, 1985).

Pulmozyme (DNase)
Genentech, Inc.
Approved for use in the management of cystic fibrosis (December, 1993).

Recombinate rAHF (recombinant antihemophiliac factor)
Baxter Healthcare
Recombinate rAHF is the recombinant version of blood clotting factor VIII, and it has been approved for the treatment of hemophilia A (December, 1992).

Recombivax HB
Merck & Co.

Approved as a hepatitis B prevention vaccine (July, 1986).

Roferon-A (recombinant alfa-interferon)
Hoffman-La Roche

Approved for the treatment of hairy cell leukemia (June, 1986) and AIDS-related Kaposi's sarcoma (November, 1988).

Biotechnology: Role in Characterisation and Conservation of Crop., Forest, Animal and Fishery Genetic Resources

On the occasion of World Food Day 2004, the United Nations Secretary-General Kofi Annan urged "individuals and institutions alike to give greater attention to biodiversity as a key theme in our efforts to fight the twin scourges of hunger and poverty and achieve the Millennium Development Goals". He also noted that the unprecedented loss of biodiversity over the past century was a major cause for alarm, where "many freshwater fish species, which can provide crucial dietary diversity to the poorest households, have become extinct, and many of the world's most important marine fisheries have been decimated. Food supplies have also been made more vulnerable by our reliance on a very small number of species: just 30 crop species dominate food production and 90 per cent of our animal food supply comes from just 14 mammal and bird species — species which themselves rely on biodiversity for their productivity and survival. There has been a substantial reduction in crop genetic diversity in the field and many livestock breeds are threatened with extinction". On the same occasion, FAO's Director-General Jacques Diouf also underlined that although forests are among the world's most important repositories of biological diversity, the world forest cover is decreasing at an alarming rate. It is in this context of declining agricultural biodiversity, that the FAO Biotechnology Forum will host this e-mail conference to consider the role that biotechnology can play in the characterisation and conservation of crop, forest, animal and fishery genetic resources in developing countries. Biotechnology is a broad collection of tools and these tools can be applied for a range of different purposes (e.g. genetic improvement of populations; disease diagnosis and vaccine development; improvement of feeds). The focus in this conference will be on biotechnology tools, such as molecular markers or cryopreservation and reproductive technologies, that can be used directly for the characterisation and/or conservation of genetic resources for food and agriculture. Genetic modification and GMOs will not be considered here. On 5-7 March 2005, as part of the preparations for this e-mail conference, an international workshop was held in Turin, Italy, entitled "The role of biotechnology for the characterisation and conservation of crop, forestry, animal and fishery genetic resources", organised by the FAO Working Group on Biotechnology, the Fondazione per le Biotecnologie, the ECONOGENE project and the Società Italiana di Genetica

Agraria. Proceedings of the workshop include 20 papers covering applications of molecular markers, cryopreservation and reproductive technologies and can be consulted by anyone looking for more detailed technical information in this area. The workshop was split into Session I on the status of the world's agricultural biodiversity; Session II on the use of biotechnology for conservation of genetic resources and Session IV on genetic characterisation of populations and its use in conservation decision-making. Session III presented results from ECONOGENE, a European Union funded project combining a molecular analysis of biodiversity, socio-economics and geostatistics to address the conservation of sheep and goat genetic resources and rural development in marginal agrosystems in Europe.

As described in Diamond (2002), domestication of crops and livestock, where species selected from the wild adapt to a special habitat created for them by humans, was a momentous development with major consequences for human societies, since "it provides most of our food today, it was prerequisite to the rise of civilization, and it transformed global demography". Domestication seems to have arisen independently on at least five different occasions in different parts of the world where, for example, hunter-gatherers in the Fertile Crescent (an area in Asia, including parts of Iran, Iraq, Israel, Jordan, Lebanon, Syria and Turkey), began domesticating barley, peas, wheat, cows, goats, pigs and sheep about 10,000 years ago. Sometimes, the same species (e.g. cow, sheep) was domesticated independently in different places. The process of domestication has continued ever since, e.g. the rabbit and strawberry were domesticated in the middle ages. Domestication had major impacts on human societies, making the transition from hunger-gathering to a settled farming existence possible. It also led to major changes in the species that were domesticated.

Since their domestication, domestic crops and livestock have been used in almost all environments of the world and many have been used in particular environments for very long periods of time e.g. Soay sheep on Hirta, off West Scotland, are thought to be the survivors of the sheep first brought to Britain by the first farmers 5,000 years ago. Each environment has a certain set of stressors that impacts the production environment. If we consider livestock, these might include climatic features (heat/cold, amount of rain, humidity); feeding conditions (quality/quantity vegetation available, access to water) or diseases (parasitic infections etc.) and, over time, populations adapted to the environment and its specific stressors. Farmers have also exercised a major influence on the domesticated species by preferentially selecting for specific morphological or production traits. Unlike crops and livestock, domestication is generally a very recent phenomenon in the fishery and forestry sectors. Only a small number of forest tree species have been, to some degree, domesticated, and such action has been taken only over the past half century. Such tree species, used in plantation forestry, are usually no more than 1-2 generations removed from their "wild relatives" (see e.g. Sigaud, 2005). For fish, apart from a few species, such as common carp domesticated about 2,000 years ago, aquaculture (fish farming) is a relatively new development (Bartley, 2005) and the majority of fish consumed today still come from wild populations, although it is predicted that by 2030 consumption from the ever-growing aquaculture industry will exceed capture fisheries. The agricultural genetic resources to be considered in this e-mail conference, therefore, include a wide range of species, from those domesticated 10,000 years ago to those domesticated in recent times and those which have not been domesticated but are nevertheless of importance for food and agriculture for humankind. As will be described in more detail in Section 3, many of these genetic resources are endangered. The need to conserve these resources is now widely accepted, generally justified for one or more of a variety of reasons, including their importance as an insurance against future changes in market needs and production conditions; as a source of material for scientific research and future germplasm development; and for cultural and historical reasons, because they are part of our heritage, passed down from previous generations (e.g. Ruane, 2000). The issue has received considerable attention at the international policy-making level. For example, it is addressed under the Convention on Biological Diversity, a legally-binding agreement with 188 Parties, through its agricultural biodiversity work programme, and under the International Treaty on Plant Genetic Resources for Food and Agriculture, a legally-binding treaty with 69 Parties that entered into force in June 2004. Two major strategies for conservation can be distinguished: in-situ conservation, where a population is maintained in its natural or agricultural habitat, or ex-situ conservation, where it is maintained outside of this habitat. Ex-situ conservation can involve living individuals (e.g. animals in zoos, fish in aquaria, crops or trees in botanical gardens and arboreta) or tissues or genetic material from individuals (such as seeds, pollen, sperm, embryos, DNA). Ex-situ conservation is important for crops, where an estimated 6 million plant, mainly crop, accessions (i.e. samples of a variety collected at a specific location and time) are stored in national, regional and international collections (FAO, 1998a, Chapter 3). Of the 6 million accessions, over 80% are in national collections and about 90% are stored in seed genebanks which, depending on the seed storage facilities, may allow short-, medium- or long-term storage. A genebank is a storage facility where germplasm of plant or animal origin is stored in forms such as seeds, pollen, semen or embryos; or in in vitro culture (germplasm kept as sterile plant tissues or plantlets on nutrient gels); in cryogenic storage; or in a field genebank i.e. as plants growing in the field. For the livestock, forestry and fishery sectors, in-situ conservation is currently more important than ex-situ conservation. Characterisation of genetic resources goes hand in hand with their conservation as it is fundamental both for understanding what is being conserved and for choosing the genetic resources that should be conserved. Characterisation enables us to identify the key features (both the strengths and weaknesses) of the available genetic resources, and this knowledge can also be used to develop breeding programmes for sustainable use of the genetic resource to harness and/or disseminate the positive attributes identified in the population. Characterisation can also play an important role regarding issues of access to, and benefit sharing from, agricultural genetic resources, as well the promotion and control of "bioprospecting" (i.e. biodiversity prospecting, the search for commercially valuable compounds, substances or genetic material in nature). If a country has characterised its genetic resources, it should be appropriately positioned to develop and implement conservation strategies for targeted species, and to promote and oversee any potential commercial or other enterprises arising from the knowledge generated; to protect the resources (or any of their products) from inappropriate bioprospecting, including that carried out by foreign companies or countries; and to negotiate appropriate compensation for use of these resources by third parties, be they national or foreign.

The kinds of features that could be characterised for the different agricultural populations include their morphological and physiological features; their phenotypic and economic performance in different environments; their interaction with, and relation to, the environment; their value as social or cultural objects; their role in scientific research; their diversity at the gene and DNA sequence level; their population size and degree of endangerment.

Crop Genetic Resources

Compared to the large numbers of wild plant species available, only very few were actually domesticated (Diamond, 2002). Although this number is small, just a sub-set of them again are of special importance globally. For example, considering plant-derived energy intake worldwide, just three crops (wheat, rice and maize) provide over 50% of the intake and 30 crops provide 95% (FAO, 1998a, Chapter 1). Splitting the world into 17 sub-regions, there are only 12 major crops which supply more than 5% of the plant-derived energy intake in one or more sub-regions i.e. wheat, rice, maize, millet, sorghum, potato, sugar cane, soybean, sweet potato, cassava, the common bean and related species (Phaseolus), banana/plantain. It should, however, be kept in mind that although some specific crops may not have any global/regional significance they may, nevertheless be important at the individual country level (e.g. tef in Ethiopia). Although, as seen, the number of major crops species is quite small, the diversity within each species can be very substantial. Within a species, cultivated crop varieties (cultivars) can be broadly categorised as farmer's varieties (also known as landraces or traditional varieties i.e. populations that are the product of breeding or selection carried out by farmers, either deliberately or not, continuously over many generations) and modern varieties (also known as high-yielding or high-response varieties, that are the products from professional breeders working in publicly-funded research institutes or private companies). Farmer's varieties tend to maintain high levels of genetic diversity and to be the focus of conservation efforts (FAO, 1998a). The first comprehensive worldwide report on the status and use of crop genetic resources was published by FAO in

1998. This State of the World's Plant Genetic Resources for Food and Agriculture (SoW-PGR) was developed through a participatory country-driven process and the primary data sources for the publication were detailed Country Reports from a total of 154 countries. In Annex 2 of the report (FAO, 1998a), the state of diversity within each of the 12 major crops is documented. It shows, for example, that the global ex-situ collection of millet contains roughly 90,000 accessions, of which 2% are wild relatives, 33% are landraces and old cultivars, 5% are advanced cultivars and breeding lines while 60% are unknown and mixed.

Although incomplete data makes it difficult to give a definitive picture of the kind of material stored in the world's ex-situ collections, it is estimated that roughly half the accessions for which the type of material is known are advanced cultivars and breeding lines, while a third are landraces and about 10% are wild species (FAO, 1998a, Chapter 3). In their Country Reports, nearly all countries said that genetic erosion (i.e. the loss of genetic diversity, generally as a result of social, economic and agricultural changes) was taking place and was a serious problem.

The main cause they cited was the replacement of local varieties or landraces by improved and/or exotic varieties and species and numerous examples were provided (e.g. displacement of traditional barley and durum wheat varieties by introduced varieties in Ethiopia). Other important causes they cited included overexploitation of plant genetic resources, including overgrazing and reduced fallow periods in shifting cultivation; deforestation and land clearance; population pressure and urbanisation; environmental degradation (e.g. desertification, flooding) and changes in agricultural systems (FAO, 1998a, Chapter 1). Preparations are underway for the 2nd report on the SoW-PGR, which should be finalised in 2008.

Forest Genetic Resources

Most forest tree species are characterised by inherently high levels of variation and extensive natural ranges. They are long-lived, frequently outcrossing organisms, with generally large distribution ranges. A high level of intra-specific genetic variation is needed to ensure present-day and future adaptability to changing environmental conditions. It is also needed to maintain options and potential for improvement to meet changing end-use requirements. Forests provide a wide range of goods and services such as timber, fibre, fuelwood, food, fodder, gum, resins, medicines, pharmaceutical products and environmental stabilisation. Similar goods and services are often provided by a wide range of genera and tree species. Despite the availability of a large number of forest tree species, less than 500 have been systematically tested for their present-day utility for human beings and less than 40 species are included in intensive selection and breeding programmes (FAO, 2000a). Estimates for the year 2000 indicate that the world's forest cover was about 3.9 billion hectares, of which 47% was in the tropics, 33% in the boreal zone (i.e. the northernmost forest zone), 11% in temperate areas and 9% in the subtropics (FAO, 2001). About 95% of the forest cover was in natural forest and 5% in forest plantations (defined as forest stands established by planting or/and seeding in the process of afforestation or reforestation). Of the roughly 190 million hectares of forest plantation, 48% had an industrial end-use (e.g. pulpwood for paper); 26% a non-industrial purpose (e.g. fuelwood, soil and water conservation); and for 26% it was not specified. Most of the forest genetic resources worldwide are therefore found in natural, largely unmanaged forests which, however, are frequently intensively used for the provision of both wood and non-wood products, for local, national and international use. Conversion of forests to other land uses represents the greatest threat to forests and their diversity. According to FAO (2001), "increasing pressure from human populations and aspirations for higher standards of living, without due concern to the sustainability of the resources underpinning such developments, heighten these concerns. While some land use changes are inevitable, it is important that such changes be planned and managed to address complementary goals. Concerns for biological and genetic conservation should be major components of land use planning and forest management strategies". Unlike the situation in crops, however, no global overview of the status of forest tree genetic resources has yet been carried out, although the idea of developing a first global assessment of forest genetic resources is currently being discussed (Sigaud, 2005).

Animal Genetic Resources

Of the 50,000 known bird and mammalian species, about 30 have been used extensively for agricultural purposes, with fewer than 14 accounting for over 90% of global livestock production (FAO, 1999). In the millennia following their domestication, animal species were influenced by both natural and artificial selection in a wide range of geographic and climatic areas and production systems, leading to the development of large numbers of genetically diverse domestic animal breeds. Many of these breeds are currently endangered. In developing countries, the introduction of exotic breeds and their spread through indiscriminate crossbreeding is a major reason for loss of local, indigenous breeds. Other factors include changes in breeders' preferences because of short-term socio-economic influences; degradation of the ecosystem in which the breeds were developed; natural disasters (e.g. drought and diseases); wars and other forms of political unrest and instability (FAO, 1998b). In 1993, FAO published the first World Watch List for Domestic Animal Diversity, providing a basic global overview of the state of the genetic resources of seven mammalian species (buffalo, cattle, donkey, goat, horse, pig and sheep). The 3rd edition, expanded to cover 30 mammalian and bird species, showed e.g. that of the over 4,000 breeds with population data, roughly 30% could be classified at a high risk of loss and that chickens and cattle have large numbers of breeds at risk while the horse and goose have the highest percentages of breeds at risk of loss (FAO, 2000b). In addition, apart from the wild boar and wild red jungle fowl (ancestors of the domestic pig and chicken respectively), the putative wild ancestors of the major livestock species are in danger of extinction or are already extinct (Hanotte and Jianlin, 2005). In a similar process to that described for the crop sector, FAO is preparing the first State of the World's Animal Genetic Resources, that is expected to be completed by 2006. So far, 151 countries have accepted to submit country reports and the objective of the country and global assessments is to provide a comprehensive analysis of the status and trends of the world's farm animal biodiversity and of their underlying causes, as well as of local knowledge regarding its management (Cardellino, 2005).

Fishery Genetic Resources

Like forestry, and unlike crops and livestock, wild populations currently play a greater role than domesticated populations in the fishery sector. When considering the status of the world's fishery genetic resources, both the aquatic species that are fished (capture fishing) as well as those that are farmed (aquaculture) can be included. Bartley (2005) gives an overview of the status of aquatic species that are fished or farmed worldwide. For capture fisheries in 2002, FAO Members reported that 974 taxa (i.e. taxonomic units such as a family, genus or species) of fin-fish, 143 taxa of crustacea, 114 taxa of molluscs, 26 taxa of plants and 73 taxa of miscellaneous animals (such as sea urchins, sea cucumbers and marine mammals) were taken from the world's capture fisheries. These numbers are, however, likely to be an underestimate as reporting is often incomplete. Although over 1000 taxa are represented, about 10 species make up about one third of capture fisheries production. Unlike the crop and animal sectors, there is no systematic effort to describe the state of the world's fishery genetic resources below the species level. Nevertheless, description of the fish genetic stocks at the within-species level is important for fisheries management and is an active research area (Bartley, 2005; Primmer, 2005). For aquaculture in 2002, FAO Members reported that, apart from a small number of aquatic plants and animals, a total of 153 species of fish, 60 species of molluscs and 44 species of crustaceans were farmed.

The relative novelty of aquaculture can be shown by the fact that its contribution to global supplies of fish, crustaceans and molluscs has grown from just 4% in 1970 to 30% in 2002 (Bartley, 2005). Aquatic science, in general, lags behind terrestrial sciences in identifying species, understanding ecosystem relationships and assessing potential uses for genetic resources. Communities of life on the ocean floor are poorly understood and, every year, some aquatic species become extinct before they have even been identified. Fish genetic resources worldwide are currently threatened by overfishing, but also by habitat destruction (e.g. dam building) and pollution from human activities (Greer and Harvey, 2004). Every 2 years, FAO publishes the State of World Fisheries and Aquaculture which, inter alia, provides a global overview of capture fisheries (marine and inland) and aquaculture. Regarding exploitation of marine fish stocks (estimated production was 84.5 million tonnes in 2002), the most recent edition indicates that there has been a consistent downward trend since 1974 in the proportion of stocks offering potential for expansion, coupled with an increase in the proportion of overexploited and depleted stocks, rising from about 10% in the mid-1970s to close to 25% in the early 2000s. The percentage of stocks exploited at, or beyond, their maximum sustainable levels varies widely among fishing regions. The report says that the information available continues to confirm that, despite local differences, the global potential for marine capture fisheries has been reached, and more rigorous plans are needed to rebuild depleted stocks and prevent the decline of those being exploited at, or close to, their maximum potential (FAO, 2004a). For inland fish stocks (estimated production was 8.7 million tonnes in 2002), unlike the major marine fish stocks, they are less well defined and occur over much smaller geographical areas, such as individual lakes, rice fields or rivers, or over vast areas such as transboundary watersheds that are often situated in areas that are difficult to access. These factors make it costly to monitor the exploitation and status of fish stocks and, in fact, very few countries can afford to do so. As a result, the majority of countries report only a small fraction of their catch of inland fisheries by species, further compounding the problem of accurate assessment. There are, however, indications that these resources are undervalued and threatened by habitat alteration, degradation and unsustainable fishing activities (FAO, 2004a).

Relevant Biotechnologies

A wide range of genetic resources are currently being used by humankind for food and agricultural purposes and many of them are in danger of being lost, due to reasons such as over-exploitation (fish), replacement of local with international germplasm (crops/livestock) or habitat change or destruction (crop/fish/forest/livestock). Here, we will give a brief overview of molecular markers and cryopreservation, in vitro culture and reproductive technologies and how they can be used for the characterisation and/or conservation of these genetic resources.

Molecular Markers

The importance of characterising genetic resources was described as well as the wide range of features that can be characterised in each population, such as morphology, phenotypic performance, degree of endangerment etc. Whereas phenotypes (e.g. yield, growth rate) or morphological traits (coat colour, seed shape) are influenced by both genetic and environmental factors, use of molecular markers reveals differences at the DNA level that are not influenced by the environment (De Vicente et al., 2005). Molecular markers usually do not have any biological effect and are normally assumed to represent neutral loci unaffected by selection. They are identifiable DNA sequences, found at specific chromosomal locations on the genome and transmitted by the standard laws of inheritance from one generation to the next. A number of types of molecular markers exist, such as RFLPs, RAPDs, AFLPs, microsatellites and SNPs, which can differ in a variety of ways, such as the amount of time, money and labour needed or the amount of genetic variation found at each marker in a given population. Microsatellites, for example, are simple DNA sequences, usually 2 or 3 DNA bases long, repeated a variable number of times in tandem. Molecular markers are used in a variety of approaches to characterise and conserve genetic resources, and here we will briefly describe the main ones. Some of the approaches are applied in each of the crop, forestry, animal and fishery sectors (e.g. estimating the genetic relationships between populations within a species) while others are more sector-specific (e.g. identifying duplicate accessions in crop genebanks or monitoring effective population sizes in capture fish populations).

Estimating the Genetic Relationships Between Populations Within a Species

This is one of the major uses of molecular markers in agricultural research. Molecular markers are typed in populations of the same species that are e.g. located in different places and, by comparing the frequencies and presence/absence of marker loci in the different populations, inferences can be made about how genetically related they are to each other. The more differences in markers found between the populations, the greater the genetic distance between them and the populations are inferred to be less genetically related to each other than to populations that have more similar marker loci frequencies. Taking a simple example for illustrative purposes (in practice many markers would be used simultaneously), if individuals in populations A, B and C are typed for a molecular marker M (with two alternative forms or alleles called M1 and M2) and all individuals typed in populations A and B have allele M1 while those in population C have M2, this suggests that A and B are genetically more similar to each other than to population C. In using molecular markers to estimate genetic distances between populations, it is assumed that they represent neutral loci (i.e. do not reflect genetic differences between populations at genes that are or have been under natural or artificial (farmer) selection) and that the use of a relatively small number of independently segregating marker loci will be a good predictor of the overall genomic diversity of a population (Hanotte and Jianlin, 2005). Typically, a genetic diversity study involve sampling biological tissue (e.g. blood, leaves, fish scales) from a certain number of individuals from a number of populations of interest and typing them in the laboratory for a number of molecular marker loci. A statistical analysis of the marker data is then carried out to estimate the genetic relationships between the populations. For example, Lanteri and Barcaccia (2005) sampled 30 individuals each from 7 populations of wild cardoon identified in Sardinia and Sicily and each individual was genotyped for 32 microsatellite markers as well as 7 AFLP primer combinations. They used a statistical analysis method called principal coordinate analysis to show that the Sardinian and Sicilian populations were clearly differentiated, representing two distinct gene pools. Such studies have been routinely applied in each of the agricultural sectors. For example, in developing a management strategy for commercially exploited fish, molecular markers are used to characterise the within-species genetic structure of the populations being harvested, to determine the units between which limited gene flow occurs i.e. to identify units which should not be overfished (Primmer, 2005). A recent questionnaire-based survey of animal diversity studies carried out during the last 10 years provided information on a total of 86 projects, involving 13 livestock species from 93 countries (FAO, 2004b). The majority of projects were for ruminants, especially cattle. Blood was the most frequently used biological sample and microsatellites were the most commonly used molecular markers. As pointed out by Lenstra et al. (2005), these kinds of studies are not only relevant for the purposes of characterisation of genetic resources, they can also provide useful insights into the history of domestication. Evidence from molecular markers has been much used to elucidate whether individual crop or livestock species were domesticated just once at a single site or independently several times in different parts of the world (Diamond, 2002).

Establishing and Managing Genebanks

As described in Section 2, genebanks are an important tool for conservation of crop genetic resources, although currently of more limited importance for livestock, forestry or fish. Molecular marker information can be used in a number of genebank-related activities, such as sampling of material, management of the collections and stimulating use of germplasm stored therein (Lanteri and Barcaccia, 2005). When sampling germplasm to create a genebank, information from the use of molecular markers to assess the within and between population genetic diversity (as described in 4.1.1) can be used in conjunction with data on other characteristics of the populations to assist decision-making regarding which material should be sampled (e.g. Simianer, 2005). The amount of germplasm to be stored may be limited, due e.g. to financial reasons, so it would be important to sample material from genetically diverse individuals. Once a genebank has been established, molecular markers can also be used to assist in a number of genebank management activities. As a first example, regeneration of seeds or other reproductive plant material in storage is an important task in a genebank, and the regeneration requirements (how frequently accessions need to be regenerated) depend on factors such as the species concerned, the storage conditions and the quality of the individual accessions (FAO, 1998a, Chapter 3). Markers can be used to check whether changes in alleles or in allele frequencies are taking place over time as a result of the adopted conservation strategies e.g. of frequent regenerations (De Vicente et al., 2005). Secondly, while safety duplication of unique accessions acts as an insurance against possible accidents, unintentional duplication or overduplication of accessions is, however, wasteful (FAO, 1998a) and markers can be used to detect them (De Vicente et al., 2005). Thirdly, to reduce costs and/or encourage greater and more efficient use by farmers and breeders, core collections (i.e. a subset of accessions selected to contain the maximum available variation in a small number of accessions) have been established for many crop species. Again, molecular markers can assist in this task. Finally, it is argued (e.g. Ferreira, 2005) that molecular markers offer opportunities to increase the use of crop genetic resources from genebanks and they will therefore stimulate increased use of genebank material for research purposes, thereby playing an important role in the sustainable conservation of these genetic resources. Since a major justification for the existence of germplasm collections is use of the conserved accessions, De Vicente et al. (2005) underline the importance of genetically characterising them so that valuable genes can be identified for use in development of new plant varieties by conventional and advanced breeding methodologies.

Gene Flow from Domesticated Populations to Wild Relatives

Wild relatives of domesticated species are of conservation interest as they represent one of the components of agricultural biodiversity. They have also proven useful for genetic improvement of a range of cultivated varieties (FAO, 1998a, Chapter 1). As described in the Background Document to Conference 7 of this Forum (on GMOs and gene flow), crossing of domesticated populations with their wild relatives has been well documented in some crop, forest tree, animal and fish species. For example, in crops, gene flow has been observed between rice and perennial rice, between maize and teosinte and between sugar beet and wild beet, while in animals there is evidence for crossing of domestic cattle with wild North American bison and of domestic pigs with European wild boars. In forestry, gene flow from intensively bred forest trees to natural populations of the same or closely related species ("wild relatives") has been a cause for concern in many species, e.g. the European black poplar (Populus nigra). For fish, crossing of escaped farmed Atlantic salmon with wild Atlantic salmon is also a much-discussed problem. Gene flow from a domesticated population will cause changes in the genetic diversity of wild populations. In cases where diversity is systematically reduced over time by such geneflow, it may potentially lead to genetic extinction of the wild population in its original genetic state (see e.g. Papa, 2005). Molecular markers can assist in conservation of the wild relatives through their use to distinguish hybrids from non-hybrid wild relatives and to monitor gene flow from domesticated populations to their wild relatives.

Estimating and Monitoring the Effective Population Size

When developing conservation strategies for wild species, accurate estimates of the effective population size (Ne) are important because Ne predicts a number of parameters such as the rate of inbreeding (Primmer, 2005), and increases in inbreeding (due to mating of genetically related individuals) can lead to the reduced abilities of individuals to survive and reproduce (a phenomenon called inbreeding depression). Ne can be estimated using pedigree information and/or knowledge about the population breeding structure (male/female mating ratio, family sizes etc.). However, for wild populations, especially of aquatic species, it can be difficult to get this information. Molecular markers can be used to estimate Ne, something which has been done, for example, in several commercial fish populations (Primmer, 2005). Similarly, molecular markers can also be used as a tool to monitor fish population sizes over time and to detect any major recent declines in Ne.

Cryopreservation, in Vitro Culture and Reproductive Technologies

As described in Section 2, there are two major strategies for conservation, in-situ and ex-situ, the latter involving e.g. storage of genetic material in genebanks or keeping live animals or plants in zoos or botanical gardens respectively. Biotechnology, through cryopreservation (freezing) technologies and in vitro culture, provides additional tools for ex-situ conservation. Cryopreservation involves the preservation of germplasm in a dormant state by storage at ultra-low temperatures, usually in liquid nitrogen (-196C) and it can be used to preserve biological material (e.g. seeds, sperm, embryos) of crop, livestock, forest or fish populations indefinitely in genebanks. It allows large quantities of genetic material to be stored in a limited amount of space. If the living populations later become extinct, they can in many instances be regenerated using the frozen genetic material.

In addition, if the living populations are declining in numbers and develop problems due to inbreeding, these problems can be alleviated by introducing unrelated genetic material from the genebank. In animals, collection of germplasm for cryopreservation and production of live offspring from cryopreserved genetic material depends on a number of associated reproductive technologies, such as embryo transfer. In vitro culture is a plant biotechnology that involves application of slow growth procedures to germplasm accessions kept as sterile plant tissues or plantlets on nutrient gels. Here, we will provide a brief overview of the current status of these biotechnologies, focusing on cryopreservation as it is applicable in all four sectors. Information provided on cryopreservation in livestock/fish and crops/forest trees is based primarily on Hiemstra et al. (2005) and Panis and Lambardi (2005), and the references therein, respectively.

Livestock and Fish

Before considering the main types of genetic material that have been cryopreserved, a brief overview of relevant terminology might be useful. In sexual reproduction, through fertilisation there is a fusion of 2 haploid gametes to form the diploid zygote, a cell which begins dividing and develops to become an embryo (note, haploid and diploid cells have one or two sets of chromosomes respectively). The female gamete is called the ovum or egg, and is derived from a cell called an oocyte that has undergone two meiotic divisions. The male gamete is called the sperm (contained in fluid called semen). For cryopreservation purposes, semen is currently the biological material of greatest importance, although embryos and, to a lesser degree, oocytes and somatic cells, have also received considerable research attention. Success in freezing these materials varies considerably from species to species, which is not surprising given the wide diversity in reproductive systems (e.g. fertilisation is usually external in fish and internal in birds, where the female stores the sperm before fertilisation). Collection of biological materials for the genebank and production of live offspring following thawing of formerly cryopreserved material is made possible through a variety of reproductive technologies, such as artificial insemination (AI) using semen, multiple ovulation and embryo transfer using embryos etc. Freezing of semen and subsequent successful AI with thawed semen was first achieved over 50 years ago and semen of most livestock species can now be frozen adequately. There are large differences between species in insemination techniques and pregnancy rates using fresh or frozen semen, where AI with frozen semen is most successful in cattle. For domesticated birds, although AI is less widely used than in mammals, reasonable success rates (albeit at times highly variable) with frozen semen have been reported for the major bird species. For fish, sperm cryopreservation has been tested in over 200 fish species with external fertilisation and "the present state of the art for many species of fish seems to be adequate for the purpose of gene banking" (Hiemstra et al., 2005). For embryos, cryopreservation in cattle is now a routine procedure. It has also been reported for other mammalian species, such as horse, pig, rabbit and sheep (ERFP, 2003). Embryos to be cryopreserved can be collected using non-surgical (cattle and horses) or surgical methods (other mammalian species). Inducing multiple ovulation using hormones can increase efficiency of the process. Alternatively, embryos can be collected through in vitro maturation and in vitro fertilisation of oocytes (a more technically demanding approach). Production of live offspring following cryopreservation involves non-surgical (only in cattle and horses and, to a lesser extent, pigs) or surgical embryo transfer to recipient animals. For bird and fish species, however, cryopreservation of embryos has not been successful, mainly because of the large size, the high lipid content and the polar organisation of the ova and early embryos.

For mammalian oocytes, live offspring have been reported in cattle and horse from embryos produced using cryopreserved oocytes, although the efficiency and reliability of using oocytes for generating offspring is still much lower today than with cryopreserved embryos. Oocytes for cryopreservation in the genebank can be collected from ovaries of dead animals or by ovum pick-up (recovery of oocytes using an ultrasound probe) on live animals. Production of live offspring following thawing of cryopreserved oocytes involves in vitro maturation and fertilisation and eventual embryo transfer to recipient animals. Cryopreservation of bird and fish oocytes has not yet been successful, mainly for the same reasons given earlier for embryos. For somatic cells (i.e. cells not involved in sexual reproduction), a number of cell types (e.g. skin fibroblasts, mammary cells) can now be cryopreserved. Collection of material for the genebank is easy and cheap. Production of live offspring (which, apart from mitochondrial DNA, are genetic clones of the individual which donated the somatic cells) is, however, complicated and has a low rate of success. It involves culturing the thawed cells and then transferring their nuclei (i.e. the organelle which contains the genetic material) to, or fusion of the somatic cells with, enucleated (i.e. without a nucleus) oocytes from another individual. The resulting embryos are then cultured and eventually transferred to recipient animals. In mammals, live offspring have been obtained from embryos generated from somatic cells in a number of mammalian species (cattle, goats, horse, pigs, rabbits and sheep) and in fish (zebrafish), but not yet in poultry. The low success rates, as well as the many developmental problems encountered, are current major limitations to application of the technology.

Crops and Forest Trees

About 90% of the 6 million plant accessions in genebanks, mainly crops, are stored in seed genebanks. However, storage of seeds is not an option for crops or trees that do not produce seed (e.g. bananas) or that produce recalcitrant or non-orthodox seed (i.e. seed that does not survive under cold storage and/or the drying conditions used in conventional ex situ conservation, e.g. mango, coffee, oak and several tropical forest tree species). Likewise, for plant species that are propagated vegetatively to preserve the unique genomic constitution of cultivars, such as fruit and several timber and ornamental trees. It also presents practical problems in most forest tree species in regard to the necessary, periodic regeneration of seedlots, as tree species usually have a long vegetative period prior to producing flowers and seed (lasting from several years to several decades), and as they require large areas to carry out such an operation, due to outcrossing and their size. Genetic resources of these species are normally conserved either in vivo, i.e. living collections, or by in vitro culture, where slow growth procedures allow the plant material to be held for 1-15 years under tissue culture conditions with periodic regeneration (subculturing), depending on the species. Normally, growth is limited using low temperatures often in combination with low light intensity or even darkness. Temperatures in the range of 0-5C are employed for cold tolerant species and 15-20C for tropical species. Growth can also be limited by modifying the culture medium and reduction of oxygen levels available to the cultures (Rao, 2004). The former option (in vivo) is the cheapest and thus the most widely adopted, but exposes the material to the harms of the external environment, e.g. contamination with pathogens or parasites. In vitro culture, on the other hand, ensures that the collections are kept free from pest and diseases and protected from adverse conditions. Maintenance of in vitro collections is, however, labour-intensive and there is still a risk of losing accessions due to contamination, human error or somaclonal variation, i.e. mutations that occur spontaneously in tissue culture, with a frequency that increases with repeated subculturing (Panis and Lambardi, 2005). In all these situations, as well as for long-term storage of seeds from orthodox species, cryopreservation offers an alternative tool or complementary strategy for ex-situ conservation. Following plant cell, tissue or organ storage at low temperatures, plants can then be regenerated and there seems to be no clear evidence so far of morphological, cytological or genetic alterations arising as a result of cryopreservation (Panis and Lambardi, 2005). They, however, conclude that, despite the fact that cryogenic procedures are now being developed for an increasing number of recalcitrant seeds and a wide range of tissues and organs, the routine utilisation of cryopreservation for the preservation of plant biodiversity is still limited. They note that the main drawback for a wider application of plant cryopreservation is the unavailability of efficient cryopreservation protocols for many plant species. They report, nevertheless, that for various herbaceous (i.e. non-woody plants), hardwood (i.e. broadleaf, deciduous trees) and softwood species (i.e. coniferous trees), cryopreservation of a wide range of tissues and organs such as cell suspensions, embryogenic cultures, pollen, meristematic tissues and seeds has been achieved. Cell suspensions (cells in culture in moving or shaking liquid medium) have been cryopreserved from banana and grape while cryopreservation of embryogenic cultures (i.e. callus or suspension cultures with potential to differentiate somatic embryos) is an advanced technology in conifers and is already being successfully applied to numerous commercial species, including pines. Methods exist for the cryopreservation of pollen from many crops, but its application is still rather limited and restricted to a few research centres. Meristematic tissues (also called meristems, i.e. plant tissues, such as shoot tips, in which the cells are capable of active division and differentiation into specialised tissues such as shoots and roots) are the most common explants (i.e. a portion of a plant aseptically excised and prepared for culture in a nutrient medium) for the cryopreservation of vegetatively propagated species, such as fruit trees and many root and tuber crops. There is large scale application of shoot tip cryopreservation in fruit crop germplasm collections, such as in plum and apple, while the number of cryopreserved herbaceous meristem samples is significantly smaller, although continuously growing. Seeds of most common agricultural and horticultural species can be cryopreserved and for orthodox seeds this can be considered as an alternative, as it offers long-term storage, to traditional storage (e.g. in celery).

Debatable

As with each conference hosted in this FAO Biotechnology Forum, the focus is on application of biotechnology in developing countries. In the debate on the role of biotechnology for the characterisation/conservation of genetic resources for food and agriculture in developing countries, some of the potential factors that should be considered are briefly described below, as they may influence applications of biotechnology for these purposes. In addition, a selection of some of the specific questions that participants might wish to address in the e-mail conference are also given:

Capacity Issues

Some of the biotechnologies described in Section 4 require a considerable amount of infrastructure and capacity. For example, application of molecular markers to marine capture fishery populations requires appropriate sampling of individuals from the populations of interest, accurate laboratory typing of the samples, good statistical analysis of the data etc. Technologies which are and have been routinely applied in developed countries may be rarely used in many developing countries.

For example, artificial insemination is a commonplace tool and is used to breed the majority of dairy cows in the Nordic countries, but is little used in many developing countries. A rough idea of the status of capacity in developing countries for some of the biotechnologies discussed in this paper can be derived from a first analysis of about 2,000 crop sector entries from 71 countries in FAO-BioDeC, a database providing information on biotechnology products/ techniques in use or in the pipeline in developing countries (Dhlamini et al., 2005).

It reports over 400 molecular marker activities, most at the research level, in 43 developing countries. Considering the different regions, most activities were reported in Latin America, with 93 trials and 165 molecular marker projects at the research phase in nine countries. Species reported to be included in molecular marker programmes in the Latin American countries are sugar cane, rice, cocoa, banana, bean, maize and Andean local roots and tubers. The survey also indicates that most countries in Asia are undertaking a wide spectrum of crop research using molecular markers. Molecular marker-related research activities in Africa are reported to be underway in only a few of the countries, such as Ethiopia, Nigeria, South Africa and Zimbabwe; the range of African crops under study with molecular markers is, however, very wide - from traditional commodities to tropical fruits. Of the different marker systems, RAPDs, microsatellites, RFLPs and AFLPs were commonly used. While the analysis does not distinguish between use of molecular markers for genetic improvement (marker-assisted selection) or for genetic characterisation/conservation, it does indicate that, in crops at least, there is a wide range of marker-based research activities ongoing in developing countries, although some countries and regions seem to have far greater capacity than others. The database also includes information on in vitro germplasm conservation and cryopreservation, indicating that there are only few activities in developing countries, although there may be substantial under-reporting. The report argues that low uptake of micropropagation techniques for in vitro germplasm conservation may also be due to the existence of established whole plant germplasm collections for species where in vitro conservation is appropriate, leading to reluctance to provide funding for in vitro facilities. The balance between in vitro and whole plant collections may change as facilities for, and capabilities in, in vitro conservation increase and existing plant collections need rejuvenation (Dhlamini et al., 2005). Some of the specific questions on this issue that participants might wish to address in the e-mail conference might include:

- How important is this issue of capacity in different countries or regions?
- What are the current limiting factors to capacity building in developing countries? How can these limiting factors be overcome?
- What role should international organisations, like

FAO or the World Bank, or the Consultative Group on International Agricultural Research (CGIAR) research centres have in this area?

- What role should public-private partnerships play in this area?
- How important should regional capacity-building projects be with respect to national initiatives?

Economic Issues

While obviously dependent on a range of factors, such as the species or the size of the initiative etc., use of biotechnology for characterisation/conservation of genetic resources can be expensive. For example, in a survey of livestock molecular marker biodiversity projects, respondents also provided information on costs of 41 of the projects (FAO, 2004b). They ranged from US$ 500 to 14 million, averaging US$ 130,000. For projects providing a breakdown of costs, it was estimated that, on average, 65% of the total project expenses were spent on genotyping, about 20% on sampling animals, 10% on the statistical analysis and 5% on project coordination. There was also considerable variation between projects, with genotyping costs ranging from 20-90% of the total costs in individual projects. Cryopreservation technologies also can bear a considerable cost. FAO (1998a, Annex 1-2) concludes "the techniques required for successful cryopreservation of non-orthodox seeds are sophisticated and implementing a cryopreservation programme requires trained technical staff, advanced plant tissue culture facilities and increased transportation/handling costs to assure fresh materials. These constraints may present a barrier to effective technology transfer to many developing countries". Some of the specific questions on this issue that participants might wish to address in the e-mail conference could include:

- In a situation where genetic resources for food and

agriculture are being lost rapidly and where financial and human resources to support conservation activities are often limited, how much emphasis should be given to the application of biotechnology in this area?

- Which applications (and in which sectors/species) should be prioritised in this situation?

Prioritisation Issues

While, in an ideal world, all available conservation options should be used, reality often dictates, for financial reasons, that tough choices have to be made. Although alternative tools or strategies can complement each other, we are therefore often forced to prioritise between them. This is also valid for the biotechnologies and conservation strategies described in this document.

Molecular Markers

Given the large numbers of animal breeds and crop varieties that are in danger of becoming extinct and given limited resources, governments may need to identify the breeds and varieties they consider to be most important for conservation purposes (for financial support, for storage in a genebank etc.). A range of factors may then be considered for the different populations, including their degree of endangerment, their economic value, their impact on the environment, their scientific value, their social and cultural importance and their genetic diversity (can be studied using DNA molecular markers). Characterising populations for any one of these factors can be time-consuming and costly. Results from FAO (2004b) suggest that many studies, at least in livestock, are characterising populations for mbre than one factor at a time. In 56 of the 86 livestock genetic diversity projects surveyed (i.e. about two-thirds), additional breed characteristics such as production performance, morphological traits, disease resistance, behavioural traits and cultural values were also recorded. If information on these different factors is available, the question is then raised of how best to prioritise the different sources of information for conservation purposes. This is a question valid for each of the agricultural sectors, where e.g. efforts have been made to develop methodologies for prioritising between brown trout populations for conservation using factors such as the relative risk of extinction, the socio-economic and scientific value and the genetic/evolutionary and ecological legacy of the different fish populations (Primmer, 2005). Some of the specific questions on this issue that participants might wish to address in the e-mail conference could include:

- How should genetic differences be weighted with respect to non-genetic differences (cultural importance, current market value, degree of endangerment etc.) when wishing to prioritise between populations for conservation purposes?
- How should differences between populations in genetic diversity at neutral loci (measured using molecular markers) be weighted respect to differences in genetic differences for traits that are or have been under selection (estimated using production/adaptation data)?
- Which kinds of molecular markers or statistical analysis methods are most appropriate for the different kinds of population of interest?

Cryopreservation, in Vitro Culture and Reproductive Technologies

As outlined earlier, in-situ and ex-situ conservation represent two major strategies. Both have their disadvantages (e.g. in-situ populations are vulnerable to disease, drought, human interference etc. while germplasm storage in ex-situ collections may be very technology-intense and thus require relatively sophisticated equipment and skilled labour) and advantages (in-situ populations can adapt to environmental changes while ex-situ collections can be stored indefinitely). Economic merits of one over the other may depend on the species involved, the kind of ex-situ collection etc. Some of the specific questions on this issue that participants might wish to address in the e-mail conference might include:

- When is it more appropriate to support biotechnology as a tool for ex-situ conservation in preference to supporting in-situ conservation?
- What kind of biological material should be cryopreserved, considering that the goal may be to eventually regenerate a living population? For example, in animals, should the focus be on semen, embryo or oocytes (or a combination)?
- The birth of the Scottish sheep Dolly in 1996, produced through somatic cell cloning using udder cells and nuclear transfer, was a major scientific breakthrough and since then, individuals from a number of other species have been cloned. How important is this biotechnology for conservation of animal genetic resources?

Impact of Genetic Engineering on Developing Countries

Genetic engineering (GE) is a recently developed technology that allows the alteration of the genetic make up of living organisms. This technology allows scientists not only to exchange genes from members of the same species, which is what farmers and nature has been doing through out history, but also the exchange of genes between completely separate species. For example genetic engendering allows scientists to insert the genes from a fish into a tomato, something that can never happen in nature. Many in the biotechnology industry claim that the recent advancements in this field of research will help solve many of the problems developing countries face. These claims have led to a massive increase in commercial growing of genetically modified organisms, (GMOs) from 1.7 million hectares in 1996 to 58.1 million hectares in 2002 worldwide. 99% of this growth has only been in four countries; Argentina, Canada, China and the USA, the USA being the largest, producing 68%. Amidst this enthusiasm there has been growing concern that there exist many hidden costs involved with GE technology. Critics of GE technology claim there are known and unknown health, social, ethical and environmental risks involved with the introduction of this technology. There are also claims that this technology has little if any benefits to the developing world and will in fact only benefit the developed world, and multinational biotech corporations such as Monsanto. Critics argue that whatever benefits developing nations gain from GE technology, these are far outweighed by the risks involved. Proponents' of genetically modified foods strongest claim is that this technology will benefit farmers in developing countries by allowing those farmers to be more productive and grow a higher yield of crops. Many studies do agree that GE technologies do give farmers a higher yield, but even this is a contested issue. Because many of these studies are sponsored and linked to the very corporations that are developing these technologies, validity of the results are questionable.

In fact, there have been certain independent studies that have concluded that genetically modified seeds in fact produce a lower yield than do conventional seeds. For example these is a two-year study by the University of Nebraska, in which Monsanto's Roundup Ready soybeans yield 6 percent less than their closest relatives and 11 percent less than high-yielding soybean varieties. This study shows that with all things being equal, genetically modified crops may in fact produce a lower yield. Because GE soy is commercially grown more than any other GE crop it will be good to take a look at why. With Roundup Ready soybeans growing to 81% of the totally soy grown within the United States in 2003 , one must ask why farmers are switching to GE soy. The reason for this is the lower costs of pesticides and herbicides. The advantage of Roundup Ready soybeans is not that they are more productive or that the seeds cost less. In fact the seeds cost about six dollars more per acre than traditional soy seeds. The advantage comes in the form of a more resistant plant. Because Roundup Ready soy has been genetically altered to be more resistant to herbicides and pesticides, specifically a Monsanto produced brand called Roundup. Because these new GE soybeans are able to withstand stronger herbicide and pesticide use at a younger age, without any damage to the crop, farmers are able to kill off weeds and pests earlier and easier. This use of stronger herbicides and pesticides in farming leads to a cleaner crop, with a lower cost of labor. A 1998 study by Mike Duffy, an economist from Iowa State University shows that all in all the costs and benefits of using GE technologies in soy and corn production do not lead to any sort of significant difference in returns compared to traditional none GE seeds. The main reasons for farmers switching to genetically altered technologies is the lower amount of labor needed for production and the cleaner crop produced with an increase of herbicides.

Clearly the fact that Roundup Ready soy, the most highly used commercial GMO product, has lower yields than traditional soy products we can dismiss the main argument given by the biotech industry that they are trying to help end world hunger. According to the United Nations and many none governmental organizations around the world the problem of world hunger is not one of a scarcity of food; it is in fact a problem of distribution of food. Today the world produces 17 percent more calories per person today than it did 30 years ago . The world does not need larger supplies of food; the world needs to address the way in which food is distributed, something that GMO technology has no effects on.

The only people that the biotech industry is trying to help are themselves. This is the reason that currently the main commercial implementation of genetically modified technology has been to increase crop resistance to pesticide use. The main producers of GE technology, firms such as Monsanto, are also the world's main producers of pesticides and herbicides. The example of soy shows that the only real impact of genetic engineering has been to transfer some of the cost of labor into capital costs.

This may be a good thing for the developing world where labor is more scarce, and capital intensive production should be sought. The developing world, on the other hand, with its high population and high unemployment would be better off using more labor intensive means of production. If GE soy technologies are applied in less developed nations, where labor is cheaper than in the developed countries, the cost of capital will not be offset as it has been in the United States by lowering labor costs. The costs of GE seeds are too high for farmers from developing countries to implement their usage.

The costs of implementing this technology will not be offset by the benefits that farmers in the US have received. Not only will farmers lose money, but unemployment, which is already a problem in many developing nations, will increase, as farmers need to hire less labor to produce the same amount of crops. The high initial cost of purchasing GE seeds makes the technology more difficult to implement by poor farmers in less developed countries. As happened during the "green revolution" these small farmers would be forced to take out loans to buy this new technology, and if the technology does not deliver higher profits these farmers may lose their land. Even if a technology was developed that would bring the cost of production down to or below that of existing production cost, there is the issue of consumer preference.

The increasing debate over genetic engineering has created a substantial difference in perception of the risks and benefits involved with GE food. Governments around the world, most notably members of the European Union have places restrictions and bans on many GMO products. Many of these countries are considering putting labels on products with GMO ingredients. Considering that many developing countries' economies are highly dependant on agricultural export, these countries can not risk the loss of major export markets.

With pressure from the biotech industry, the United States, and the World Trade Organization some countries are become more lax on their restrictions on GE imports and regulations. The most recent example is the lifting of a moratorium on commercial GMOs in New Zealand on October 29th, 2003. While the governments of many countries are slowly lowering their restrictions on GE technology, many of the consumers in these countries are still highly opposed to the consumption of GMOs. The highest consumer opposition to this technology comes from Western Europe and Japan. With many consumers in the developed world being highly opposed to GMOs and willing to pay a different, higher price for GMO free food, GE crops stop being a substitute for traditional crops, and two separate markets are formed, with different demand curves.

Even if a GE technology is developed that allows higher productivity at equal or slightly lower costs, this may still not be a profitable investment for farmers that export to locations such as Western Europe where there is high consumer resistance to GMOs. In a market where GE foods are not substitutes for traditional foods, many consumers will be unwilling to purchase GE products. Also, if GE technology does become more productive than traditional food, those who are willing to substitute GE food for traditional food will have a larger supply of both genetically modified and traditional food to chose from. With the lower demand, and higher supply, the price of genetically modified foods will fall. What benefits the farmers of GMOs received in switching to this technology will be accompanied by a loss of price of their goods. The option of growing a limited amount of genetically modified products, and keeping the rest of the market GMO free, is a very costly, if not impossible task. Fear of GMOs spreading to the wild and having negative effects on the local ecosystems is one of the main environmental arguments against GE technology. Some countries have attempted to stop this by creating "buffer zones" between genetically altered plants and traditional plants.

The problem with this is most of these buffer zones are too small in size. Genetically altered plants have been found to spread their pollen over 800 meters , it is highly unlikely and would be extremely costly for farmers to have to implement buffer zones this large around their farms to make sure their crop does not contaminate any outside crops. While this is currently an argument environmentalists are using to show that GMOs are a threat to the ecosystem, this is not only a threat to the environment, but also to other farmers who wish to farm using traditional seeds. Farmers who try to sell their products to the none GMO market and have their fields contaminated by pollen from their neighbor's GE crop will not be able to sell their products as GMO free. If the market for GMO product goes bad it will be close to impossible for a country to stop production of GMOs once they get out of their contained areas.

One technological innovation that the biotech industry has come up with that does not have this problem is the terminator technology. Industry wide research has been devoted to expanding this technology. Terminator seeds are seeds which create plants that are sterile and cannot produce new seeds. With this technology farmers are forced to purchase new seeds every year from biotech corporations, unlike traditionally where farmers were able to use seeds from the previous harvest to plant the next year's crop. The reason for developing this technology is simply to protect the patent on the corporations genetically altered product. Forcing the purchase of new seeds every season would hurt farmers in poorer developing nations most. For generations farmers around the world have been harvesting seeds from their best plants every year, naturally evolving their crops to be better. The ability to breed the best plants with one another is taken away when farers plant sterile seeds.

This technology will force farmers from developing nations to be more dependant on multinational biotech corporations. While terminator technology has been met with large criticisms and biotech firms have been slow to implement its uses in the United States, because of fears of their patents not being enforced in developing countries, to ensure that their technology is not used by anyone without their permission, biotech companies are more likely to use terminator technologies in developing countries.

Critics of GMOs claim that the long term health effects of these technologies are not known yet. The economic risks involved are also not all known. "Super weeds" that are not stopped by herbicides can cause a lower crop yield. Many scientists argue that usage of higher amounts of herbicides will create resistance in certain types of weeds, and these "super weeds" will not be stopped by herbicide use. Another, more alarming trend is that certain traits of genetically altered crops have crossed into weeds and those weeds now posses the same resistance to herbicides that the genetic alterations gave the crop. Under monoculture a farmer's crops are at higher risk of being destroyed by a disease. Because a farmer grows all the same species, if a disease breaks out, that farmers whole crop can be ruined. This is the same danger with GMOs only to a higher extent. Because genetically modified crops are exactly the same genetically, the risk from diseases is much higher.

Unlike traditional crops which may be divers enough to avoid a totally disaster, GE crops have no diversity. Not only is GE implementation a bad idea for farmers from developing countries, it is already threat to many farmers who produce things such as sugar. Biotech firms are altering the genetic makeup of certain crops grown in northern climates to produce sugar and other derivatives, traditionally only obtained from crops grown in developing countries. With the development of this technology developed countries in the north will be able to grow products that they otherwise would have had to trade for.

For example, coconut oil is naturally high in lauric acid. However it has become threatened by genetically engineered high-lauric acid canola oil grown in developed countries. While genetic engineering has been attacked on environmental, health and ethical grounds, it is clear that economically this technology will harm the developing world more than it can ever help. The technology is not being used to feed the world's hungry, nor does it need to be, distribution is the problem. Through patens and higher use of their own pesticides, GE technology has so far only been used to make biotech companies more money. The costs of implementing this technology are too high. With a higher investment in capital, and unknown returns in not something a low income farmer can afford. This would be especially costly if terminator seeds are implemented in developing countries, due to fear of patents not being honored in those countries. Developing countries should focus on more labor intensive production that does not leave them dependant on multinational corporations and the developed world.

Bibliography

Asahara T, Takahashi T, Masuda H, Kalka C, Chen D, Iwaguro H, Inai Y, Silver M, Isner JM. VEGF contributes to postnatal neovascularization by mobilizing bone marrow-derived endothelial progenitor cells. EMBO J 1999; 18:3964- 3972.

Assady, S., *et al.,* "Insulin production by human embryonic stem cells," Diabetes 50: 1691-1697 (2001).

Atkinson, M. A. and Leiter, E. H., "The NOD mouse model of type 1 diabetes: As good as it gets?" Nature Medicine 5: 601-604 (1999).

Brivanlou, A. H., *et al.,* "Stem cells. Setting standards for human embryonic stem cells," Science 300: 913-916 (2003).

Bush, G.W., "Stem Cell Science and the Preservation of Life," *The New York Times*, August 12, 2001, p. D13.

Callahan, D., *What Price Better Health: The Hazards of the Research Imperative.*

Carpenter, M.K., et al., "Characterization and Differentiation of Human Embryonic Stem Cells," Cloning and Stem Cells 5: 79-88 (2003), and Pittenger, *M. F. et al.,* "*Multil*ineage potential of adult human mesenchymal stem cells," Science 284: 143-147 (1999).

Chen, Y., *et al.,* "Embryonic stem cells generated by nuclear transfer of human somatic nuclei into rabbit oocytes," Cell Research 13: 251-264 (2003).

Childress, J., "Federal Policy Toward Embryonic Stem cell research," *American Journal of Bioethics* 2(1): 34 (2002).

Chu, K., et *al.,* "Human neural stem cells can migrate, differentiate, and integrate after intravenous transplantation in adult rats with transient forebrain ischemia," Neuroscience Letters 343: 129-133 (2003).

Clark, J., "Squandering Our Technological Future," *The New York Times*, August 30, 2001, p. A19. See also the presentation of Thomas Okarma, President and CEO of Geron Corporation, before the Council on September 4, 2003.

Daley, G. Q., *et al.*, "Realistic Prospects for Stem Cell Therapeutics," Hematology American Society for Hematology Education *Program: 39*8-418 (2003).

Daley, G., "Cloning and Stem Cells—Handicapping the Political and Scientific Debates," *New England Journal of Medicine* 349(3): 211-212 (2003).

Doerflinger, R., "Ditching Religion and Reality," *American Journal of Bioethics* 2(1): 31 (2002).

Drukker, M., et al., "Characterization of the expression of MHC proteins in human embryonic stem cells," Proceedings of the National Academy of Sciences of the *United States of America 99: 9864-9869 (2002).*

Elefanty AG, Robb L, Birner R, Begley CG. Hematopoietic-specific genes are not induced during in vitro differentiation of scl-null embryonic stem cells.

Englund, U., *et al.,* "Transplantation of human neural progenitor cells into the neonatal rat brain: extensive migration and differentiation with longdistance axonal projections," Experimental Neurology 173: 1-21 (2002).

Faden, *et al.*, "Public Stem Cell Banks: Considerations of Justice in Stem Cell Research and Therapy" *Hastings Center Report* 33:6 (2003).

Faraci, M., *et al.*, "Severe neurologic complications after hematopoietic stem cell transplantation in children," Neurology 59: 1895-1904 (2002).

Folkman, J. Therapeutic angiogenesis in ischemic limbs. Circulation 1998; 97:108- 110.

Gianessi, Leonard P. and Janet E. Carpenter, "Agricultural Biotechnology: Insect Control Benefits," National Center for Food and Agricultural Policy, 1999. Available on Biotechnology Industry Organization at www.bio.org.

Hogan, P., et al., "Economic Costs of Diabetes in the US in 2002," Diabetes Care 26: 917-932 (2003).

Hori, Y., et al., "Growth inhibitors promote differentiation of insulin-producing tissue from embryonic stem cells," Proceedings of the National Academy of Sciences of the *United States of America 99: 16105-16110 (2002).*

Ivanova, N. B., *et al.*, "A Stem Cell Molecular Signature," Science 298: 601-604 (2002).

Jaffredo T, Gautier R, Eichmann A, Dieterlen-Lievre F. Intraaortic hemopoietic cells are derived from endothelial cells during ontogeny. Development 1998;125:4575-4583.

James, Clive, "Global Review of Commercialized Transgenic Crops: 1998," *ISAAA*, No. 8, 1998.

Kahn, J., "Missing the mark on stem cells," *Bioethics Examiner* 5:3, Fall 2001, p. 1.

Kalka, C. et al. Transplantation of ex vivo expanded endothelial progenitor cells for therapeutic neovascularization. Proc. Natl. Acad. Sci. USA 2000; 97:3422-3427.

Kass, L., "The Meaning of Life - In the Laboratory," *The Public Interest*, Winter 2002. Also see the Council's July 2002 report *Human Cloning and Human Dignity: An Ethical Inquiry,* Chapter 6.

Kawano H, Do YS, Kawano Y, Starnes V, Barr M, Law RE, Hsueh WA. Angiotensin II has multiple profibrotic effects in human cardiac fibroblasts. Circulation 2000;101:1130-1137.

Kennedy M, Firpo M, Choi K, Wall C, Robertson S, Kabrun N, Keller G. A common precursor for primitive erythropoiesis and definitive haematopoiesis.

Kennedy, D., "Stem Cells: Still Here, Still Waiting," *Science* 300: 865 (2003).

Kerr, D. A., et al., "*Hum*an Embryonic Germ Cell Derivatives Facilitate Motor Recovery of Rats with Diffuse Motor Neuron Injury," The Journal of Neuroscience 23: 5131-5140 (2003).

Kerr, D. A., *et al.,* "Human Embryonic Germ Cell Derivatives Facilitate Motor Recovery of Rats with Diffuse Motor Neuron Injury," The Journal of Neuroscience 23: 5131-5140 (2003).

Labastie M-C, Cortes F, Romeo P-H, Dulac C, Peault B. Molecular identity of hematopoietic precursor cells emerging in the human embryo. Blood 1998;92:3624-3635.

Latham, S., "Ethics and Politics," *American Journal of Bioethics* 2(1): 46 (2002).

Lechner, A. and Habener, J.F., "Stem/progenitor cells derived from adult tissues: potential for the treatment of diabetes mellitus," American Journal of Physiology—Endocrinology and Me*tabolism* 284: E259-266 (2003).

Lewis, C. S. The Abolition of Man. New York: The Macmillan Company, 1947.

Liker, M., et al., "Human neural stem cell transplantation in the MPTP-lesioned mouse," Brain Research 971: 168-177 (2003).

Liu, Z., and Martin, *L. J.,* "Olfactory bulb core is a rich source of neural progenitor and stem cells in adult rodent and human," Journal of Comparative Neurology 459: 368-391 (2003).

Liu, Z., and Martin, L.J., "Olfactory bulb core is a rich source of neural progenitor and stem cells in adult rodent and human," Journal of Comparative Neurology 459: 368-391 (2003).

Los Angeles, CA.: University of California Press, 2003; also see Daniel Callahan's presentation before the Council on July 24, 2003, available on the Council's website at www.bioethics.gov.

Lumelsky, N., *et al.,* "Differentiation of embryonic stem cells to insulin-secreting structures similar to pancreatic islets," Science 292: 1389-1394 (2001).

Macklin, Ph.D., Ruth. "Ethics, Politics, and Human Embryo Stem Cell Research." Women's Health Issues, vol. 10, no. 3 (May/June 2000): 111-15.

Magnus, David, Arthur Caplan, and Glenn McGee, ed. In Who Owns Life? Amherst, New York: Prometheus Books, 2002.

Majumdar, M. K., et al., "Characterization and functionality of cell surface molecules on human mesenchymal stem cells," Journal of Biomedical Science 10: 228-241 (2003).

Marquis, D., "Stem cell research: The Failure of Bioethics," *Free Inquiry* 22(1): Winter 2002.

McCormick, R. A. "Who or What is the Preembryo?" In Corrective Vision: Explorations in Moral Theology. Kansas City: Sheed & Ward, 1994.

McKenny, Gerald P. "Enhancements and the Ethical Significance of Vulnerability." In Enhancing Human Traits: Ethical and Social Implications. Washington, D.C.: Georgetown University Press, 1998. 222-37.

McKibben, Bill. Enough: Staying Human in an Engineered Age. New York: Henry Holt and Company, 2003.

McLean, Margaret. "Stem Cells: Justice at the Gate." Dialog, vol. 41, no. 3 (fall 2002).

Meilaender, Gilbert. "Terra es animata: On Having a Life." Hastings Center Report, vol. 23, no. 4 (July-August 1993): 25-32.

Murray, T., "Hard Cell," *The American Prospect,* September 24, 2001.

Ogawa M, Kizumoto M, Nishikawa S, Fujimoto T, Kodama H, Nishikawa SI. Blood 1999;93:1168-1177.

Okarma, T., Presentation at the September 4, 2003, meeting of the President's Council on Bioethics, Washington, D.C., available at www.bioethics.gov.

Okarma, T., Presentation at the September 4, 2003, meeting of the President's Council on Bioethics, Washington, D.C., available at www.bioethics.gov.

Onyango, P., *et al.,* "Monoallelic expression and methylation of imprinted genes in human and mouse embryonic germ cell lineages," Proceedings of the National Academy of Sciences of the *United States of America* 99: 10599-10604 (2002).

Orlic D, Kajstura J, Chimenti S, et al. Bone marrow cells regenerate infarcted myocardium. Nature 2001, 410:701-705.

Orr, R., "The Moral Status of the Embryonal Stem Cell: Inherent or Imputed?" *American Journal of Bioethics* 2(1): 57-59 (2002).

Pursley, W.H., Presentation at the September 4, 2003, meeting of the President's Council on Bioethics, Washington, D.C., available at www.bioethics.gov.

R. Alta Charo, of the University of Wisconsin Law School, quoted in Coyle, M., "The Clone Zone," *The National Law Journal*, May 15, 2002.

Rafii S, Shapiro F, Rimarachin J, Nachman R, Ferris B, Weksler B, Moore AS, Asch AS. Isolation and characterization of human bone marrow microvascular endothelial cells: hematopoietic progenitor cell adhesion.

Rideout, W., *et al.,* "Correction of a genetic defect by nuclear transplantation and combined cell and gene therapy," Cell 109: 17-27 (2002).

Ryan, E.A., et al., "Clinical outcomes and insulin secretion after islet transplantation with the Edmonton protocol," Diabetes 50: 710-719 (2001).

Sato, N., *et al.,* "Molecular signature of human embryonic stem cells and its comparison with the mouse," Developmental Biology 260: 404-413 (2003).

Soria, B., *et al.,* "Insulin-secreting cells derived from embryonic stem cells normalize glycemia in streptozotocin-induced diabetic mice," Diabetes 49: 157-162 (2000)

Strong, C., "Those Divisive Stem Cells: Dealing with Our Most Contentious Issues," *American Journal of Bioethics* 2(1): 39-40 (2002).

Takahashi, T. et al. Ischemia- and cytokine-induced mobilization of bone marrowderived endothelial progenitor cells for neovascularization. Nat. Med. 1999; 5:434-438.

Tsai FY, Keller G, Kuo FC, Weiss M, Chen J, Rosenblatt M, Alt FA, Orkin SH. An early hematopoietic defect in mice lacking the transcription factor GATA- 2. Nature 1994; 371:221-225.

Zhao, M., et al., "Amelioration of streptozotocin-induced diabetes in mice using human islet cells derived from long-term culture in vitro," Transplantation 73: 1454- 1460 (2002).

Index

U

V

W